UTAH
TRAVEL✦SMART®

S0-BTE-252

THE ORGAN AT ARCHES NATIONAL PARK

Steve Mulligan

UTAH
TRAVEL✧SMART®

Michael R. Weibel

John Muir Publications
Santa Fe, New Mexico

Acknowledgments
With thanks to my wife Lora, who put up with me and the deadlines for a second book during the first year of our marriage.

John Muir Publications, P.O. Box 613, Santa Fe, New Mexico 87504

Printed in the United States of America.
First edition. First printing May 1999.

ISSN: 1520-8001
ISBN: 1-56261-458-4

Editors: Marybeth Griffin, Lizann Flatt
Graphics Editor: Heather Pool
Production: Janine Lehmann
Design: Marie J. T. Vigil
Cover design: Janine Lehmann
Typesetting: Melissa Tandysh
Map style development: American Custom Maps—Jemez Springs, New Mexico
Map illustration: Kathleen Sparkes, White Hart Design
Printing: Publishers Press
Front cover photo: *Inset:* © Leo de Wys, Inc./Masahura Uemar—Temple Square in Salt Lake City
               Large: © Leo de Wys, Inc./Fridmar Damm—Dead Horse Point State Park
Back cover photo: © Frank Jensen—Snowboarding in Utah

Distributed to the book trade by
Publishers Group West
Berkeley, California

UTAH TRAVEL•SMART:
A GUIDE THAT GUIDES

Most guidebooks are basically directories, providing information but very little help in making choices—you have to guess how to make the most of your time and money.

Utah Travel•Smart is different: By highlighting the very best of Utah and offering various planning features, it acts like a personal tour guide rather than a directory.

TAKE THE STRESS OUT OF TRAVEL

Sometimes traveling causes more stress than it relieves. Sorting through information, figuring out the best routes, determining what to see and where to eat and stay, scheduling each day in order to get the most out of your time— all of this can make a vacation feel daunting rather than fun. Relax. We've done a lot of the legwork for you. This book helps you plan a trip that suits you—whatever your time frame, budget, and interests.

SEE THE BEST OF UTAH

Author Mike Weibel lives and works in Utah. He has hand-picked every listing in this book, and he gives you an insider's perspective on what makes each one worthwhile.

So while you will find many of the big tourist attractions listed here, you'll also find lots of smaller, lesser known treasures, such as the fascinating George S. Eccles Dinosaur Park in Ogden, the Great Basin Museum in Delta, . or the spectacular cold-water Crystal Geyser in Castle Valley. And each sight is described so you'll know what's most—and sometimes least—interesting about it.

In selecting the restaurants and accommodations for this book, the author sought out unusual spots with local flavor. While in some areas of the state chains are unavoidable, wherever possible the author directs you to one-of-a-kind places.

We also know that you want a range of options: One day you may crave fancy Italian food served in an artsy and cosmopolitan atmosphere, while the next day you would be just as happy (as would your wallet), with a good old-fashioned burger from a popular local diner. Most of the restaurants and accommodations listed here are moderately priced, but the author also includes budget and splurge options, depending on the destination.

CREATE THE TRIP YOU WANT

We all have different travel styles. Some people like spontaneous weekend jaunts, while others plan longer, more leisurely trips. You may want to cover as much ground as possible, no matter how much time you have. Or maybe you prefer to focus your trip on one part of the state or on some special interest, such as skiing, nature, the venues of the 2002 Winter Olympic Games, or arts and culture. We've taken these differences into account.

Though the individual chapters stand on their own, they are organized in a geographically logical sequence, so that you could conceivably fly into Salt Lake City, drive chapter by chapter to each destination in the book, and end up close to where you started. Of course, you don't have to follow that sequence, but it's there if you want a complete picture of Utah.

Each destination chapter offers ways of prioritizing when time is limited: In the Perfect Day section, the author suggests what to do if you have only one day to spend in the area.

Every Sightseeing Highlight is rated, from one to four stars: ★★★★—or "must see"—sights first, followed by ★★★ sights, then ★★ sights, and finally ★—or "see if you have spare time"—sights.

At the end of each sight listing is a time recommendation in parentheses. User-friendly maps help you locate the sights, restaurants, and lodging of your choice.

And if you're in it for the ride, so to speak, you'll want to check out the Scenic Routes described at the end of chapters 4, 10, 11, and 14. They take you through some of the most scenic parts of Utah.

In addition to these special features, the appendix has other useful travel tools:

- The Planning Map and Mileage Chart help you determine your own route and calculate travel time.
- The Special Interest Tours show you how to design your trip around any of seven favorite interests.
- The Calendar of Events provides an at-a-glance view of when and where major events occur throughout the state.
- The Resource guide tells you where to go for more information about national and state parks, cities and counties, local bed-and-breakfasts, and more.

HAPPY TRAVELS

With this book in hand, you have many reliable recommendations and travel tools at your fingertips. Use it to make the most of your trip. And have a great time!

WHY VISIT UTAH?

From the mountains to the desert to the Great Salt Lake, Utah is alive with culture and a vibrant history. You can stand where dinosaurs once roamed, or walk the same trails that carried mountain men to their favorite haunts and a rendezvous or two. You can raft the same river that John Wesley Powell once navigated, or watch the sunrise from an alcove decorated by ancient Fremont or Anasazi artwork. Every corner of the state deserves to be explored.

Most people have heard about the state's predominant religion. Mormons are often synonymous with Utah itself. Their unique contribution to the expansion of the American West extends far beyond religion and the famous Mormon Tabernacle Choir.

Utah's early people were able to make a lush oasis out of a sandy desert, and that same pioneering spirit is alive today. Groundbreaking technological advances are being made every day in the state's colleges and universities, as well as in the many businesses and laboratories that have sprung up as a result of that research. The first artificial human heart was designed and developed at the University of Utah. Young school children have planned and designed tests that were used on the space shuttle. Utah will host the 2002 Olympic Winter Games. Plans are in the works for Utah's western desert to become a landing strip for space vehicles carrying the next generation of explorers back from other planets and galaxies.

But Utah hasn't forgotten its roots. Small town life is celebrated with

I

parties and festivals paying tribute to everything from sauerkraut to raspberries, mountain men to Mormon pioneers, and cars to quilts.

Past, present, and future merge in Utah. Modern rocket systems are tested just a few miles from where the golden spike was driven to complete the first transcontinental railroad. You can leave the bustling metropolis of Salt Lake City and in hours be in the nearly untouched wilderness of any one of more than a dozen national parks, monuments, or forests throughout the state.

Brigham Young was right when he first arrived in Utah and said, "This is the place."

THE LAY OF THE LAND

Looking at a map of Utah, you'll see that the state is divided by north-south-running mountain ranges. Most of the state lies on a plateau higher than 4,000 feet above sea level. In fact, Utah is the nation's rooftop if you measured only the highest peak in each county. The average elevation of these peaks is 11,222 feet. Compare that to second-place Colorado, with 10,791 feet. Utah also has one of the greatest elevation differentials in the nation. Beaver Dam Wash, in the southwest corner of Utah, is the lowest point in the state, at 2,350 feet. Compare that to the state's highest point, 13,528-foot Kings Peak in the Uinta Mountains of northeastern Utah. That's a 11,178-foot difference in elevation.

In the shadow of Utah's mountains are two mighty rivers, the Colorado and the Green. In the southeastern part of the state, John Wesley Powell and his party scaled cliffs, mapped rivers and side canyons, made a variety of scientific observations, and named several topographical features. To the north, of course, is the Great Salt Lake. The desert of the Great Basin lies to the west.

State officials have divided Utah into four geographical and geological provinces: Rocky Mountain, Red Rock, Wasatch Front, and Great Basin.

The Rocky Mountain province spans the heart of the state for 300 miles from north to south. It includes the Wasatch Mountains, which form a backdrop for the state's largest cities, which are between Provo and Ogden. To the east are the Uinta Mountains, Utah's most rugged and highest mountains. The Uintas include several peaks reaching well above 12,000 feet, including the state's highest. The Uintas are the only large mountain range in North America that runs east-west.

To the southeast is Utah's Red Rock province, located on the Colorado Plateau, a high tableland of eroded sedimentary rock. It's famous for its red rock canyons, arches, domes, and buttes, as well as for the Green and the Colorado Rivers. All of Utah's national parks are located in this province.

The Wasatch Front province includes Utah's largest cities—such as Ogden and Salt Lake City—which are located along the west base of the Wasatch Mountains. The rural areas to the west of those cities slide away to the remote mountain ranges and wide open spaces of the Great Basin Desert.

The Great Basin province covers a large portion of northwestern Utah, including the Great Salt Lake and the Bonneville Salt Flats.

FLORA AND FAUNA

Utah's deserts, rivers, wetlands, and mountains are home to a diverse collection of plants and animals. When canyon hillsides come alive in the fall with the bright reds, oranges, and yellows of maples and quaking aspens, Utah rivals New England for spectacular color. But other parts of Utah may appear quite plain and barren. After all, much of the state is a desert. The Great Basin Desert in Utah is called a cold desert because it has long periods of cold weather and gets more precipitation than some other deserts (10 to 20 inches), often in the form of snow. A National Biological Survey shows that Utah's vegetation is dominated by sagebrush, grasses, and pinyon pine and juniper forests. The state tree is the blue spruce. Bristlecone pines, which are found on several Utah mountains, are the longest living tree species on earth. Mountain mahogany, sub-Alpine fir, and Englemann spruce are common tree species.

Wildflowers are abundant, including the sego lily, which is the state flower. Indians taught the early Mormons to eat the sweet, nutritious bulb. Some say it tastes like a potato when it's boiled. I'll have to take their word for it.

Mule deer, elk, moose, and rabbits are common sights throughout Utah. Lucky travelers may get to see or hear a coyote or two. Mountain lions and black bears are also found throughout the state, particularly in some of the remote mountain ranges, but they make few public appearances.

Ask any Audubon Society member about the birds that live in Utah, and they'll tell you that Utah has an enormous number of feathered residents. Raptors—including hawks, falcons, and eagles—are regularly seen in Utah's skies. California gulls (similar to sea gulls) were named the state birds because they saved the crops of early pioneers from ravenous crickets in 1848 and 1849. The Bear River Migratory Bird Refuge, near Brigham City, is an occasional home to loons, grebes, pelicans, herons, swans, geese, ducks, pheasants, cranes, and hundreds of other birds. Mountain goats inhabit the upper reaches of the Tusher Mountains in south-central Utah, while bison roam freely in the Henry

Mountains in the southeastern part of the state and on Antelope Island in the Great Salt Lake.

HISTORY

When many people think about Utah's history, they conjure up images of Mormon pioneers making the grueling trek west across the plains and mountains to the shores of the Great Salt Lake. But Utah was inhabited long before the Mormons found their modern-day Zion. Native Americans were the first to leave their mark throughout most of Utah. The Clovis and Folsom paleo-Indians lived on this land from approximately 500 A.D. to 5000 B.C., during the time the enormous Lake Bonneville was receding to the size of its present-day successor, the Great Salt Lake. Later, the Anasazi and Fremont cultures, dating back from 1298 A.D. to 2 B.C., settled in southern Utah. They carved petroglyphs and painted pictographs in the red rock walls of Utah's desert canyons—telling the tales, perhaps, of successful hunts and other aspects of their everyday lives. You can still see many of those scenes today.

In the mid-eighteenth century, Juan Maria Antonio de Rivera, a Spaniard, was the first European known to have ventured into Utah. He traveled from New Mexico and found the Colorado River near Moab. Rivera was followed 11 years later, in 1776, by two Franciscan friars, Atanasio Dominguez and Silvestre Valéz de Escalante, who were in search of an overland route between Santa Fe and Monterey, California. Their journals were later used by traders and explorers who ventured into what is now Utah. Étienne Provost, Antoine Robidoux, Peter Skene Ogden, William Ashley, Jedediah Smith, and Jim Bridger were among the traders and trappers who made a living along Utah's rivers in the early nineteenth century.

It was the call to "go west" that brought thousands of immigrants to Utah. John C. Fremont's explorations between 1843 and 1853, and his subsequent maps, helped pave the way for westward migration. Parts of Fremont's reports found their way into Joseph Ware's The Emigrant Guide to California. And a few years later, Mormons learned of the Dominguez-Escalante expedition into Utah through Fremont's reports. It was the Mormons who shaped much of present-day Utah.

In the 1820s Mormon-church founder Joseph Smith, while pondering which church he should join, was reportedly visited by the angel Moroni. It is said that this angel, who is depicted in a sculpture atop the Mormon Temple in Salt Lake City, told Smith where to uncover some golden plates inscribed with a history of early American Christians. Those plates were transcribed into the Book of Mormon in 1830. Smith established the Church of Jesus Christ of

Latter-day Saints, which is often called the Mormon Church by "LDS" and non-LDS people. Mormons believe that Jesus Christ was the son of God and that Christ visited the Americas after his crucifixion and resurrection.

The Mormons practiced polygamy and believed they were the true "chosen of God," which inflamed many of their non-Mormon neighbors. Fleeing from persecution, Smith, the son of a New York farmer, led his followers from New York to Kirtland, Ohio, to Independence, Missouri, and to Nauvoo, Illinois. After Smith was assassinated in Nauvoo, Brigham Young led the Mormons to Utah. They arrived in the Salt Lake Valley on July 24, 1847. The day is celebrated today as a state holiday with fireworks and parades, much like the Fourth of July. They called their land "Deseret," a Book of Mormon term meaning "honey bee." The term symbolized industry and activity.

In 1850 the federal government declared a portion of Deseret as Utah Territory, named after the Ute Indians. Statehood was granted to Utah in 1896, after the Mormon agreed to denounce the practice of polygamy and the church began to encourage its members to participate in national political parties.

The transcontinental railroad in northern Utah, completed in 1869, brought non-Mormon settlers into the territory. People of many different ethnicities and nationalities, including Irish and Chinese, helped build the railroad, and when it was finished, they stuck around. The railroad also made travel to the West much easier, prompting people from various backgrounds to try life on the Western frontier. Many of those folks got off the train in Utah.

Today, Utah is home to a diverse population, but the Mormon influence is still strong in daily life and politics. A booming film industry has introduced many non-Utahns to the state, where spectacular scenery abounds. And, Utah continues to grow.

CULTURES

The Mormon culture is predominant throughout Utah. The percentage of Mormons living in many communities throughout the state exceeds 60 percent.

The faith discourages drinking, smoking, and cussing. Mormons are known for being teetotalers—they abstain from drinking alcohol and many do not drink caffeinated beverages. While it may be tough to find any blue laws remaining on the books in Utah, it's not uncommon to find many businesses closed and the sale of alcohol restricted on Sundays. For those who are not church goers, take advantage of the fact that, on Sundays, there are fewer people on the ski slopes during the winter and golf courses during the summer, most of which remain open.

"Wholesome," activities like going to the movies (with G and PG ratings) and on family camping trips, are popular throughout the state. Many Mormons even set aside Monday nights as a time to spend with their families.

Mormons do not have professional clergy. Instead, they rely on lay members of each congregation to serve in various church positions. LDS missionaries are sent all over the world as well as throughout Utah. They, and all Mormons in general, are encouraged to tell others about their church and its doctrines. Because so many people have served on LDS missions, it's not uncommon to find someone in any Utah community who can speak another language.

The Mormon Church is broken down into neighborhood "wards," where small chapels are built for weekly services. Ward buildings are also used for community events such as lectures and concerts. Unlike Midwestern communities, which are often built around a county courthouse or city hall, several Utah communities are built around their Mormon tabernacles—much larger than ward chapels, these are assembly halls used for meetings and occasionally services. Mormon temples, on the other hand, are sacred buildings where LDS members are married and participate in other "ordinances." Non-Mormons are rarely allowed in Mormon temples. In fact, only those Mormons that are in good standing with the church are allowed in.

The church and the state government outlawed polygamy more than 100 years ago, just prior to statehood. Few Mormons practice polygamy today, but there are a few remote sects in Utah that participate in and encourage plural marriage.

The church owns and operates the state's largest university—Brigham Young University in Provo. It also owns KSL radio and television stations, as well as the Deseret News newspaper in Salt Lake City and a chain of bookstores and thrift stores, and has numerous landholdings throughout the state.

In the political arena, the state is predominantly conservative. But there are a few areas, namely Price, where liberals feel right at home. Mining attracted many non-Mormon, foreign-born immigrants to Price, as well as to other communities throughout the state.

But as the railroads and mines brought more diversity to the state's population, a deep division formed between Mormons and non-Mormons, especially on social and cultural levels. More recently, the influx of military personnel, college students from other states, and the relocation of high-tech businesses to Utah have stirred the pot more. Utah continues to struggle with its growth and increasing diversity. Some of the state's non-Mormons criticize the way Mormon culture is evident in nearly every aspect of life. But, non-Mormons remain in Utah because they recognize the benefits of living, working, and raising kids in a clean, safe, and wholesome environment.

THE ARTS

Utahns are quite proud of their arts. A handful of wealthy patrons, like the Eccles family, have made countless donations to ensure that the various collections and performances throughout the state continue to grow and that more people—primarily youngsters—are exposed to many forms of art and creativity.

Utah boasts several fine art museums, which house priceless paintings, sculptures, pottery, and other works by Utah artists as well as international artists, including the masters. In June downtown Salt Lake City comes alive during the annual Utah Arts Festival, which features more than 100 performers in music, dance, and theater, as well as culinary artists and street performers.

An internationally recognized symphony, a ballet company, and two opera companies make their homes in Utah. A Shakespeare festival takes place every summer in Cedar City, while young pianists compete every four years during the prestigious Bachauer International Piano Festival in the capital city. Independent filmmakers from around the world descend upon Park City and nearby Sundance resort for Robert Redford's annual Sundance Film Festival.

Utah's strong Mormon influence is seen in its art and music. Of course, there's the Mormon Tabernacle Choir, which performs in the tabernacle and makes special appearances throughout the state and the world. While touring the tabernacle, you will likely learn of the resourcefulness of Mormon pioneers and their pride in making things with their hands. Unable to find or afford prime lumber, they mastered a technique of painting pine and other cheaper lumber to look like expensive oak and walnut. This technique was not only used to decorate the tabernacle, but it was used to paint home furniture. Antique hunters with a sharp eye may find some examples. Perhaps the best place to see Mormon art is the Museum of Church History and Art in Salt Lake City, next to the church's Family History Library (the largest repository of genealogical records in the world).

A group called the Daughters of Utah Pioneers maintains museums in every major community throughout the state, as well as in many small towns. Their museums and "relic halls" feature a variety of artifacts, from clothing and quilts to furniture and books from the state's early pioneers. These museums are staffed by volunteers, and their hours of operation are usually limited.

The most common figure in Utah, particularly southern Utah, is a hump-backed flute player. His name is Kokopelli, and he's found on rocks and canyon walls as petroglyphs (carved or pecked images) and pictographs (painted images). He is believed to have been a fertility symbol, roving minstrel or trader, rain priest, hunting magician, and a trickster. Only the Anasazi knew for sure who this mythical character was. But modern day Utahns have adopted

Kokopelli as a mascot of sorts. His image adorns T-shirts and jewelry that can be purchased in almost every city in the state. Other Native American figures, particularly Navajo, are also common in Utah and throughout the American Southwest. Native American influences are also found in ceramics, baskets, and textiles.

CUISINE

Like the United States as a whole, Utah is a melting pot of cuisines. This can be partly attributed to the Mormon missionary program, which sends young people to cities around the globe. They bring back the knowledge of and the craving for different kinds of food. You can find just about any kind of food in the state if you know where to look. Of course, the most diverse culinary choices can be found in Salt Lake City, primarily because of its large population. Nearly every city has at least one Chinese restaurant, while Salt Lake City has Thai, Cambodian, Vietnamese, Japanese, and several other types of Asian restaurants. There are also numerous Mexican and Italian restaurants throughout the state. Utah is landlocked, so you won't find many seafood restaurants. But because hunting and outdoor recreation are quite popular, you might run across elk, pheasant, grouse, or venison on a menu.

Surprisingly, there's only a few true Greek restaurants left in Utah. But, if you're lucky, you'll get a chance to try some delectable Greek cuisine at any one of a handful of Greek festivals that take place each year in Price and in Salt Lake City. Festivals, as a matter of fact, are a great way to sample foods from around the world. Check with local tourism offices to see if there will be any festivals taking place during your stay in Utah.

Because the state's ski slopes attract people from many different countries, several of the resorts go the extra mile to provide world-class cuisine. Of course, you can still find a good hamburger at most ski resorts, but resorts like Snowbird, Park City, and Deer Valley are also known for their fine dining.

There really isn't any one particular cuisine unique to the state. Utah was settled primarily by hardy farmers and ranchers—people who grew up eating meat and potatoes. Maybe that's as close as anything to Utah's cuisine. However, one thing found in Utah that you may not see anywhere else is a peculiar concoction called fry sauce. This light-orange sauce is a mixture of ketchup and mayonnaise, and it's gobbled up by the denizens of Utah on French fries and just about anything else that people might otherwise use ketchup, mustard, or mayonnaise on. It's available at most fast-food restaurants. Be sure to give it a try.

OUTDOOR ACTIVITIES

If it can be done outdoors, it most likely can be done in Utah. The state is a playground for outdoors people.

Every winter, skiers and snowboarders flock to Utah's mountain resorts, which boast of "the best powder on earth." Even one of the state's license plates touts Utah's largest outdoor recreation industry—"Ski Utah! Greatest Snow on Earth" Olympic and World Cup skiers share the slopes with beginners at Utah's world-class ski resorts.

People who like the solitude of the backcountry enjoy cross-country skiing and snowshoeing in remote areas throughout all of Utah's mountain ranges. Those who prefer horsepower to human power can jump on a snowmobile and explore hundreds of miles of groomed trails throughout the state. But there's more to Utah's outdoor activities than snow.

Moab is the mountain bike capital of the United States. Thousands of people venture to this southeastern Utah city every year to ride the Slickrock Trail and other routes in beautiful red rock country. Mountain biking is also popular at many of the state's ski resorts, where riders can get an easy lift to the top of the mountain.

You might remember John Wayne as he rode through Utah's Monument Valley. Today, you too can climb atop a saddle and experience the state's backcountry from the same vantage point the Duke had. Hikers can find easy, moderate, and difficult trails within minutes of most cities. More adventurous people enjoy long backpacking trips in the Uinta Mountains or in any one of a number of smaller ranges in the state. There are many peaks above 12,000 feet for people of mountaineers to conquer. Rock climbing has become a popular outdoor activity for people of all ages and skill levels. Some of the finest limestone, granite, and quartzite sport climbs are found just outside of Logan and Salt Lake City. You can get rowdy in off-highway vehicles like jeeps and four-wheelers. Daredevils will find a frozen waterfall or two to climb in the winter. But when the ice thaws, Utah's wild rivers attract kayakers and rafters. You can enjoy sailing, waterskiing, and Jet skiing at Utah's lakes and reservoirs—the most popular of which is the enormous Lake Powell. But there are also plenty of quiet and relaxing waters for canoes.

And no place can top Utah when it comes to fishing. There are numerous lakes and ponds from which you can reel in a big lunker, as well as many blue-ribbon trout streams for anglers willing to tempt their fish with a fly. Come let Utah reel you in.

PLANNING YOUR TRIP

Before you set out on your trip, you'll need to do some planning. Use this chapter in conjunction with the tools in the appendix to answer some basic questions. First of all, when are you going? You may already have specific dates in mind; if not, various factors will probably influence your timing. Either way, you'll want to know about local events, the weather, and other seasonal considerations. This chapter discusses all of that, while the Calendar of Events in the appendix provides a month-by-month view of major area events.

How much should you expect to spend on your trip? This chapter addresses various regional factors you'll want to consider in estimating your travel expenses. How will you get around? Check out the section on local transportation. If you decide to travel by car, the Planning Map and Mileage Chart in the appendix can help you figure out exact routes and driving times, while the Special Interest Tours provide several focused itineraries. The chapter concludes with some reading recommendations, both fiction and nonfiction, to give you various perspectives on Utah. If you want specific information about individual cities or counties, use the Resource Guide in the appendix.

HOW MUCH WILL IT COST?

You will find that Utah can be both affordable and pricey. It all depends on what you decide to do.

It's not uncommon to find hotels in the $35 to $60 range in each destination in this book. Some of these places may be bare bones in terms of amenities, while others provide first-class accommodations. Contrary to what you might believe, bed-and-breakfast inns are not necessarily the most expensive places to stay. Many fine bed-and-breakfasts charge rates well under $100 a night, especially in the off-seasons (see When To Go section).

In Park City and at the major ski resorts, you'd be hard pressed to find a room below the $60 to $90 price range. In fact, many hotels and inns will top $100 a night in these locations. Rooms in mountain lodges and luxury hotels may have price tags well above $300 a night. However, there is an alternative—camping. Utah's spectacular scenery provides a backdrop that can't be matched by any hotel walls. Recreational vehicle parks are located in most cities, as are private campgrounds like KOA. Campgrounds for people willing to rough it in tents in exchange for a cheap price are located throughout Utah's national forests, national parks, and state parks.

Cheaper still, there are numerous areas in the parks and forests where campers can stay for free, but don't look for the few amenities offered at other campgrounds, like drinking water and restrooms. Adventurous campers should check with the nearest U.S. Forest Service office or parks office to see if there are any special restrictions. People who use primitive campsites should follow "Leave No Trace" practices to ensure that future campers in the same area will enjoy a pristine wilderness. Pamphlets that describe proper camping procedures are available from the Forest Service.

Restaurant prices vary as much as hotel prices. But there are very few restaurants in Utah that fall into the extremely high-priced category. Dinner for two will run under $30 at most eateries. Expect to pay more at the ski resorts near Salt Lake City—a hamburger could cost between $5 and $10. And a fine, world-class dinner could easily cost more than $40 per person at some of the posh restaurants along the Wasatch Front, in the canyons, or in Park City.

Most attractions in Utah are free or very reasonably priced. Many of those that do charge offer discounts to students and seniors. In addition, some restaurants and hotels offer various discounts.

Entrance fees for national parks, monuments, and historic sites in Utah range from $4 to $10 per carload. If you plan on spending a lot of time in the parks, you might want to invest in a Golden Eagle Passport, which lets you enter any national park in the country. The pass costs $50 and is good for one year. Golden Age Passports, which are lifetime passes, are available for people 62 and older for a one-time $10 fee.

Sales tax varies from city to city. A portion of the sales tax in many cities supports things like the arts, recreation, and public transportation.

WHEN TO GO

The tourist areas in different parts of Utah have different off-seasons, so if you want to take advantage of cheaper routes, you can always find a destination that is experiencing its low season. Ski season generally runs from Thanksgiving to Easter. Special rates for accommodations may be available at the beginning and end of the ski season. But don't wait too long if you're expecting to get out on the slopes. Many ski resorts close their lifts before the snow has melted off their mountains. Presidents' Day weekend is often the busiest time on the slopes. If you don't want to wait in long lift lines, avoid skiing this weekend.

You can also escape the lines by skiing at the lesser-known resorts. Skip Snowbird and Park City, and try Beaver Mountain, Powder Mountain, or Brian Head. It might be a longer drive from Salt Lake City, but you're likely to get more skiing in.

While the ski slopes are crowded in the winter, the desert is usually empty at that time of year. The season down south begins around Easter, when off-highway vehicle (OHV) enthusiasts gather in Moab for the annual Jeep Safari. Thousands of mountain bikers also descend upon Moab for races in April. As if that weren't enough, the streets of Moab are congested in April with street rods that rip up and down Highway 191 during the annual Rod Benders Car Show.

When it gets really hot during the summer, Utahns and tourists alike flock to Lake Powell. Memorial Day weekend signals the start of summer fun on Utah's lakes, and Powell is the state's biggest attraction for people who like water skiing, jet skiing, boating, and sailing. Three to four million people visit the lake each year, and as many as half a million conclude their summer on the lake during Labor Day weekend. If you want to avoid crowds, avoid holiday weekends or try another lake.

Summer is also a prime time to get outdoors and enjoy Utah's mountains. But, if you're looking for a secluded campsite, you may have some problems. Fortunately, many campgrounds accept reservations.

Utah can be very brown during the summer and very white during the winter. If you're looking for a colorful treat, visit the state in the fall, when the trees provide a show of color unsurpassed in the West. Or, visit in the late spring, when everything is green and starting to bloom.

CLIMATE

Utah's weather is more a guessing game than a science. A winter snowstorm that causes all sorts of problems in Ogden, for example, may not have touched Brigham City, some 30 miles away. In fact, it might be sunny in

Brigham City. And on a bright, sunny afternoon in the Uinta Mountains, a dark, dangerous thunderstorm can appear with very little warning.

Utah is probably best known for its snow. Mother Nature's white blanket falls on every region of the state, and although Utah receives most of its snow during the winter and early spring, snow has fallen during every month of the year in the mountains, at one time or another. A lot of snow can drop at one time—105 inches fell in one storm at Alta in January 1965. And yes, it even snows in the desert.

One thing is certain about Utah's weather: visitors should be prepared for anything.

TRANSPORTATION

Salt Lake International Airport is the only major airport in Utah. Commuter airlines serve other cities including Cedar City, Vernal, and St. George. Delta Airlines has established a western hub at Salt Lake International, which is also served by several regional, national, and international airlines. The airport is a few miles west of downtown Salt Lake City. Buses, cabs, and rental cars are available at the airport. If you're going to spend more than a day in Utah, especially if you're planning to see more than Salt Lake City, rent a car. But if your stay is going to be short and you're not planning to leave downtown Salt Lake City, take one of the shuttles. Many major hotels provide transportation to and from the airport. Shuttles are also available at the airport to carry passengers to cities like Logan and Moab that aren't served by airlines.

Utah Transit Authority (UTA) buses serve most of the Wasatch Front, and in 1998, construction began on a light rail system that will serve Salt Lake City. Amtrak stops in Salt Lake City, at the historic Rio Grande depot, providing primarily east-west travelers with an alternative to driving or flying. Other cities served by the railroad include Green River, Helper, and Provo. Greyhound buses run daily on most of the state's major freeways.

The capital city is a crossroads for two major interstate freeways: I-80 and I-15. Interstate 80 crosses the state east to west from Evanston, Wyoming, through Salt Lake City and across the west desert (near the Bonneville Salt Flats) to Wendover, Nevada. Interstate 15, on the other hand, stretches the full 402-mile length of the state from Portage in the north to St. George in the south. Most of Utah's major cities lie along I-15, which also runs along the foot of many of the state's mountain ranges. Interstate 70 runs into the state just above Moab from Grand Junction, Colorado. It passes through Green River, then ends in a junction with I-15 near Cove Fort, about halfway between Fillmore and Beaver.

It's almost impossible to get lost in most Utah cities because the streets are set out in a grid system. Nearly all streets are numbered according to their relation to a central point in the city. For instance, in Salt Lake, the central point is the Mormon Temple—ground zero, as it were. The street running on the north side of Temple Square is North Temple, the next street to the north is 200 North, the next, 300 North, and so on. The same numbering system is used for streets running south, west, and east of the Temple. So, for example, if you needed to find a building with the address 125 South 1300 East, you would go 13 blocks east of the Temple to 1300 east (or "Thirteenth East," as the locals call it). The building would be between 100 south and 200 south (the first two streets directly south of the Temple) on 1300 East. This may sound complicated at first, but you will quickly get the hang of it.

CAMPING, LODGING, AND DINING

Utah boasts a variety of restaurants and lodgings. This book focuses on unique bed-and-breakfast inns and restaurants with local character. National chain hotels and motels are provided on occasion, as are bare-bone alternatives to pricey accommodations and eateries—a budget motel and a greasy spoon that local folks frequent. Of course, you can't get much cheaper than setting up a tent and eating homemade sandwiches.

Every attempt was made to ensure the accuracy of the details in each chapter, including prices. But Utah's recent and rapid growth, as well as the upcoming 2002 Winter Olympics, has contributed to a number of changes that might not be reflected in this book. Tourism-related businesses seem to have been particularly affected by this growth spurt, and many have changed hands, expanded, or simply faded away.

Because the popularity of outdoors activities has grown dramatically in Utah, campers should secure campground reservations, whenever possible—this can't be stressed enough. Even backcountry permits may be limited for primitive camping in some forests and national parks.

Yes, you can get a drink in Utah. Utah's liquor laws are very complex, and they are likely to change before and after the world descends upon the state in 2002 for the Olympic Winter Games. In 1998 you could buy package liquor and wine only in state liquor stores. Beer was available in many grocery and convenience stores. Most bars served only beer. Liquor, beer, and wine were available mostly in private clubs, where weekly memberships were available to tourists. Some restaurants had licenses to serve only beer, some to serve all types of alchohol. But many restaurants opted not to sell any alcohol. It might be best to call ahead if you want a drink to make sure the place where you're planning to eat serves alcohol.

Smoking is not allowed in most public buildings in Utah, including restaurants.

RECOMMENDED READING

For a general overview of the people, landscapes, and history of the state, read a couple of the books that were published as part of Utah's centennial celebration in 1996. *Faces of Utah: A Portrait*, edited by Shannon R. Hoskins (Gibbs Smith, 1996), is a pictorial documentary of Utah's people. Some of the most spectacular Utah scenery, photographed by Tom Till, is found in *Utah: A Centennial Celebration*, by Brooke Williams (Westcliffe, 1995).

Great and Peculiar Beauty: A Utah Reader (Gribbs Smith, 1995) is a collection of essays about Utah, edited by Thomas Lyon and Terry Tempest Williams. *Utah: The Right Place/The Official Centennial History* (Gribbs Smith, 1995), written by Thomas Alexander, is a comprehensive history book.

Each of Utah's 29 counties commissioned separate books detailing their history to celebrate the centennial. Other books with a historical perspective of the state include: Kathleen Thompson's *Utah* (Raintree, 1986) which is from the series "Portrait of America," Milton Hunter's *Utah in Her Western Setting* (Deseret News Press, 1946), and Charles Peterson's *Utah* (Norton, 1977) which was published as part of a national bicentennial series. A detailed history of Utah can be found in the *Utah History Encyclopedia*, edited by Allan Kent Powell (University of Utah Press, 1994). But it may be difficult to find outside Utah—it's not the kind of book you'd read cover to cover.

Another hard-to-find, but worth-the-effort book is *The Restored Church*, by William Berrett (Deseret Book Co., 1974). This book is written like a junior high school textbook, but it describes and explains the Mormon Church better, perhaps, than any other publication. Another author, Leonard Arrington, has spent decades documenting the state's history, including it's Mormon pioneers. Three of his books worth note are: *Brigham Young: American Moses* (A.A. Knopf, 1985), *Great Basin Kingdom: An Economic History of the Latter-Day Saints 1830–1900* (Harvard University Press, 1958), and *The Mormon Experience: A History of Latter-Day Saints* (University of Illinois Press, 1992).

Wallace Stegner spent a great deal of time in Utah and the West. You can see their influence in his writing, especially in his 1964 book *The Gathering of Zion: The Story of the Mormon Trail*. Zane Grey fans are already familiar with his famous *Riders of the Purple Sage*, which was set in southwestern Utah in 1871. Acclaimed author Norman Mailer also featured Utah when he wrote *The Executioner's Song* (Little Brown, 1979) about the last year of Gary Gilmore's life before he was executed in early 1977 for murdering two people.

Women are often forgotten in Utah's history, but Colleen Whitley made up for it with the book *Worth Their Salt/Notable But Often Unnoted Women of Utah* (Utah State University Press, 1996).

If you're looking for something about the Great Salt Lake, try either of two books with the same title: *Great Salt Lake*, edited by J. Wallace Gwynn (Utah Geological and Mineral Survey, 1980) and *Great Salt Lake* by Dale Morgan (Bobbs-Merrill, 1947) which was part of the "American Lakes" series. The fantastic rock formations that cover the state are explained in *Roadside Geology of Utah* by Halka Chronic (Mountain Press, 1990). One of the best books about the first Utahns is *Canyon Country Prehistoric Indians* by Barnes and Pendleton (Wasatch, 1979). It covers the native American cultures, ruins, artifacts, and rock art in Utah.

Edward Abbey is legendary in Utah. He described life as a ranger at Arches National Park in *Desert Solitaire*, and wrote the book that inspired many of today's active environmentalists, *The Monkey Wrench Gang*. Terry Tempest Williams is the naturalist in residence at the Utah Museum of Natural History on the University of Utah campus. A sampling of her works include: *Desert Quartet* (Pantheon Books, 1995), *Pieces of White Shell: A Journey to Navajoland*, (Scribner, 1984), and *Refuge* (Pantheon Books, 1991).

Of course, there are numerous hiking, climbing, biking, and skiing guides to Utah, some of which cover portions of the state, some of which cover all of it. One of the best overall hiking books is *Hiking Utah*, by Dave Hall (Falcon, 1996).

I
SALT LAKE CITY

Utah's capital city is, in many ways, a small model of the entire state. The Mormon pioneers made their way across the plains and over the mountains to arrive in Utah in 1847 in what historian John McCormick said was their "religious utopia in the wilderness." Shortly after the first pioneers arrived in Utah, Mormon converts, mostly from European countries, started arriving in Salt Lake City.

Salt Lake City streets, like those in many Mormon communities throughout the West, were laid out in a grid system based on Mormon Church founder Joseph Smith's ideas for the city of Zion. The Salt Lake City LDS Temple was completed in 1892, about 23 years before the capitol was built. That illustrates the important role the Mormon Church has always played in Salt Lake City, which remains the world headquarters for the church.

The city was a crossroads for many travelers, beginning with the California gold rush. After that, prospectors moved into Utah's mountains (Brigham Young discouraged Mormons from prospecting for precious metals). Then, the transcontinental railroad brought even more non-Mormons to the Mormon Zion. Although a majority of Salt Lake City's residents are non-Mormons, the LDS faith is the largest single faith in the capital city and throughout most of the state.

Salt Lake City's economy slowed during the Great Depression and boomed during World War II. In the 1960s the city joined the growing trend to establish suburban areas. Two decades later, efforts to beautify the city got underway. Ranked as one of the best environments for business, today the Salt Lake City area has a high concentration of biomedical, high-tech, and software firms. The world will get a close look at Salt Lake City during the 2002 Winter Olympics.

A PERFECT DAY IN SALT LAKE CITY

The best place to start is Temple Square. Guides, usually Mormon missionaries, provide tours and offer brief explanations about the church's history and doctrine. Next, you should tour other historic buildings, monuments, and museums downtown that are related to the Mormon Church. The Beehive House, the Eagle Gate, and the Museum of Church History and Art are a few examples. Don't forget to visit the State Capitol, up on the hill. Its hallways are a museum, with exhibits from a Mormon race car to the USS *Utah* memorial. If you have time, drive out to Saltair and take a quick look at the Great Salt Lake. At the end of the day, enjoy a sumptuous Italian dinner at Al Fornos.

GETTING AROUND

Like most Utah cities, Salt Lake City was designed on a grid system of streets. They are numbered with corresponding directions. The center of Salt Lake City's grid is South Temple Street and Main Street, at the southeast corner of Temple Square. Although Main Street is one baseline for the grid system, a parallel street one block east, State Street, is the city's main north-south street.

Buses are easy to catch and soon the city will be served by a light rail system. Don't waste your time trying to find a place to park on the streets. There are many affordable parking garages downtown.

SIGHTSEEING HIGHLIGHTS

★★★★ STATE CAPITOL
Capitol Hill, 801/538-3000
After Utah territory leaders realized that Fillmore was too far away and too isolated to serve as the capital city, they decided to build the capitol in Salt Lake City. Completed in 1915 and built of Utah granite at a cost of $2.7 million, the state capitol overlooks most of the city. It houses the governor's office, house and senate chambers, and the state supreme court. The hallways are filled with numerous

---

exhibits, including photographs and statues. Visitors are welcome in the fourth-floor galleries in each legislative chamber during sessions, which run for 45 days in January and February.

Details: Located at the northernmost end of State St. Guided tours every half hour Mon–Fri 9–4. Free. (2 hours)

★★★★ TEMPLE SQUARE
Bounded by North Temple, South Temple, West Temple, and Main Sts., 801/240-2534

The mecca for members of the Mormon Church, Temple Square is the most-seen tourist attraction in Utah. The 10-acre city block, enclosed by 15-foot walls, is home to the Salt Lake City LDS Temple. Construction of the six-spired temple started in 1853 and took 40 years to complete. The building is sacred to Mormons, and it is not open to the public. The tabernacle, however, is open to the public. It is home to the world-famous Mormon Tabernacle Choir. It seats 6,500 people under the world's largest domed roof without center supports. The building has incredible acoustics, and, if you're lucky, your tour guide will demonstrate this with the drop of a pin.

The square is illuminated with more than 300,000 lights at Christmas time, making it a worthwhile visit during the yuletide season.

Details: Guided tours begin at the flagpole, every 10 minutes daily, 9 a.m.–9 p.m. Free. (45 minutes). The public is invited to the choir's rehearsals, Thu 8 p.m. Organ recitals during the summer Mon–Sat noon and 2 p.m., Sun 2 p.m.; in winter Mon–Sat noon, Sun 2 p.m. (2 hours)

★★★ BEEHIVE HOUSE
67 East South Temple St., 801/240-2671

Imagine a home that is decorated with beehives—Utah's symbol for industry—right down to the doorknobs. Salt Lake City has such a house. It was Brigham Young's home and office when he was second president of the Mormon Church and governor of the Utah territory. **The Lion House**, next door, which is not open to the public, housed 26 of Young's wives and his children. Nearby, at South Temple and State Street, is the **Eagle Gate**, which served as the entrance to Brigham Young's estate when it was erected in 1859. It has been moved several times since then.

Details: Tours Jun–Aug Mon–Fri 9:30–6:30, Sat 9:30–4:30, Sun 10–1; the rest of the year Mon–Sat 9:30–4:30, Sun 10–1. Free. (1 hour)

DOWNTOWN SALT LAKE CITY

★★★ PIONEER MEMORIAL MUSEUM
300 North Main St., 801/538-1050

This Daughters of Utah Pioneers museum houses 38 rooms of exhibits detailing Utah's past, from a polygamist family's spoon collection to a model of the city's Salt Palace made out of—what else—salt. You can also see wreaths made from women's hair. The museum contains historic vehicles and farm machinery, too.

Details: Open Mon–Sat 9–5. Free. (1 hour minimum)

★★ FAMILY HISTORY LIBRARY
35 North West Temple St., 801/240-2331

This library is the largest repository for genealogical records in the world. Mormons are active in genealogical research because they believe their sacred ordinances, such as baptism, can be given retroactively, so to speak, to deceased ancestors. But you don't have to be a member of the Mormon Church to take advantage of this useful library. The genealogical records are open for anybody to use for research.

SIGHTS
Ⓐ Beehive House
Ⓑ Catholic Cathedral of the Madeleine
Ⓒ Children's Museum of Utah
Ⓓ Family History Library
Ⓔ Fort Douglas
Ⓕ Governor's Mansion
Ⓖ Greek Orthodox Church and Hellenic Cultural Museum
Ⓗ Hansen Planetarium
Ⓘ LDS Church Office Building
Ⓙ Pioneer Memorial Museum
Ⓚ Red Butte Garden and Arboretum
Ⓛ Rio Grande Depot Railroad and Utah Historical Society
Ⓜ State Capitol
Ⓝ Temple Square
Ⓞ Tracy Aviary
Ⓟ Utah Museum of Fine Arts
Ⓠ Utah Museum of Natural History

FOOD
Ⓡ Al Fornos
Ⓢ Baci Trattoria
Ⓣ Barking Frog
Ⓤ Bill and Nada's Cafe
Ⓥ Market Street Grill
Ⓦ Mikado
Ⓧ Old Salt City Jail
Ⓨ Pierpont Cantina
Ⓩ Red Iguana
ⓐ RedRock Brewing Company
ⓑ Squatter's

LODGING
Ⓧ Anniversary Inn
Ⓒ Armstrong Mansion Historic Bed-and-Breakfast
ⓓ Brigham Street Inn
ⓔ Perry Hotel
ⓕ Royal Executive Inn

Note: Items with the same letter are located in the same place.

Details: An orientation program is available. Mon 7:30–6, Tue–Sat 7:30 a.m.–10 p.m. Free. (1–2 hours)

★★ GOVERNOR'S MANSION
603 East South Temple St., 801/538-1005

Silver-mining executive Thomas Kearns built this home in the late 1800s or early 1900s. His widow gave the 36-room mansion to the state in 1937. It is now the official residence of Utah's governor, as well as the venue for a variety of public events. This restored home offers visitors a glimpse of how the rich and famous lived in the early twentieth century.

Details: Tours available by reservation. (1 hour)

★★ GREEK ORTHODOX CHURCH AND HELLENIC CULTURAL MUSEUM
279 South 300 West, 801/328-9681

Built in 1923, this cathedral was once in a section of the city called Greek Town. The Hellenic Cultural Museum is located in the lower level of the cathedral. It includes artifacts made by Greek immigrants in Utah. You'll find out about such things as the grueling work they did underground as miners in Castle Valley. It is the first museum in the United States devoted exclusively to Greek immigrants.

Details: Open Wed 9–noon, Sun about an hour after church. Also open by appointment. (1 hour)

★★ HANSEN PLANETARIUM
15 South State St., 801/538-2098

The planetarium features a space science museum with hands-on exhibits. See white dwarfs and red giants, and learn the difference between them during the planetarium's popular daily star shows. Laser/music concerts are also offered.

Details: Open Mon–Sat 9:30–9:30, Fri–Sat 9:30 p.m.–midnight, Sun 12:30–6 p.m. Museum is free. Star shows $4.50 adults, $3.50 kids. Laser shows $6.50 adults, $5 kids, $7.50 after 9 p.m. (2 hours)

★★ RIO GRANDE RAILROAD DEPOT AND UTAH HISTORICAL SOCIETY
300 South Rio Grande St., 801/533-3500

Marie J.T. Vigil

GREATER SALT LAKE CITY

N

40
189
248
224
Snyderville
Park City
Wasatch
National
Forest
WASATCH MOUNTAINS

B Brighton
Brighton Ski Area
E Solitude Ski Area
A
J D Alta Ski Area
Snowbird Ski Area

Mt. Olympus Wilderness Area

Cottonwood Canyon
Twin Peaks Wilderness Area
Little Cottonwood Canyon
Lone Peak Wilderness Area
190
210

65
Mill Creek Canyon
Emigration Canyon
L
Pioneer Trail State Park
80
C
186
F
University of Utah
1300 S ST
2300 E ST
3300 S ST
3900 S ST
4500 S ST
I
7000 S ST
HOLLADAY BLVD
Holladay
G
209
K
Sandy
10600 S ST
700 E ST
1300 E ST
H
M
700 E ST
VAN WINKLE EXPWY
71
STATE ST
Midvale
9400 S ST
15
89
South Salt Lake City
286
173
48
151
N
1700 W ST
REDWOOD RD
15
68
215
West Jordan
11800 S ST
2100 N ST
Salt Lake City International Airport
BANGARTER HWY
171
154
4700 S ST
6200 S ST
7800 S ST
172
2100 S ST
West Valley City
5600 W ST
8400 W ST
3500 S ST
4100 S ST
5400 S ST
111
BINGHAM HWY
OLD BINGHAM HWY
48
NORTH TEMPLE ST
201
Copperton
80
202
Kennecott Copper's Bingham Canyon Mine

Great Salt Lake

SCALE
0   6
KILOMETERS   MILES
0   6

PARK BOUNDARY
PLACE OF INTEREST
× PLACE OF INTEREST
HIGHWAY
ROAD

This historic railroad depot was built in 1910, shortly after the Union Pacific Depot down the street was completed in 1909. The Denver and Rio Grande Railroad donated the building to the state in 1978 to house the Utah Historical Society. Numerous changing exhibits on the state's history and prehistory, with an emphasis on the various ethnic groups that settled here, are on display. The society's offices and a research library are also located in the building.

Details: Open Mon–Fri 8–5, Sat 10–2. Free. (30 minutes–1 hour)

★ CATHOLIC CATHEDRAL OF THE MADELEINE
331 East South Temple St., 801/328-8941

This Catholic church is a Roman gothic–styled masterpiece, complete with magnificent stained-glass windows and elaborate artwork. It was built in 1909 and restored in 1993.

Details: You can see the cathedral during mass, which is still held in the historic building, or call to make a tour appointment. (1 hour)

★ CHILDREN'S MUSEUM OF UTAH
840 North 300 West, 801/328-3383

This is a hands-on discovery museum for kids as well as adults. Features here include a *Light Touch* exhibit where children can freeze their shadow with a light beam; a *Miniaturized Grocery Store* exhibit where children can pretend that they are buying groceries; and a *Nine-Mile Canyon* exhibit which provides a detailed summary of

SIGHTS
Ⓐ Alta
Ⓑ Brighton
Ⓒ Hogle Zoo
Ⓓ Snowbird
Ⓔ Solitude

FOOD
Ⓕ Bangkok Thai
Ⓖ La Caille
Ⓗ Salt Lake Pizza and Pasta

LODGING
Ⓘ Alpine Chalet
Ⓐ Alta Peruvian Lodge
Ⓙ Blacksmith Condominium Lodge
Ⓑ Brighton Lodge
Ⓓ Cliff Lodge
Ⓔ Inn at Solitude
Ⓚ Mountain Hollow Bed-and-Breakfast
Ⓚ Pinecrest Bed-and-Breakfast Inn
Ⓜ Wildflowers Bed-and-Breakfast

CAMPING
Ⓝ Camp VIP

Note: Items with the same letter are located in the same place.

Utah's history, as well as an excavation site where children can search for woolly mammoth bones.

Details: Open Mon–Thu and Sat 10–6, Fri 10–8. $3 adults and children, kids under 2 are free. (3 hours)

★ **HOGLE ZOO**
2600 East Sunnyside Ave., 801/582-1631
Near the mouth of Emigration Canyon, this small but wonderful zoo is home to a wide variety of exotic animals and plants. See monkeys and wolves as well as butterflies and gophers.

Details: Open in summer daily 9–6; spring and fall 9–5; Nov–Feb 9–4:30. $5 adults, $3 ages 4–14. (3–4 hours)

★ **LDS CHURCH OFFICE BUILDING**
50 East North Temple St., 801/240-2190
This is the tallest building in Salt Lake City. It serves as the world headquarters for the Mormon Church. Two observation decks are open to the public on the 26th floor.

Details: Tours Mon–Sat 9–4:30. Free. (1 hour)

★ **TRACY AVIARY**
589 East 1300 South, 801/596-8500
There are more than 1,000 birds on display here in the southwest end of Liberty Park. It's like a zoo, but all the animals have feathers. In addition to the exhibits, Free-flying bird shows are presented daily, as are several educational programs.

Details: Open in the summer 9–6; in the winter 9–4:30. $3 adults, $1.50 ages 5–12, kids under 4 are free. (2–3 hours)

UNIVERSITY OF UTAH SIGHTSEEING HIGHLIGHTS

This is Utah's oldest and largest public institution of higher learning. It was established by Mormon pioneers in 1850, just a few years after they arrived in the Salt Lake Valley. Originally called University of Deseret, it underwent numerous changes until 1894, when the name was changed to University of Utah. The institution moved to its present location in 1900, on land donated by the federal government. Utah's only medical school is located on campus, and it has received worldwide recognition for research and development in the field of artificial organs.

★★★ FORT DOUGLAS
32 Potter St., 801/588-5188
Federal land from this site was donated to the university at the turn of the century. The fort was built in the mid-1800s to house federal troops that were sent to Utah to keep the "Mormon threat" under control. A military museum features exhibits of U.S. and Utah military history from 1858 through Desert Storm.
Details: Open Tue–Sat 10–4. Free. (30 minutes)

★★★ UTAH MUSEUM OF FINE ARTS
1530 East 400 South, 801/581-7332
This museum may be the only general art museum in the state. It houses a permanent collection of paintings, sculpture, furniture, and tribal art from Europe, Asia, Africa, and the Americas. You can see Flemish paintings, Louis XIV furniture, Micronesian canoes, Mayan masks, and a Roman sarcophagus.
Details: Open Mon–Fri 10–5, Sat–Sun noon–5. Free. (2 hours)

★★★ UTAH MUSEUM OF NATURAL HISTORY
President's Circle, 801/581-4303
This is the museum where Utah school kids get to see bones. In fact, they can dig up a real mastodon skull in one of the museum's several hands-on exhibits. The building holds many exhibits about the plants and animals that are found throughout the state, as well as about the animals that roamed here long, long ago.
Details: Open Mon–Fri 9:30–5:30, Sat–Sun noon–5. $3 adults, $1.50 kids. (2 hours)

★★★ RED BUTTE GARDEN AND ARBORETUM
East of the university's research park, 801/581-5322
This is the state's premiere botanical garden. It contains four miles of nature trails and about 20 acres of tended flower and rock gardens. Tours are available.
Details: Open in summer daily 9–8; in winter Tue–Sun 10–5. $3 adults, $2 kids. (1–2 hours)

SKI RESORTS SIGHTSEEING HIGHLIGHTS
Utah's license plates call it the "greatest snow on earth." More than 500 inches of snow falls on Utah's mountains each year. The four resorts in Big Cottonwood Canyon

---

and Little Cottonwood Canyon, just above Salt Lake City, make a business out of that fresh white powder all year-round.

Little Cottonwood Canyon is home to Alta and Snowbird; Big Cottonwood Canyon is home to Brighton and Solitude. People have been skiing in these canyons, named for their abundance of cottonwood trees, long before skiing became a popular recreation industry. No one knows who first traversed the deep white powder in Utah's Wasatch Mountains. It's possible that mountain men used skis, as well as snowshoes, to hunt game and check their traps during the winter. Their skis were likely modeled after ones used by Norwegian immigrants, who had learned the value of using skis in their native country.

The establishment of the Wasatch Mountain Club in 1912 marked the beginning of organized touring groups that explored the local mountains for recreation. A few years later, the club started sponsoring winter outings into the surrounding canyons. The Brighton area was a popular destination for skiers on two- to four-day trips in the 1920s. About the same time, ski jumping became popular in the Salt Lake City foothills. Alf, Sverre, and Corey Engen's daring skills on skis attracted even more Utahns to the fledgling sport.

By the late 1930s, rope and cable tows were dragging skiers to the tops of hills and mountains from Logan to Provo. One of the first cable tows was in the Brighton area—a well-known summer resort for the well-to-do. But it was in Little Cottonwood Canyon that Utahns built their first aerial ski lift—it was the second one built in the country. The nearly dead mining town of Alta was reborn as a ski resort.

Solitude was added in the 1950s, and Snowbird opened in the 1970s. Today, Snowbird is also a summer resort, proving that the ski slopes can be enjoyed any time of year. The rich combination of history, heritage, modern facilities and amenities, and the beautiful Wasatch Mountains makes the Cottonwood Canyons a prime destination for locals as well as travelers from around the world.

★★★★ SNOWBIRD
Hwy. 210 in Little Cottonwood Canyon, 801/742-2222

Less than 30 minutes from downtown Salt Lake City, Snowbird has grown to become one of the most famous ski resorts in the world. California native Ted Johnson started acquiring property in the canyon (mostly abandoned mining claims, including the old Snowbird mine) in the mid-1960s. The resort opened in 1972, and two years later Johnson was bought out by Texas businessman Dick Bass—who later became the first person to climb the highest mountain on each continent. Bass wanted the resort to be the biggest and the best, perhaps a result of his Texas heritage. The resort's growth has been criticized by some people for its lavish use of concrete and the large structures that have been built.

Snowbird offers more than 2,500 acres of skiable terrain, served by one aerial tram, one high-speed detachable quad lift, and seven double lifts. The resort also offers snowcat and helicopter skiing on nearby slopes. It's not uncommon to find skiers on Snowbird's slopes as late as the Fourth of July.

In the summer, Snowbird is the place to go for hiking, mountain biking, volleyball, and tennis. The resort even stocks trout in Austin Pond so kids ages 12 and younger can try their luck at fishing. The resort also offers rock climbing clinics, a ropes course and an orienteering course, and paragliding. Snowbird can even make arrangements to fly you by helicopter to a nearby golf course. The resort sponsors a summer camp for kids ages 4 to 12, and team-building adventure programs for groups and businesses.

Details: (full day–1 week)

★★★ ALTA
Hwy. 210 in Little Cottonwood Canyon, 801/359-1078 or 801/742-3333

This resort is located at the upper end of Little Cottonwood Canyon, above Snowbird. The town of Alta was established a few years after silver was discovered in the area in 1864. At one point this mining town had 26 notorious saloons. But economic trouble in the late 1800s took its toll on this community. The population dropped from 3,000 in 1872 to 300 in 1880. By 1930 there were only six registered voters in Alta.

But all that soon changed. The Salt Lake City Winter Sports Association was formed by a group of businessmen and skiers. Using Sun Valley, Idaho as a model, they built Utah's first ski lift. On January 15, 1939, the lift carried 350 skiers up Collins Hill at a price of 25¢ a ride or $1.50 for a full day. Prices have increased since then, but locals still consider Alta one of the best ski resorts for the price ($28 for an adult all-day lift ticket in 1997).

Alta's 2,200 acres of skiable terrain are accessed by six double lifts, two triple lifts, and five surface tows.

Alf Engen directed the resort's ski school from 1948 to 1989. He had set world ski-jumping records and coached the U.S. Olympic Team in 1948. Engen and his two brothers helped bring attention to

RADIO STATION 550 AM

Little Cottonwood Canyon has its own radio station, 530 AM, which provides a looped message about traffic, road, and canyon conditions. It is cooperatively managed by the town of Alta, Alta Ski Lift Company, Snowbird, and the Utah Department of Transportation. Its message is intended to serve as a tool for making travel plans. If the highway is temporarily closed for avalanche control, for example, the station will try to broadcast that at least half an hour in advance.

the fledgling sport of skiing in Utah in the 1930s. Today, the ski school is run by his son Alan.

Details: *(full day–1 week)*

★★★ BRIGHTON

Hwy. 190 in Big Cottonwood Canyon, 801/532-4731

A rope tow was pulling skiers up the mountain here in 1936, two years before the first lift at Alta was built. In the late 1800s and early 1900s, the Brighton area was a well-known summer resort for affluent people from the Wasatch Front. During the winter of 1937/1938, county officials agreed to plow the road in Big Cottonwood Canyon. At the same time, members of the Alpine Ski Club fashioned a cable tow, which evolved into a T-bar tow, to pull skiers up the mountainside.

Today, Brighton has two high-speed quad lifts, two triple lifts, and three doubles serving 64 runs on 850 acres at the top of Big Cottonwood Canyon. It has 18 runs open for night skiing. Brighton was one of the first resorts in Utah to be fully open to snowboarders.

Hiking and mountain biking are popular activities at the resort during the summer, but the lifts don't run.

Details: *(full day–1 week)*

★★★ SOLITUDE

Hwy. 190 in Big Cottonwood Canyon, 801/534-1400

This Big Cottonwood Canyon resort was built in 1958. After a decade of ups and downs, it grew to become a respected resort. It is advertised as a family-oriented ski resort, with 63 named runs and three bowls covering 1,200 acres. The adjacent **Honeycomb Canyon**, served by the Summit Lift, provides another 400 acres of off-piste skiing with mostly expert runs. Solitude has one high-speed quad lift, two triple lifts, and four doubles.

Solitude is also home to the state's oldest Nordic skiing center. It has 20 kilometers of groomed trails, including a trail for kids.

Details: *(full day–1 week)*

SCENIC DRIVES

The highways that wind through both Big Cottonwood and Little Cottonwood Canyons have been designated as scenic byways. The seven-mile byway through Little Cottonwood Canyon affords motorists views of the sheer ruggedness and beauty of the glacier-carved corridor. Granite from the mouth of the canyon was quarried for construction of the Salt Lake City LDS temple. The church also uses the granite on the north side of the canyon to house its records vaults. The bombproof vaults, which are not open to the public, hold more than 5 million rolls of microfilmed geneological and other records. Albion Basin, at Alta, is famous for its wildflowers. The 15-mile byway in Big Cottonwood Canyon provides motorists with spectacular views of the erosive power of the rivers that carved this canyon. Because the canyon is a watershed area, no pets are allowed.

FITNESS AND RECREATION

There are lots of hiking and mountain biking trailheads just minutes away from downtown Salt Lake. The **Lake Blanche Trail**, in Big Cottonwood Canyon, is a fun and popular hike, while the trail leading to the **Pfeifferhorn**, or **Little Matterhorn**, in Little Cottonwood Canyon, provides a challenging hike and rewards hikers with views of Utah's spectacular rugged alpine country. There are also numerous rock climbing areas in the local mountains, and there are climbing gyms in town. Check with a local outdoor sporting goods store for information and guidebooks. The mountain rivers and streams are also popular among fly fishers.

In town, the **Jordan River Parkway**, which follows the Jordan River from the state fairgrounds to Rose Park Golf Course, is frequented by runners and joggers. Another favorite park among joggers is **Sugarhouse Park**, 2100 South 1300 East. The **Steiner Aquatic Center**, 801/583-9713, has an indoor and an outdoor pool near the University of Utah. Also check with the parks and

THE GREAT SALT LAKE AND KENNECOTT COPPER MINE

The Great Salt Lake is the largest lake west of the Mississippi River, and only the Dead Sea has a higher salt content. For the most part, it smells bad and is often infested with brine flies. It wouldn't be mentioned in this book if it weren't such a popular landmark in Utah. **Saltair Resort**, *about 17 miles west of the city on Interstate 80, Exit 104, 801/250-1822, was built in 1893 over the edge of the Great Salt Lake. It burned to the pillars in 1925 but was then rebuilt and abandoned in the 1950s. It suffered another fire in 1970 and was rebuilt, only to be flooded in the 1980s. Today, it has been renovated again and hosts concerts, dances, and receptions. Large historic photographs of the building can be found on the walls of the ballroom. Saltair is adjacent to* **Great Salt Lake State Park**, *801/531-8102. South of the lake is* **Kennecott Copper's Bingham Canyon Mine**. *Prospectors in the mid-1800s sought gold and silver here. But it wasn't until the late 1800s that they started mining copper. Today, this is the world's largest open-pit copper mine. Nearly 300,000 tons of copper are excavated here each year. The hole is more than half a mile deep and two and a half miles across. The visitors center has exhibits and a video presentation on the history, geology, and operation of the mine. Take the 9000 South Exit off Interstate 15, west of Salt Lake City, 801/252-3234. It's open April to October. Admission is $2 for motorcycles, $3 for cars, $15 for mini tour buses, and $30 for regular tour buses.*

recreation departments in the city, 801/972-7800, and the county, 801/468-2560. They operate 14 pools in the area. Most of the city and county parks also have tennis courts.

Each of the ski resorts offers—of course—skiing. The **Ski Utah Interconnect Adventure Tour**, 801/534-1907, offers a day-long, guided ski trip that hits each of the four resorts in the Cottonwood Canyons. **Wasatch Powderbird Guides**, 801/742-2800, offers helicopter skiing and snowboarding from Snowbird's helipad. Snowcat skiing is also available at Snowbird. In the back country in and around the

Cottonwood Canyons, cross-country skiing (both touring and telemark skiing) is very popular. **Solitude Nordic Center**, 801/534-1400, has 20 kilometers (about 12 miles) of cross-country skiing trails. It's even open some nights for moonlight skiing.

People still flock to the slopes at **Snowbird**, even during the summer. Rides are available on the tram year-round ($12 for adults, $9 for kids ages six to 16, $16 for an all-day mountain biking pass). The resort also has paragliding, tennis, volleyball, squash, racquetball, swimming pools, and a spa. There's an extensive network of trails at the resort. Hike the Gad Valley Trail to the top of Hidden Peak (where you can turn around and hike down or pay for a half-price ticket and ride the tram down). The Barrier-Free Interpretive Trail is wheelchair-accessible.

Mountain biking is allowed on many trails in the Wasatch and at the ski resorts. Snowbird and Solitude offer lift service for bike riders to the tops of their mountains. Rock climbing is another popular sport in the Cottonwood Canyons. One of the largest man-made climbing walls in the world is built onto the side of the Cliff Lodge at Snowbird.

If you can stand the smell, the Great Salt Lake is a good place for sailing. The beach at **Great Salt Lake State Park** is also popular among kite flyers.

There are several golf courses in the Salt Lake City area. **Bonneville**, 954 Conner Street, 801/583-9513, was built in 1929. This is a challenging course that requires accuracy on many drives. **Forest Dale**, 2375 South 900 East, 801/483-5420, is another of Utah's historic golf courses. Originally the Salt Lake Country Club, this course has small tabletop greens. **Glendale**, 1603 West 2100 South, 801/974-2403, is an open, beautiful course, but beware of the water—three lakes and the Jordan River are features here. **Mountain Dell**, in lower Parley's Canyon, 801/582-3812, has both a lake and a canyon course. The lake course is narrow, with lots of scrub oak along the boundaries. The canyon course is relatively new. It is very hilly, but not as difficult as other courses. **Nibley Park**, 2730 South 700 East, 801/483-5418, is a short nine-hole course with plenty of water hazards. **Wingpointe**, 3602 West 100 North, 801/575-2345, consistently ranks as one of the top golf courses in the state. Located next to Salt Lake International Airport, this nearly treeless course has several bunkers to keep play quite challenging.

FOOD

There are a lot of people who will drive more than an hour just to eat in Salt Lake City, mostly because it has such a large selection of excellent and diverse restaurants. **Al Fornos**, 239 South 500 East, 801/359-6040, is a fantastic

Italian restaurant, without exorbitant prices. But you'd never know it was a fine restaurant from the outside of its building (I've driven past it a number of times looking for it). Kids can draw on the tablecloths with crayons. **Salt Lake Pizza & Pasta**, 1063 East 2100 South, 801/484-1804, is another great and inexpensive Italian restaurant. It serves beer from several local microbreweries. Ask about their homemade ravioli. **Baci Trattoria**, 134 West Pierpont Avenue, 801/328-1500, is a fancier Italian restaurant with an artsy, cosmopolitan atmosphere. Its food is excellent, but the prices are a bit higher than other Italian eateries.

The **Market Street Grill**, 54 Market Street, 801/322-4668, is one of the best places to get fresh seafood—by itself or in omelets and sandwiches. There are always lots of specials here. Just down the street is the **Barking Frog**, 39 West Market Street, 801/322-3764, a trendy Southwestern restaurant that knows how to use chiles.

The **Red Iguana**, 736 West North Temple Street, 801/322-1489, is an excellent Mexican restaurant with moderate prices. Don't let the bullet holes in the windows scare you. It looks like a dive from the outside, but it has incredible food. Its specialty is molés, which are rich sauces concocted with chocolates and other Mexican and pre-Hispanic ingredients. The **Pierpont Cantina**, 122 West Pierpont Avenue, 801/364-1222, is another popular Mexican restaurant with slightly higher prices. It features fish tacos and more of a Tex-Mex variety of fajitas.

Squatter's, 147 West Broadway, 801/363-2739, was Salt Lake City's first brewpub. The food—mostly upscale, healthy pub fare—and beer are great, so don't be surprised if there's a crowd. Just down the street is **RedRock Brewing Company**, 254 South 200 West, 801/521-7446, popular for its woodburning pizza ovens and, of course, beer.

Mikado, 67 West 100 South, 801/328-0929, is a traditional Japanese restaurant and a favorite among downtown symphony and theater-goers. It offers a fine selection of fresh and cooked sushi. If you ever wanted to eat in jail, you can try the **Old Salt City Jail**, 460 South 1000 East, 801/355-2422, where you'll get to hear the sheriff sing on weekends while you dine on seafood and steaks. **Bangkok Thai**, 1400 South Foothill Drive, 801/582-THAI, is a favorite among vegetable lovers. Try the tea-smoked prawns. Be warned—some dishes can be quite spicey.

Bill and Nada's Cafe, 479 South 600 East, 801/359-6984, is a 24-hour coffee shop right out of the 1950s. But unlike the trendy, retro restaurants that are popping up in many cities, this restaurant's nostalgic setting is the real thing. A list of Salt Lake City restaurants wouldn't be complete without mentioning **La Caille**, 9565 South Wasatch Boulevard, 801/942-1751. This restaurant, one of the most expensive in town, is in a building that looks like a French chateau. This is "the" place to bring someone you want to impress with good food in a fantastic setting.

LODGING

A favorite among honeymooners and young couples in love is the somewhat pricey **Anniversary Inn**, 460 South 1000 East, 801/363-4900, which has themed rooms for that special getaway. Sleep in a covered wagon in Jackson Hole, or try a pirate ship or lighthouse. Each of the suites also offers guests an opportunity to bathe under a waterfall.

Other moderate to high-end lodging choices include the **Armstrong Mansion Historic Bed-and-Breakfast**, 667 East 100 South, 801/531-1333, which has 14 luxury suites in a Queen Anne–style mansion. **Brigham Street Inn**, 1135 East South Temple, 801/364-4461, with eight rooms and one suite in a more than 100-year-old Victorian home. **Wildflowers Bed-and-Breakfast**, 936 East 1700 South, 801/466-0600, is also in a Victorian. This quaint, comfortable home is tucked away in a sleepy little Salt Lake City neighborhood.

More moderately priced accommodations include the **Pinecrest Bed-and-Breakfast Inn**, 6211 Emigration Canyon, 801/583-6663, which is a historic home on a six-acre estate surrounded by pine trees and a spring-fed stream. **Mountain Hollow Bed-and-Breakfast**, 10209 South Dimple Dell Road, Sandy, 801/942-3428, is on a two-acre estate. It has 10 rooms ranging from simple "country style" rooms to the Mountaindew Suite, which has a living room and fireplace. The **Alpine Chalet**, 4235 South Lynne Lane, Holladay, 801/277-9300, look like—what else—a Swiss Alpine cottage. The somewhat fancy, historic **Perry Hotel**, 110 West 300 South, 801/521-4300, is yet another option among the moderately priced accommodations.

But if you just need a bed to sleep on—nothing fancy—try the **Royal Executive Inn**, 121 North 300 West, 801/521-3450. As some people have said, there's certainly nothing royal about it. It's just an ordinary motel, but it's the closest lodging facility to the Delta Center.

At the ski resorts, the **Alta Peruvian Lodge**, at Alta, 801/742-3000, has an outoor pool and hot tub, a bar, and a big-screen television on which movies are shown nightly during the winter. The 80 rooms are simple, but the management believes you don't spend a lot of time in your room anyway. Prices tend to be moderate to high for winter accommodations (rates are lower in the summer); the price includes three full meals a day. **Blacksmith**

Condominium Lodge, 801/742-3200, is on the ridge between Alta and Snowbird. Rather than offering meals, Blacksmith provides kitchens in each room. Prices here are moderate to expensive. The **Cliff Lodge**, 801/742-3300, Snowbird's flagship hotel, has a variety of rates ranging from budget to extravagant. You can't miss it. It's the one with the climbing wall up one side of the building. Rates at the **Inn at Solitude**, 801/536-5700, a 46-room full-service hotel, range from moderate to expensive. **Brighton Lodge**, 800/873-5512, is a rustic 20-room mountain lodge offering moderate prices.

CAMPING
There are a handful of Forest Service campgrounds in the mountains just above Salt Lake City (see Utah Valley chapter). Otherwise, you can stay at **Camp VIP**, a commercial campground at 1400 West North Temple Street, 801/328-0224, that has 500 RV and tent sites.

SHOPPING
There are several shopping malls in Salt Lake City. Three of the most popular are **ZCMI Center Mall**, 36 South State Street, **Crossroads Plaza**, 50 South Main Street, and **Trolley Square**, 600 South 700 East. The ZCMI department store is the centerpiece of the ZCMI mall. It was established by Mormon pioneers as a co-op called Zion's Cooperative Mercantile Institution. Crossroads is a multilevel shopper's paradise occupying the next block west of ZCMI. Trolley Square is farther east. The city's street cars were housed in this building during the first part of the twentieth century. Today it is a dining and entertainment center with unique shops and two theaters.

NIGHTLIFE
The **Zephyr Club**, 301 South West Temple, 801/355-5646, features nationally touring bands such as Los Lobos and Mojo Nixon and has good sound, balcony seating, and a dance floor. The **Dead Goat Saloon**, 165 South West Temple, 801/328-GOAT, looks like a typical smokey tavern, but the back room has a stage for local bands and, on a regular basis, nationally touring groups—particularly jazz and blues bands. It's got good hamburgers too. **Brewvies**, 677 South 200 West, 801/322-3891, is a unique business that combines a movie theater with a pub. Play pool, drink beer, and watch a movie. **Confetti**, 909 East 2100 South, 801/486-4261, is a dance club in what appears to be a converted garage. Alcohol is not

served at this club. **The Bay**, 404 South West Temple, 801/363-2623, is another dance club that does not serve alcohol. It has three levels, each featuring a different style of music. There's even a patio and a pool here. If you want to dance and you like the music loud, The **Holy Cow**, 241 South 500 East, 801/531-8259, is the place for you. But if you just want to catch up on your favorite sports action, stop by **Iggy's Sports Grill**, 677 South 200 West, 801/532-9999. They've got great food there too, but save room for the dessert.

PERFORMING ARTS

Salt Lake City is home to numerous art galleries. It is also home to the **Utah Symphony**, 123 West South Temple, 801/533-5626, which features a special pop series in addition to their regular orchestral presentations; the **Utah Opera Company**, 801/355-ARTS; and **Ballet West**, 801/355-ARTS.

Other Salt Lake City performing art highlights include **Desert Star Playhouse**, 4861 South State Street, 801/266-7600, which presents musical comedy melodramas; **Hale Centre Theatre**, 3333 South Decker Lake Drive, 801/984-9000, which offers a variety of plays; **Off Broadway Theatre**, 272 South Main Street, 801/355-4628; and the **Salt Lake Community College Grand Theatre**, 1575 South State Street, 801/957-3322, which presents a variety of musical productions.

PROFESSIONAL SPORTS

Sports fans can catch the **Utah Jazz** basketball team at the Delta Center, 801/325-2500; the **Salt Lake Buzz** baseball team, a AAA affiliate of the **Minnesota Twins**, at Franklin Quest Field, 801/485-3800; and the **Utah Grizzlies** hockey team, 801/530-7166.

2
OGDEN AREA

Nestled between the Great Salt Lake and the northern end of the Wasatch Mountains, Ogden has been an important crossroads for fur trappers, railroads, and, more recently, the military. It is Utah's largest city north of Salt Lake City, and its rich history is filled with the stuff that conquered the Wild West.

Ogden is full of history. You can visit the region's first settlement, Fort Buenaventura, which was built in the 1830s along the Weber River to serve westbound immigrants. Miles Goodyear built and lived in a cabin there that still stands—although it has been moved—and today it is part of a pioneer museum collection. A few blocks away, you can see the guns that gave the West its rip-roarin' reputation at the Browning Firearms Museum. And, just outside the building are the mighty railroad engines that pulled trainloads of people and supplies to Ogden and the West.

The city thrived as a railroad center from 1869, the year the golden spike was driven into the ground. In fact, the transcontinental railroad was built through nearby Weber Canyon, and Ogden's Union Station was the hub of railroad traffic for half a century.

Since the decline of the railroad after World War II, Ogden has grown as a military town. Hill Air Force Base employs thousands of military and civilian personnel. Many of the air force's historic warbirds are on display at the base's Aerospace Museum. Ogden is also the home of regional offices for the Internal Revenue Service and the U.S. Forest Service.

To the north, Ogden Canyon is the gateway to three ski resorts—Snowbasin, Nordic Valley, and Powder Mountain. To the south, Ogden serves as a gateway to Antelope Island—the largest island in the middle of the Great Salt Lake.

A PERFECT DAY IN THE OGDEN AREA

If you've got kids and you're driving north from Salt Lake City, you may not make it any farther than Ogden's southern neighbor, Farmington—home of Lagoon amusement park and Pioneer Village. That's okay. Enjoy a ride on Utah's only wooden roller coaster. But try to make it to Ogden to take in the Hill Aerospace Museum and marvel at the giant warbirds. Then head west across the Great Salt Lake's causeway to Antelope Island, where buffalo (actually, bison) roam and deer play. After taking a short hike, drive back to the city and see Union Station's railroad and firearms museums. Finish the day on 25th Street, just east of the station, where many restaurants, bars, and nightclubs line the historic street.

SIGHTSEEING HIGHLIGHTS

★★★★ **HILL AEROSPACE MUSEUM**
7961 Wardleigh Rd. (Exit 341 off I-15), 801/777-6818
Several historic aircraft are on display at the museum, including an SR-71 Blackbird spy plane, a B-17 Flying Fortress, a giant B-52, and a sleek P-51D Mustang. Aircraft, missiles, engines, bombs, and other artifacts are on display inside the 52,000-square-foot building and outside surrounding the building. Self-guided walking tours let visitors view the aircraft up close. An eight-minute film about the history of adjacent Hill Air Force Base is shown continuously. Keep your eye to the skies—you might see squadrons from the air force's 388th Fighter Wing and the air force reserve's 419th Fighter Wing.
Details: *Open daily 9–4:30. A gate pass for Hill Air Force Base is not required to visit the museum. Free. (3 hours)*

★★★★ **UNION STATION**
2501 Wall Ave., 801/629-8444 or 801/629-8535
Built in 1924, this was the hub for transcontinental rail traffic for more than half a century. Today, it houses a restaurant and several museums, and serves as a civic center and exhibition hall. In addition to housing the **Utah State Railroad Museum**, which features films

and railroad memorabilia, Union Station is home to the **Wattis-Dumke Model Railroad Museum**, which features HO scale model railroads with a dozen trains running on eight different layouts, and the **Spencer S. and Hope F. Eccles Railroad Center**—an outdoor pavilion featuring historic Union Pacific engines and cabooses.

But Union Station is about more than just railroad museums. The building is also home to the **Browning Firearms Museum**, featuring the Winchesters, Colts, Remingtons, and other guns that John Browning and three subsequent generations of Brownings designed and manufactured. Many prototypes are on display, as are modern weapons that are being built and used today. Historical photographs and artifacts of John Browning accompany the exhibits, and an informative slide show illustrates the Browning legacy.

Union Station is also home to the **Browning-Kimball Car Collection**, featuring classic automobiles from the early 1900s ranging from a single-cylinder 1901 Oldsmobile to a 16-cylinder, three-ton Cadillac. The **Myra Powell Gallery** is located on the second floor. It features rotating shows by local and world-renowned artists, and traveling exhibits from national collections. As if that weren't enough, Union Station is also home to a small natural history museum, where you can see "The Lady," the largest crystal ever faceted—44,472 carats. And don't miss the table where rocks resembling food are being served.

Details: Open Mon–Sat 10–6; also open Sun noon–5 in summer. $3 adults, $1 kids under age 12. (3 hours)

★★★ ANTELOPE ISLAND STATE PARK
Call 801/625-1630 for recorded info.

At 28,000 acres, this island in the middle of the Great Salt Lake is Utah's largest state park. The island was named after the pronghorn antelope found on the island in 1845 by Captain John C. Fremont. The island was inaccessible in the 1980s because high water in the lake made the causeway dangerous. The seven-mile causeway has since been rebuilt, and the island is once again a popular destination for tourists and locals alike. One of the biggest attractions on the island is a herd of bison that has grown from 12 head in 1893 to more than 600 head today. Several other types of animals also inhabit the island, including deer, bobcats, coyotes, and numerous shorebirds and waterfowl. Camping, hiking, biking, horseback riding, swimming,

DOWNTOWN OGDEN

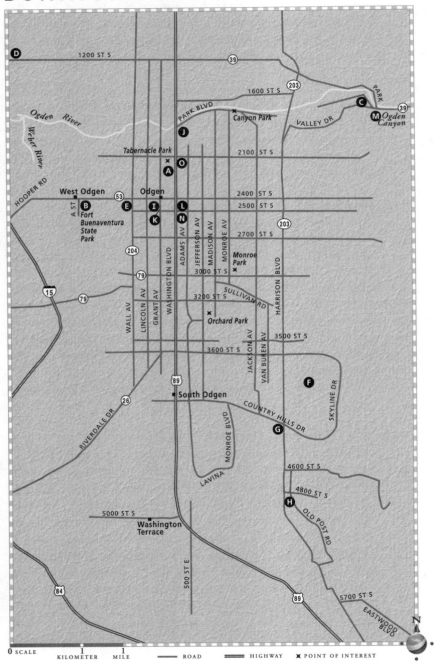

and sunbathing are popular activities on Antelope Island. It also provides a unique vantage point from which to see the Great Salt Lake.

Details: Exit 335 off I-15, drive west on Hwy. 127 across the causeway. Open summer daily 7 a.m.–10 p.m. $7/vehicle, $3 bikers and walkers. (2 hours)

★★★ GEORGE S. ECCLES DINOSAUR PARK
1544 East Park Blvd., 801/393-DINO or 801/629-8290

Imagine a park filled with more than 100 different dinosaurs and other prehistoric creatures from the Cretaceous, Jurassic, and Triassic periods. But unlike the real creatures, these creatures are perfectly harmless because they are only life-size metal sculptures. The park is a wonderful educational outing and offers a unique backdrop for a family picnic.

Details: Open May–Labor Day Mon–Sat 10–8, includes holidays; late May–early Sep Sun noon–6; Mar–May and Sep–Oct shorter hours. $3.50 adults, $1.50 kids, $2.50 seniors. (1–2 hours)

★★★ LAGOON
375 North Lagoon Dr. (Exit 327 off I-15), Farmington 801/451-8000

About 15 miles south of Ogden, a giant Ferris wheel beckons motorists to Utah's largest amusement park. Its predecessor, Lake Park, was built in 1886 as a bathing resort on the Great Salt Lake. It closed in 1893 and was rebuilt three years later on the outskirts of Farmington—two miles inland from the lake. One of the first rides was

---

SIGHTS
Ⓐ Daughters Utah Pioneers Museum and Miles Goodyear Cabin
Ⓑ Fort Buenaventura State Park
Ⓒ George S. Eccles Dinosaur Park
Ⓓ Odgen Nature Center
Ⓔ Union Station
Ⓕ Weber State University

FOOD
Ⓖ Bavarian Chalet
Ⓗ Berconi's
Ⓘ La Ferrovia
Ⓙ Prairie Schooner
Ⓚ Roosters
Ⓛ Señor Frogs Mexican Place
Ⓜ Timber Mine
Ⓔ Union Grill

LODGING
Ⓝ Historic Radisson Suite Hotel
Ⓣ Ogden Marriott Hotel
Ⓞ Travelodge

CAMPING
Ⓑ Fort Buenaventura State Park

Note: Items with the same letter are located in the same place.

---

a carousel, which is still in operation today. The park also features Utah's only wooden roller coaster, a restored pioneer village, and a water park.

Details: *Open Memorial Day–Labor Day Sun–Fri 11 a.m., Sat 10 a.m.; closing time varies from Sun at 10:30 p.m. to Fri and Sat at midnight. The park is open only on weekends in Apr, May, and Sep. It is closed the rest of the year except for special events. $26.95 adults over 51 inches in height, $20.95 kids over age 4 and under 51 inches, $13.95 toddlers and seniors. (full day)*

★★ DAUGHTERS OF UTAH PIONEERS MUSEUM AND MILES GOODYEAR CABIN
2148 Grant Ave., 801/393-4460

Goodyear was Ogden's first permanent settler. His cabin was originally located at Fort Buenaventura. The cabin, which was built in 1845, is believed to be the oldest homestead in Utah. In 1848, when he moved to California, he sold the cabin to Mormon settlers. He died the following year. In 1928 the cabin was moved to Ogden's LDS Temple Square. Today, it is part of the Daughters of Utah Pioneers Museum collection, which includes photographs, artifacts, and memorabilia from Utah's pioneer era in a building adjacent to the cabin.

Details: *Open summer Mon–Sat 10–5. Tours can be arranged during the off-season. Free. (1 hour)*

★★ FORT BUENAVENTURA STATE PARK
2450 South A Ave., 801/392-5581

A replica of the fort built by Miles Goodyear is the centerpiece of this 84-acre state park along the Weber River. Facilities include a trading post, visitors center, and a picnic area. Guides in mountain-man costumes explain the history of the fort and the lifestyles of the people who lived in the area when the fort was used.

Details: *Open Mar–Nov 8–dark. $3/vehicle, $1 bikers and walkers. (1 hour)*

★★ OGDEN NATURE CENTER
966 West 12th St., 801/621-7595

This facility, nestled between the Internal Revenue Service's regional office and the Ogden Defense Depot, is a 127-acre wildlife sanctuary with nature trails, six ponds, and educational programs. The center provides wild animals with a refuge from nearby urban development. A gift shop and visitors center were built at the sanctuary using wood from pilings that once supported a railroad trestle across a section of the Great Salt Lake. Tours are available.

Details: *Open Mon–Sat 10–4; closed Sun, major holidays, and the last two weeks of Dec. $1 general admission. (1–2 hours)*

★★ OUR LADY OF THE HOLY TRINITY ABBEY
1250 South 9500 East, Huntsville, 801/745-3784

Catholic monks have been living and working at this monastery since 1947. They raise cattle and crops on an 1,800-acre farm, and sell honey, peanut butter, and whole-wheat cereal from a bookstore and gift shop to cover their expenses.

The monks belong to the Cistercian Order, popularly called "Trappists," which dates back to the seventeenth century, when reforms were made in the Cistercian monastery of La Trappe in northern France. They are "white monks," in contrast to the traditional black-clad Benedictine monks.

Their day starts with a prayer service at 3:30 a.m. Throughout the rest of the day, they gather several times for prayers, a morning mass, and meals. They also work and devote themselves to study and meditation. Unlike monks in other religious orders, who are engaged in teaching or the ministry, the monks at Holy Trinity Abbey are devoted to a life of communal and private prayer.

Visitors of all faiths are welcome to attend daily mass at the monastery and to participate in individual retreats. At one time, only men were allowed to participate in these retreats, but in recent years, women have been welcomed at the monastery when the nearby guest house is not being used by relatives of the monks.

Details: *Mass daily at 6:20 a.m. (1 hour)*

★★ WEBER STATE UNIVERSITY
Between 3700 and 4400 Harrison Blvd., 801/626-6000

Founded in 1889, WSU is renowned for its health professions, education, technology, and business fields. Weber State was the first higher education institution to build a satellite and have it sent into space. The campus is graced by landmarks such as the 100-foot Stewart Carillon Bell Tower and the Ada Lindquist Plaza Fountain. The **Dee Event Center**, on campus, is host to a wide variety of events, from theatre and performing arts to concerts and sporting events. For ticket and schedule information, call 801/626-8500. The **Ice Sheet**, 4390 Harrison Boulevard, next to the Dee Event Center, 801/399-8750, is an Olympic-size ice arena built for the 2002 Winter Olympics and is open to the public.

Weber State University is also home to the **Collett Art Gallery**, which features ongoing exhibits and lectures on contemporary art. Call the Department of Visual Arts, 801/626-7689, for more information. The **Museum of Natural Science**, in Lind Lecture Hall, 801/626-6653, features free exhibits, from prehistoric animals to open-heart surgery. Upstairs from the museum is the **Layton Ott Planetarium**, 801/626-6855, which offers star shows on Wednesday nights at 6:30 p.m. and 7:30 p.m. during the fall, winter, and spring. Admission is $2.

Details: (half day)

FITNESS AND RECREATION

The Ogden area is a paradise for outdoor recreation. Camping, hiking, hunting, and fishing opportunities abound in the region. Numerous hiking trails crisscross the northern part of the Wasatch Mountains between Mount Ogden and Ben Lomond Peak—including easy hikes in the foothills and difficult treks to the mountain peaks. Two of the most popular trails are **Indian Trail** and **Skyline Trail**. Mountain biking and rock climbing are also popular activities in the local mountains, where many trailheads and climbing crags can be reached from Ogden and Weber Canyons. The **U.S. Forest Service**, 801/625-5306, and **Utah State Parks**, 801/538-7220, can provide details on trails, roads, facilities, and regulations.

The mountains are also popular for cross-country and alpine skiers. Recently, **Snowbasin**, 801/399-1135, had five lifts serving 1,800 skiable acres. But work was under way to improve the ski resort, which will host Olympic athletes during the 2002 Winter Games. Nearby **Powder Mountain**, 801/745-3771, has seven lifts serving 1,600 skiable acres and offers rides on snowcats for the best of skiing in untracked powder. And **Nordic Valley**, 801/745-3511, has two lifts serving 85 skiable acres. All three resorts are accessible from Ogden Canyon and allow snowboarders.

Antelope Island is a playground for people who like to hike, bike, horseback ride, and swim.

Pineview Reservoir is a popular fishing and boating spot. Streams are also strong attractions for people with rods and reels. Trout are abundant in the Ogden, Weber, and South Fork Rivers. Rocky Mountain whitefish can also be found in the Weber and South Fork Rivers. Small-mouth bass are stocked in the lower Weber River, west of Interstate 15.

In town the **Ogden River Parkway** attracts all sorts of fitness-minded people. The three-mile parkway follows Ogden River from the mouth of Ogden Canyon to Washington Boulevard. It links six separate parks with scenic walkways and bike trails. Ice-skating is possible year-round at the **Ice Sheet**, 801/399-8750, next to the Dee Events Center on the Weber State University campus. And several area golf courses lure people to the links—including **Mount Ogden Golf Course**, 3000 Taylor Avenue, 801/629-8700, which is perhaps the toughest course in the region. **Ben Lomond Golf Course**, 1800 North U.S. Highway 89, Harrisville, 801/782-7754, is a relatively flat course with fine greens. **Riverside Golf Course**, 5460 South Weber Drive, 801/399-4636, is neither long nor tough, but it's fun.

FOOD

There are several Italian restaurants in the Ogden area. One of the best is **La Ferrovia**, 234 25th Street, Ogden, 801/394-8628. It's a quaint, family-run business on a historic street, offering a modest selection of pastas and calzones without a big price tag. There's nothing fancy here, but the food is great. The restaurant features authentic southern Italian recipes and an excellent house salad dressing. Another great Italian restaurant is **Berconi's**, 4850 Harrison Boulevard, 801/479-4414. Complete with red gingham tablecloths and candles, this eatery features several varieties of pasta and pizza and is near the Weber State University campus.

Across the street from La Ferrovia is a popular brewpub, **Roosters**, 253 25th Street, 801/627-6171, featuring hand-crafted beers and upscale pub fare. At the end of the block, in historic Union Station, is **Union Grill**, 2501 Wall Avenue, 801/621-2830. It's easy to imagine the customers who may have grabbed a bite to eat in the old depot before climbing aboard one of the trains nearly half a century ago. This grill features upscale sandwiches, soups, and salads. Southwestern foods like fajitas are available at the popular **Señor Frogs Mexican Place**, 455 25th Street, 801/394-2323.

If you're looking for a steak in a western setting, try either the Timber Mine or Prairie Schooner. The **Timber Mine**, 1701 Park Boulevard, 801/393-2155, offers steak and seafood. It is surrounded by old mining decor and is located near the mouth of Ogden Canyon. The **Prairie Schooner**, 445 Park Boulevard, 801/392-2712, is renowned for its large portions. It also serves diners in covered wagons. Check the daily seafood special.

OGDEN AREA

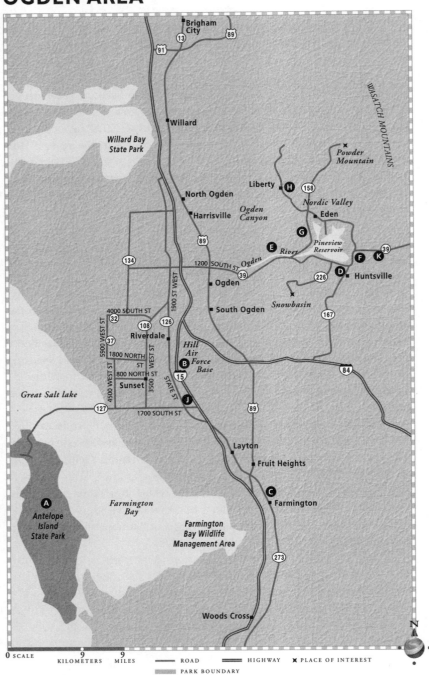

Brigham City
89
13
91

Willard

Willard Bay
State Park

WASATCH MOUNTAINS

Powder Mountain ✕

Liberty H 158

Nordic Valley

North Ogden

Ogden Canyon

Harrisville

Eden

G

Pineview Reservoir

E River F K 39

1200 SOUTH ST Ogden 39

134

1900 ST WEST

Ogden

226 D Huntsville

South Ogden

Snowbasin ✕

167

4000 SOUTH ST

32

108 126

37

Riverdale

Hill Air Force Base

84

1800 NORTH ST

800 NORTH ST

Sunset

B

5900 WEST ST

4500 WEST ST

3500 WEST ST

STATE ST

15

J

Great Salt lake

127

1700 SOUTH ST

89

Layton

Fruit Heights

C

A

Antelope Island State Park

Farmington Bay

Farmington

Farmington Bay Wildlife Management Area

273

Woods Cross

N

0 SCALE   9   9
KILOMETERS   MILES   ━━━ ROAD   ═══ HIGHWAY   ✕ PLACE OF INTEREST
▨ PARK BOUNDARY

If German fare is what you're looking for, go to the **Bavarian Chalet**, 4387 Harrison Boulevard, 801/1479-7561. This establishment is run by two German immigrants. The dinner-only restaurant features authentic schnitzels, sauerbraten, and sausage—as well as homemade *apfelstrudel*.

LODGING

Moderately priced accommodations include the **Alaskan Inn** bed-and-breakfast, 435 Ogden Canyon, 801/621-8600, which has 12 rooms, each with a different Alaskan theme. The inn is surrounded by mountains and a nearby river. Another option is the **Heritage Inn** bed-and-breakfast, 7355 East 200 South, Huntsville, 801/745-3226, which has two rooms and is near Pineview Reservoir on the eastern side of the Wasatch Mountains. It even offers a babysitting service. It may be a bit out of the way—11 miles east of Ogden—but the quiet, rural setting is worth it if you want to relax.

Also in Huntsville is the reasonably priced **Jackson Fork Inn**, 7345 East 900 South Highway 39, 801/745-0051. The rustic dairy barn has been renovated into a dinner house and eight-room inn. The two-story rooms have beds in a loft area accessible by a spiral staircase.

On the other side of Pineview Reservoir are the small towns of Eden and Liberty. Reasonably priced options in that area include the five-room **Snowberry Inn**, 1315 North Highway 158, Eden, 801/745-2634. It is a quaint bed-and-breakfast with spectacular views of the pastoral valley. The outdoor hot tub is an inviting feature after a long day. Golfers like the 30-room **Wolf Creek Resort**, 3720 North Wolfcreek Drive, Eden, 801/745-0222, because it is adjacent to Wolf Creek Golf Course in the rolling hills below Powder Mountain Ski Resort.

Farther north, in Liberty, the two-room **Vue De Valhalla** bed-and-breakfast, 2787 Nordic Valley Road, 801/745-2558, is priced right. It is also a favorite

SIGHTS	LODGING	CAMPING
Ⓐ Antelope Island State Park	**Ⓔ** Alaskan Inn	**Ⓘ** Century RV Park
Ⓑ Hill Aerospace Museum	**Ⓕ** Heritage Inn	**Ⓗ** North Fork Park
Ⓒ Lagoon	**Ⓕ** Jackson Fork Inn	**Ⓒ** Lagoon
Ⓓ Our Lady of the Holy Trinity Abbey	**Ⓖ** Snowberry Inn	**Ⓙ** National Forest Campgrounds
	Ⓗ Vue de Valhalla	**Ⓙ** Weber Memorial Park
	Ⓖ Wolf Creek Resort	

Note: Items with the same letter are located in the same place.

among duffers because it is located on the second fairway of the Nordic Valley Golf Course.

Closer to downtown Ogden is the moderately priced **Historic Radisson Suite Hotel**, 2510 Washington Boulevard, 801/627-1900, which dates back to 1890. The 11-story hotel boasts the original staircase that led to its luxurious ballrooms. It's easy to imagine its heyday—when 25th Street was alive with the hustle and bustle of a vibrant young city.

Additional downtown hotels include the reasonably priced, eight-story **Ogden Marriott Hotel**, formerly the Ogden Park Hotel, 247 24th Street, 801/627-1190, which is the city's largest full-service luxury hotel. Thrifty travelers might want to save some money and stay at the well-kept **Travelodge**, 2110 Washington Boulevard, 801/394-4563.

CAMPING

On a six-mile stretch of Utah Highway 39, near Huntsville, there are 10 National Forest campgrounds providing numerous tent and RV sites. All of them have restrooms and most have drinking water. The largest of the 10 campgrounds is **Anderson Cove**, two and a half miles southwest of Huntsville. It has 29 RV sites and 74 tent sites. The other National Forest campgrounds are: **Botts, Hobble, Jefferson Hunt, Lower Meadows, Magpie, Perception Park, South Fork**, and **Upper Meadows**. These campgrounds are open generally between May and September. For more information call 800/280-2267.

Weber County operates another campground along the same stretch of highway, **Weber Memorial Park**, 800/280-2267 which has 38 RV and 150 tent sites. The county also operates **North Fork Park**, near Liberty, 800/407-2757, which has 150 trailer and tent sites.

The state offers group camping only at **Fort Buenaventura**, 800/322-3770. It also has 64 RV sites and 11 tent sites that are available year-round on Antelope Island.

Century RV Park, 1399 West 2100 South, 801/731-3800, is a commercial facility with a pool, Laundromat, and showers. If you're planning to visit **Lagoon** in Farmington, 801/451-8000, the amusement park has its own commercial campground with 205 RV sites and 10 tent sites.

NIGHTLIFE

The clubs and restaurants along 25th Street have a long and bawdy history, dating back to a time when Ogden was a major hub for railroad traffic. The once infamous hotels and brothels have been transformed into a number of shops, bars, clubs, and restaurants. **City Club**, upstairs at 264 25th Street, 801/392-4447, is popular among Beatles fans because its decor is a hodge-podge collection of Fab Four memorabilia. Other popular hangouts include **Beatnik's**, 240 25th Street, a biker bar that has become popular for its live bands, and **Brewski's**, 244 25th Street, 801/394-1713.

The rip-roaring Wild West is still alive in Huntsville at the **Shooting Star Saloon**, 7350 East 200 South, 801/745-2002. This is one of the oldest operating taverns in the state. Much of the saloon's historic character is still intact, including a hitching post and a mounted Saint Bernard's head.

If you're looking for another kind of wildlife, head out to the ballpark and catch a game with the **Ogden Raptors**, a minor-league baseball team associated with the Milwaukee Brewers. Call 801/393-9313 for tickets.

PERFORMING ARTS

Catch a movie, play, or concert at the ornate **Egyptian Theater**, 2415 Washington Boulevard, 801/627-2117. The restored theater hosts a variety of performances, including those by Ballet West, the Utah Symphony and the Sundance Film Festival. The **Utah Musical Theater at Weber State University**, 801/626-8500, also offers performances in the Egyptian Theater.

WSU's Dee Events Center, 3750 Harrison Boulevard, 801/626-8500, is home to sporting events, concerts, plays, and other productions throughout the year. Performances by the **WSU's Department of Performing Arts**, 801/626-6437, and the **Ogden Symphony and Ballet Association**, 2580 Jefferson Avenue, 801/399-9214, are often listed on the center's marquee. The **Golden Spike Arena Events Center**, 1000 N. 1200 West, 801/399-8544, is home to the Weber County fair, as well as sporting events, concerts, conventions, and other shows. Another venue for live entertainment is the **Terrace Plaza Playhouse**, 99 W. 4700 South, South Ogden, 801/393-0070, which is renown for its repertory theater.

3
GOLDEN SPIKE
REGION

Tens of thousands of people have flocked to Promontory, a small section of the desert just north of the Great Salt Lake, to see gold—not a nugget, but a spike. Actually, the ceremonial gold and silver spikes that used to commemorate the completion of the first transcontinental railroad aren't on display. But replicas of the original steam engines that met on May 10, 1869, are there where east and west came together with the Union Pacific and Central Pacific railroads about 32 miles west of Brigham City.

Brigham City was settled by Mormons 18 years before the railroad's completion. They named their city after Mormon Church leader Brigham Young. It remains a primarily agricultural community today, with a typical small-town Main Street fronted by many homegrown businesses. It's hard to believe that just a short drive away, in Thiokol, the solid-fuel rocket motors that propel America's space shuttles into orbit are built.

Brigham City's rural heritage included a cooperative association that was developed to help the community sustain itself. That association, which included a store, woolen mill, sheep and dairy herds, and a hat factory, was used as a model for other cooperatives that were established in many Mormon communities throughout the state. A remnant of that original association, the woolen mill, remains in operation today. Its fine wool blankets are still the product of a program where finished goods are traded for raw wool and other supplies from producers in several states.

Several abandoned buildings, just off U.S. Highway 89, stand as a landmark in the city. They were used between 1950 and 1984 as a school for Native Americans. Before that, the site was home to Bushnell Hospital, where wounded veterans were treated during World War II. Today, a golf course winds its way around the buildings, which have captured the eyes of several developers who hope to convert the abandoned buildings to better uses.

Bathers have been attracted to the region's natural hot springs for decades.

A PERFECT DAY IN THE GOLDEN SPIKE REGION

Start at dawn in the Bear River Migratory Bird Refuge, where winged creatures begin a new day with the rising sun. From there, head farther west to Promontory and see where the final spike was driven into the ground to complete the transcontinental railroad. If time permits, stretch your legs on the Big Fill Hike. On the way back to town, stop at Thiokol to see the rocket display before visiting Corinne and touring the historic Methodist Church. After an early Mexican dinner at Ricardo's, drive north on old Highway 38, where charming stone homes are built at the base of the Wellsville Mountains. Complete the day with a relaxing dip in the warm mineral waters at Crystal Hot Springs.

SIGHTSEEING HIGHLIGHTS
★★★★ BEAR RIVER MIGRATORY BIRD REFUGE
15 miles west of Brigham City on Forest St., 435/723-5887
An arch spanning Main Street in downtown Brigham City touts the splendor of this refuge. Located west of Brigham City, the refuge provides a seasonal home for migrating birds on nearly 74,000 acres of marshes, uplands, and open water where the Bear River flows into the Great Salt Lake. More than 200 species of birds regularly utilize the refuge, including the 62 species that have been known to nest here. Spring is a good time to visit. Birds are generally in their brightest and most colorful plumage for courtship and mating. Flooding and the ice action of the Great Salt Lake destroyed much of the refuge in 1983. But the 12-mile automobile tour loop, which offers access to various vantage points to see wildlife at fairly close range, was restored in 1989, and plans are under way to develop a new educational center.
Details: *Open daily dawn to dusk except Jan–mid-Mar. Free. (1–2 hours minimum)*

★★★★ GOLDEN SPIKE NATIONAL HISTORIC SITE
32 miles west of Brigham City (I-15 Exit 368) on Hwy. 83
435/471-2209

The rails of the Union Pacific and Central Pacific railroads met here on May 10, 1869, and the first transcontinental railroad was established. The event that brought east and west together is commemorated on the anniversary each year with a re-enactment of the driving of the last spike. Working replicas of Union Pacific's "119" and Central Pacific's "Jupiter" steam engines are on display in the summer and fall. Special interpretive programs are offered Memorial Day to Labor Day. The annual **Railroader's Festival** is held the second Saturday in August, with a number of demonstrations, games, and contests. Railroad buffs also gather at the site between Christmas and New Year's Day for the annual **Railroader's Film Festival** and **Winter Steam Demonstration**. A booklet available at the visitors center provides information for a self-guided, interpretive driving tour at the site. National Park Service rangers at Golden Spike can also direct you to the **Central Pacific Railroad Trail Backway**, which follows the old Central Pacific Railroad grade (a four-wheel-drive vehicle is recommended). The three-quarter-mile **Big Fill Hike** starts at the eastern end of the self-guided driving tour and continues to a deep ravine. Central Pacific crews spent two months filling the ravine to maintain the maximum two percent railroad grade.

Details: Visitors center open Memorial Day–Labor Day daily 8–6; the rest of the year 8–4:30. $7/vehicle mid-Apr–mid-Oct, $4 the rest of the year. (2–3 hours)

★★★ BARON WOOLEN MILLS
56 North 500 East, Brigham City, 435/723-1087

Lorenzo Snow, one of the early fathers of Brigham City, realized that a local industry was essential for the city's survival. Thus, the Brigham City Mercantile and Manufacturing Association was created. It was used as a model for other cooperative associations in many Mormon communities in Utah. The woolen mill, which was later purchased from the association by an English immigrant, continues to produce fine wool blankets that can be bought by the general public. The mill is unique because it still relies on barter and trade. Finished goods, for example, are traded for raw wool and other supplies from producers in several states.

Details: Open Mon–Fri 9–5. Tours are available. Free. (1 hour)

GOLDEN SPIKE REGION

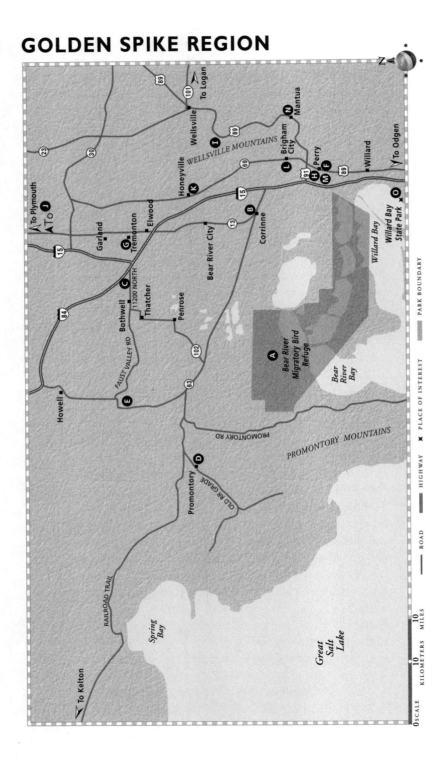

★★★ ELI ANDERSON'S WAGONS
8790 West Hwy. 102, Bothwell, 435/854-3760
Anderson, a farmer and Utah legislator, spent several years collecting old horse-drawn wagons as a hobby. Today, he has what is possibly the largest private collection of wagons in the West. There are more than 150 wagons in his collection, and no two are alike. Most date from the late 1800s, and the collection includes horse-drawn sleighs, farm wagons, a stagecoach, and a yellow wagon that once carried tourists through Yellowstone National Park. They are stored in barns and warehouses on his property northwest of Brigham City, but efforts were under way in 1998 to develop a theme park centered around his collection. They are shown by appointment only, and Anderson can explain much of the rich history behind each wagon.

Details: By appointment only. Free. (1–2 hours)

★★★ THIOKOL ROCKET GARDEN
5 miles north of Golden Spike National Historic Site on Hwy. 83, Promontory
See examples of the solid-fuel rockets that propel the space shuttle into orbit. The defense contractor has a display of rockets at its facility just north of Golden Spike National Historic Site, with interpretive signs explaining how many of the rockets were used. Occasionally, rocket tests can be seen from the highway.

Details: (1 hour)

SIGHTS
A Bear River Migratory Bird Refuge
B Corinne Methodist Church
C Eli Anderson's Wagons
D Golden Spike National Historic Site
E Thiokol Rocket Garden

FOOD
F Fruitway
G JC's Country Diner
G Lucky's
H Maddox Ranch House

LODGING
I Best Western Sherwood Hills Resort
G Sandman Motel
G Western Inn

CAMPING
J Belmont Hot Springs
K Crystal Hot Springs
L Golden Spike RV Park
M KOA Campground
N Mountain Haven Campground
O Willard Bay State Park

Note: Items with the same letter are located in the same place.

BRIGHAM CITY

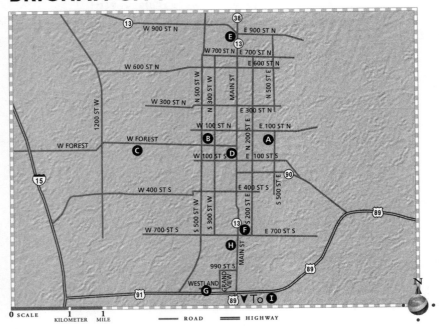

SIGHTS

A Baron Woolen Mills
B Brigham City Museum-Gallery
C Brigham City Railroad Depot

FOOD

D Idle Isle Cafe
E Railhead Supper Club
D Ricardo's

LODGING

F Bushnell Motel
G Crystal Inn
H Galaxie Motel
I Howard Johnson

Note: Items with the same letter are located in the same place.

★★ BRIGHAM CITY MUSEUM-GALLERY
24 North 300 West, Brigham City, 435/723-6769

This history, art, and cultural center features items relating to the city's past, particularly between 1850 and 1900. Compare how much or how little the city has changed. Artifacts from local pioneers as well as historic and contemporary handicrafts, ceramics, photographs, and paintings are on display in the center. Hands-on exhibits in the museum and gallery also help entertain and educate kids. Various rotating exhibits are on display here, primarily featuring local artists and regional art competitions.

Details: Open Tue–Fri 11–6, Sat 1–5. Free. (1 hour)

★ BRIGHAM CITY RAILROAD DEPOT
833 West Forest St., Brigham City, 435/723-2989
Once a large shipping center for the Union Pacific Railroad, the depot is now an educational center for railroad history. Built in 1906, it sat empty for more than 20 years, until a group of people convinced the railroad to give it to Box Elder County in 1994. It has been completely restored.

Details: Open in winter Mon–Tue and Thu–Sat 1–5; summer noon–6. Free. (1 hour)

★ CORINNE METHODIST CHURCH
On Hwy. 83 in Corinne, west of Brigham City
This was the first Protestant church in Utah. It outlived the many saloons and bordellos that once thrived in this town when the transcontinental railroad was completed. Corinne is four miles from Brigham City. Now fully restored, the church is complete with a pot-bellied stove, kerosene lamps, and the original pedal organ—which still works. It is used for weddings and recitals. Tours are available by appointment.

Details: For tours call DeVerle Wells, president of the Corinne Historical Society; 435/744-2442. Free. (30 minutes)

FITNESS AND RECREATION
Just down Interstate 15, south of Brigham City, is **Willard Bay**. The man-made, freshwater reservoir is adjacent to its more famous saline neighbor, the Great Salt Lake. A 15-mile-long dam separates the two bodies of water. The bay, which is also a state park, holds 9,900 acres of water. It is popular for all sorts of boating, water skiing, Jet skiing, and fishing. The shoreline trees are also the focus of birders watching for bald eagles.

Belmont Hot Springs, 435/458-3200, and **Crystal Hot Springs**, 435/547-0777, are both north of Brigham City and offer soothing, warm mineral water in swimming and wading pools. You can camp at both resorts.

Brigham City also has an indoor pool at the **Box Elder Natatorium**, 380 South 600 West, and an outdoor pool at **Pioneer Park**, 800 West Forest Street.

There are several golf courses in the Golden Spike Region, including **Eagle Mountain**, 960 East 700 South, Brigham City, 435/723-3212; **Brigham Willows**, at the junction of Highways 89 and 30, Brigham City, 435/723-5301; and **Skyway**, 450 North Country Club Drive, Tremonton, 435/257-5706.

The **Box Elder County Tourism Council**, 435/734-2634, publishes a guide to a few local road and mountain bike routes, including the 16-mile road to Inspiration Point near Willard Peak, which overlooks the valley and is a popular destination for people with four-wheel drives.

FOOD

Peaches, cherries, and other fruits grown in the fertile alluvial Bear River delta soil are sold at roadside stands along Highway 89 in the late summer and early fall. This highway, the "Fruitway," was the main thoroughfare between Ogden and Brigham City before the interstate freeway was completed.

If you're looking for a full, sit-down meal, try **Maddox Ranch House**, along the Fruitway at 1900 South Highway 89, 435/723-8545. It's a steakhouse that meets the high expectations of local ranchers. The **Railhead Supper Club**, 900 North Main Street, Brigham City, 435/723-1188, offers a unique, members-only experience. A $5 pass gives you a 14-day membership. **Ricardo's**, 84 South Main Street, Brigham City, 435/723-1811, provides good Mexican food that's priced to fit most anyone's budget. The **Idle Isle Cafe**, 24 South Main Street, Brigham City, 435/734-2468, has an interesting history. Many of the World War II veterans who were being treated at nearby Bushnell Hospital were amputees. The 1920s-era restaurant offered a free steak dinner to each patient outfitted with artificial legs as soon as they were able to walk through the door on their own. Be sure to try their homemade candy.

Farther north, in Tremonton, good homecooked meal is available at **Lucky's**, 55 West Main Street, 435/257-7261, and **JC's Country Diner**, 10260 North Highway 13, 435/257-1867.

LODGING

Most accommodations in the Golden Spike Region are motels. **Crystal Inn**, 480 Westerland Drive, Brigham City, 435/723-0440, is reasonably priced and has the newest and most modern accommodations in the city. **Howard Johnson**, 1167 South Main Street, Brigham City, 435/723-8511, is always a bargain. This one is situated on a hill with some rooms providing a nice view of the valley and surrounding mountains. The budget-priced **Bushnell Motel**, 115 East 700 South, 435/723-8575, and **Galaxie Motel**, 740 South Main Street, 435/723-3439, are both in Brigham City and are older roadside motels with nothing fancy or spectacular except a cheap bed when it's needed. The same goes for the **Sandman Motel**, 585 West Main Street, 435/257-7149, and **Western Inn**, 2301 West Main Street, 435/257-3399, both in Tremonton.

For a fun getaway, try the reasonably priced **Best Western Sherwood Hills Resort**, which is tucked in the forest along U.S. Highway 89-91 between Brigham City and Logan, 435/245-5054. It is expensive if all you want is a hotel room, but the resort has a pool, tennis courts, hiking trails, an outdoor theater, an adjacent golf course, and horseback riding.

CAMPING

Belmont Hot Springs, one mile south of Plymouth on Highway 13, 435/458-3200, and **Crystal Hot Springs**, 8215 North Highway 38, Honeyville, 435/547-0777 or 435/279-8104, have sites and hookups near their warm mineral pools. Close to town is **Golden Spike RV Park**, 905 West 1075 South, Brigham City, 435/723-8858. There's a **KOA Campground** south of Perry off U.S. Highway 89, 435/723-5503, and **Mountain Haven Campground** is in the small community of Mantua (pronounced "Man-a-way") in Box Elder Canyon east of Brigham City on U.S. Highway 89-91, 435/723-7615.

There's also tent and RV camping at the north and south marinas at **Willard Bay State Park**, off Interstate 15 between Ogden and Brigham City, 801/734-9494 or 800/322-3770.

NIGHTLIFE

Cowboy boots and a Western hat might be common attire, but a strong thirst and a hankering for Western music is all you need to belly up to the bar at **B & B Billiards**, 21 West Forest, Brigham City, or the **Draw Bar**, 52 West Main Street, Tremonton. And **Mim's Bar & Grill**, 4020 West 2450 North, Corinne, 435/744-2206, is a great local joint that serves up fantastic hamburgers along with their beer.

PERFORMING ARTS

The **Palace Playhouse**, 10 North Main Street, Brigham City, 435/723-7202, and the **Heritage Theatre**, 2505 South Highway 89, Perry, 435/723-8392, offer a variety of live theater productions.

4
CACHE VALLEY

Nestled between the Wellsville and Bear River mountain ranges in northern Utah is Cache Valley. The first Europeans to settle the valley were early Mormon pioneers, whose names are still prominent in the towns they founded. Originally called Willow Valley, the name changed in 1826, after a trapper was accidentally buried and killed in a cave where furs were cached for safe keeping—hence the name, Cache Valley.

The largest city in Cache Valley is Logan, which is surrounded by 18 smaller cities and towns. These communities are scattered over 30 miles of the valley floor and mountain benches formed by the ancient Lake Bonneville, predecessor of the Great Salt Lake. The earliest settlement in the valley was Maughan's Fort, now called Wellsville. It was established in 1856 by Mormon pioneer Peter Maughan, whose descendants still live in the small city. Three years later he had a hand in the selection of the site for Logan near the mouth of Logan Canyon and along Logan River. The name "Logan" comes from another trapper from the area, who was killed by Indians.

Most of the valley remains predominantly agricultural with a strong emphasis on dairy industries. In 1888 Utah's land-grant agricultural college was established in Logan. Today, Utah State University is the valley's largest employer. The area's strong pioneering heritage continues at USU, where internationally recognized research in fields ranging from agriculture to space exploration is conducted.

A PERFECT DAY IN CACHE VALLEY

Cache Valley has one "main" street, U.S. Highway 89, which runs smack through the middle of Logan and several other communities. Stop along the highway at the American West Heritage Center, which is built around the Jensen Living Historical Farm—a 1917 working farm. After tasting the flavor of Cache Valley's rural past, drive into Logan, park your car downtown, and pick up a little booklet called *Get to Know Logan's Historic Main Street*. Many of the buildings on this walking tour were built around the same time period represented at the Jensen Farm, when Logan was a young and growing city. Complete the day with a drive past Utah State University and through Logan Canyon, a 41-mile scenic byway through the mountains to Bear Lake.

SIGHTSEEING HIGHLIGHTS

★★★★ AMERICAN WEST HERITAGE CENTER

6 miles southwest of Logan on U.S. Hwy. 89-91
435/245-4064

The center combines the **Festival of the American West**, the **Jensen Historical Farm**, and the **Man and His Bread Museum**. The concept of the living-history farm was to train USU graduate students in outdoor museum studies, folklore, and history, and to preserve the agricultural life of a bygone era—1917, to be exact. Guides in period costumes lead people around this operating farm. Sheepshearing, canning, threshing, and other activities are demonstrated. Special events are held throughout the year. The annual Festival of the American West celebrates the valley's rich history with a replica Western frontier town, cowboy poetry, and a Dutch oven cook-off.

Details: $5 adults, $3 children 12 and under, $4 students and seniors, $15 per family. Annual passes are available. (1–3 hours)

★★★ HISTORIC DOWNTOWN LOGAN

Chamber of Commerce, 160 North Main St.
435/752-2161

Pick up a copy of *Get to Know Logan's Historic Main Street* at the tourist information center in the Chamber of Commerce Building. The pamphlet outlines a self-guided walking tour that winds around 14 buildings on the three historic blocks of downtown Logan. Another prominent historic building, which is not listed in the pamphlet, is the **Logan LDS Temple**, just up the hill from downtown at 200 North and 200 East. The temple, which is not open to visitors, is one of only four Mormon temples that were built during the nineteenth century. The others are in St. George, Manti, and Salt Lake City.

Details: *(1 hour)*

★★★ UTAH STATE UNIVERSITY
North of U.S. Hwy. 89, roughly between 700 and 1400 East Logan, 435/797-1000

Utah's land-grant agricultural college, founded in 1888, has developed into a major center for learning and research. Located on the hill overlooking downtown Logan, the university offers music, theater, art, workshops, and other activities year-round. The most prominent building on campus is the tower of **Old Main**, which was completed in 1902. This landmark, which still houses classrooms as well as administrative offices, was once featured on the city of Logan official seal and continues to be portrayed in numerous local artworks and business logos.

Aggie Ice Cream, made at the university, is available in the Nutrition and Food Sciences Building on the northeast corner of 700 North and 1200 East. Be prepared for long lines on hot summer days. The **Discovery Center**, in room 132 of the Science and Engineering Research Building in the middle of campus between the library and business buildings, is a free, hands-on science exploration center for children and adults. During the summer, free outdoor band concerts are held on the patio at the **Taggart Student Center**, on 800 East at approximately 600 South. The student center is also home to USU's bookstore, several conference rooms, and a food court.

Details: *General information, 435/797-1158 upcoming events, and 435/797-0305 tickets. (1 hour–full day)*

★★ DAUGHTERS OF UTAH PIONEERS MUSEUM
160 North Main St., Logan, 435/752-5139 or 435/753-1635

This museum houses Mormon pioneer artifacts and a collection of musical instruments from the Logan and Cache Valley area. The DUP Museum is located in the Chamber of Commerce Building.

Details: *Open Jun–Sep Tue–Fri 10–4; by appointment the rest of the year. Donations accepted. (1 hour)*

CACHE VALLEY

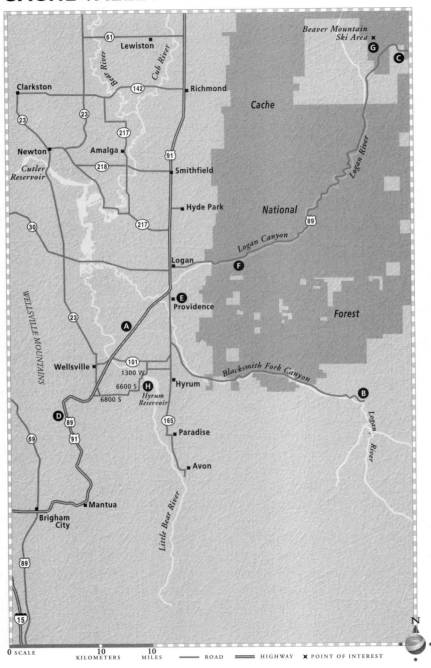

Beaver Mountain Ski Area

G
C

61
Lewiston

Bear River
Cub River

Clarkston
142
Richmond

Cache

23
23

217

Newton
Amalga
91

Cutler Reservoir
218
Smithfield

30
217
Hyde Park

National

89

Logan
Logan Canyon

F

E
Providence

A

Forest

Logan River

WELLSVILLE MOUNTAINS

23

Wellsville
101
1300 W

6600 S
H
6800 S
Hyrum
Hyrum Reservoir

Blacksmith Fork Canyon

B

Logan River

D
89
165
Paradise

69

91
Avon

Little Bear River

Mantua

Brigham City

89

15

N

0 SCALE   10   10
           KILOMETERS   MILES   ROAD   HIGHWAY   ✖ POINT OF INTEREST

★★ HARDWARE RANCH
435/753-6168

This ranch is a popular place in the winter, when visitors in horse-drawn sleighs can view herds of elk feeding at the ranch. The visitors center and restaurant are open year-round. During the summer the ranch offers overnight horseback-riding trips in the Bear River Mountains.

Details: South from Logan on Hwy. 165 to Hyrum, turn left (east) on Hwy. 101 and drive up Blacksmith Fork Canyon for 18 miles. (2 hours)

★★ NORA ECCLES HARRISON MUSEUM OF ART
650 N. 1100 East, Logan, 435/797-0163

Located on the USU campus, this museum features changing exhibitions from its permanent collection of twentieth-century American ceramics, paintings, sculptures, prints, photographs, and American Indian arts. The curator isn't afraid to put items on display that might be somewhat unusual in an art museum, like automobile grills and hood ornaments. The museum also organizes temporary and traveling exhibitions and serves as a venue for exhibitions of national and international stature.

Details: USU campus next to the Chase Fine Arts Center. Open Tue, Thu, Fri 10:30–4:30, Wed 10:30–8, Sat–Sun 2–5, closed Mon and holidays. Free. (1–3 hours)

★★ WILLOW PARK ZOO
419 West 700 South, Logan, 435/750-9877

The city-owned zoo has more than 600 animals, including coyotes, bald eagles, monkeys, and birds—lots of birds. It is adjacent to the Cache County Fairgrounds and Logan's Willow Park, which includes

---

SIGHTS
Ⓐ American West Heritage Center
Ⓑ Hardware Ranch

LODGING
Ⓒ Beaver Creek Lodge
Ⓓ Weston Sherwood Hills Resort
Ⓔ Providence Inn B&B
Ⓕ Zanavoo Lodge

CAMPING
Ⓖ Beaver Mountain Ski Resort
Ⓗ Hyrum State Park

picnic and playground areas as well as softball diamonds and horse-shoe pits.

Details: *Open daily 8–dusk; closed major holidays. Donations accepted. (1–3 hours)*

FOOD TOUR

Several businesses produce food in Cache Valley and have shops where you can sample their delectable morsels and buy some to take home. Call ahead for hours. **Cache Valley Cheese** makes, of course, cheese. It's located at 6351 North 2150 West in Amalga, northwest of Logan, 435/563-3281. **Gossner Foods** makes cheese and other dairy products at 1000 West 1000 North in Logan, 435/752-9365. **Cox Honey** produces honey and sells a variety of gifts made in Utah. Find it at 1780 South Highway 89-91 in Logan, 435/752-3234. **Pepperidge Farm** has a cookie and cracker factory north of Logan. It's found at 901 North 200 West, Richmond, 435/258-2491. **Bluebird Candy Company** makes hand-dipped chocolates at 75 West Center, Logan, 435/753-3670.

FITNESS AND RECREATION

There's an unlimited number of outdoor activities to pursue in Logan Canyon, which is in the mountains east of Logan along U.S. Highway 89 and the Logan River.

Hikers of all levels enjoy the **Riverside Nature Trail**, an easy three-mile loop trail with interpretive signs between Spring Hollow and Guinavah-Malibu campgrounds, just a few miles into the canyon. The **Crimson Trail** is another popular, but more difficult, hike from Spring Hollow. It climbs part way up the mountain and runs along the rugged cliffs overlooking Logan River. Call or stop by the Logan Ranger District office for more information, 1500 East Highway 89, just before driving into the canyon, 435/755-3620. Steeper hikes can be found on the other side of the valley, west of Logan, in the Wellsville Mountains.

Pamphlets and guidebooks describing local hiking and biking trails are available at the Logan Ranger District office, the Chamber of Commerce, and some outdoor stores. One of the free pamphlets describes a few mountain-bike trails and road-bike routes in the area. Make sure the trail you plan to ride is open to bicycles.

Fishing is also popular along Logan River and in any one of three small reservoirs formed by dams along the river. Camping and horseback riding are also popular in the canyon.

During the winter, snowmobiling and cross-country skiing are popular on groomed trails and in the back country. Downhill skiers often find good packed powder on the slopes at **Beaver Mountain Ski Resort**, 435/753-0921, 27 miles east of Logan.

The limestone outcroppings throughout the canyon attract many rock climbers. During the winter you can continue to climb indoors at **Adventure Sports Climbing Gym**, 51 South Main, 435/753-4044.

Golfers will find several links to play in Cache Valley. There are two municipal courses, **Logan River Golf Course** in Logan, 435/750-0123, and **Birch Creek Golf Course** in Smithfield, 435/563-6825. Logan River is a very challenging course straddling the river and surrounded by old willow trees. Birch Creek is a bit easier to play, with spectacular views of Cache Valley. The **Logan Golf and Country Club** is a private club near the university in Logan, 435/753-6050. **Sherwood Hills Golf Course** is adjacent to a hotel and resort in Wellsville Canyon, 435/245-6055. Its wide, open fairways are relatively easy to play.

There are several recreation facilities in Logan, including the **Recreation Center**, 195 South 100 West, which has indoor and outdoor tennis courts, and indoor basketball and racquetball courts. The city also maintains an indoor swimming pool called the **Municipool**, 1000 North and 200 East. Call the Parks and Recreation Department for more information, 435/750-9877.

FOOD

Most restaurants in Cache Valley are in Logan. **Angies**, 690 North Main, 435/752-9252, is a very popular café among locals, especially at breakfast time on weekends. It also features several vegetarian items and is cooperative about substitutions. The **Cottage Grill**, 51 West 200 South, 435/752-5260, also offers a wide range of menu selections for breakfast, lunch, and dinner. You might want to try its eggs Benedict or a sumptuous seafood omelet. But if all you need is coffee, stop by **Café Ibis**, 52 Federal Avenue, 435/753-4777. Church Street and Federal Avenue are unusual streets in downtown Logan, with a few specialty shops and restaurants off Main Street between 100 and 200 North. The **Italian Place**, 48 Federal Avenue, 435/753-2584, is a small restaurant, adjacent to a basket shop, that is willing to make sandwiches out of any combination of ingredients it has on hand. The **Copper Mill**, 55 North Main, 435/752-0647, and **Bluebird**, 19 North Main, 435/752-3155, are full-service restaurants in the middle of downtown. The Bluebird is worth a visit just for the old soda fountain. Nearby, the

LOGAN

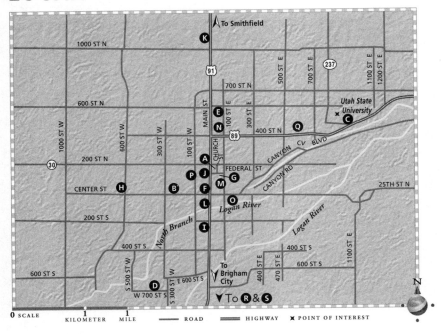

SIGHTS
Ⓐ Daughters of Utah Pioneers Museum
Ⓑ Historic Downtown Logan
Ⓒ Nora Eccles Harrison Museum of Art
Ⓒ Utah State University
Ⓓ Willow Park Zoo

FOOD
Ⓔ Angies
Ⓕ Bluebird
Ⓕ Blue Goose
Ⓖ Café Ibis
Ⓗ Café Habanero
Ⓘ Cottage Grill
Ⓙ Copper Mill
Ⓚ El Toro Viejo

FOOD (continued)
Ⓛ The Factory/Gias
Ⓜ Grapevine
Ⓖ Italian Place
Ⓝ Mandarin Garden

LODGING
Ⓞ Center Street B&B
Ⓟ Logan House Inn

CAMPING
Ⓠ Phillips 66
Ⓡ Riverside
Ⓢ Traveland RV Park

Note: Items with the same letter are located in the same place.

Blue Goose, 1 North Main, 435/752-0619, offers a healthy selection of sandwiches.

For Mexican food, try **El Toro Viejo**, 1079 North Main, 435/753-4084, or **Café Habanero**, 600 West Center, 435/753-8880, in the historic railroad depot. Owners of the Café Habanero are quite proud of their automated tortilla maker. It's an upscale restaurant, while El Toro has a more casual café atmosphere. **Gias** upstairs and **The Factory** downstairs at 119 South Main, 435/752-8384, offer Italian fare. The pizza is really good. There are several Chinese restaurants in Logan. One of the popular ones is **Mandarin Garden**, 432 North Main, 435/753-5789. For fine dining, there's no substitute for the **Grapevine**, 129 North 100 East, 435/752-1977. It is located in an old house and has both indoor and patio seating.

LODGING

Logan House Inn, 168 North 100 East, Logan, 435/752-7727, has six moderately priced rooms in a turn-of-the-century home, while **Center Street B&B**, 169 East Center, Logan, 435/752-3443, has 16 rooms, including theme rooms, in a Victorian house that range in price from budget to somewhat expensive. **Zanavoo Lodge**, 4888 East Highway 89 in Logan Canyon, 435/752-0085, is a log lodge that was built in 1948 to give Cache Valley residents a quiet getaway from the nearby city. It offers 11 simple budget rooms along the river and has an adjoining restaurant.

For moderately priced accommodations, try the **Beaver Creek Lodge**, farther up the canyon, 28 miles east of Logan, 435/753-1076, with 11 rooms in a rustic setting near Beaver Mountain Ski Resort. Rooms are reasonably priced. **Weston Sherwood Hills Resort** (Best Western) is in Wellsville Canyon, between Brigham City and Wellsville on U.S. Highway 89-91, 800/532-5066, with 85-plus rooms, including some theme rooms. Prices here tend to vary. Country charm is available at the **Providence Inn B&B**, 10 South Main, Providence, southeast of Logan, 435/752-3432. It has 15 rooms and is adjacent to the historic Old Rock Church which is used for parties and receptions.

CAMPING

There are numerous Forest Service campgrounds in Logan Canyon. The most popular areas include Spring Hollow, Sunrise, Tony Grove, and Malibu. None of the Forest Service sites have electrical hookups for RVs. Call the **Logan**

Ranger District, 435/755-3620, for more information or to make reservations for the few sites that allow reservations.

Beaver Mountain Ski Resort in Logan Canyon, 435/753-0921, also has several tent and RV sites, some with hookups, for summer use. **Hyrum State Park** at Hyrum Reservoir, south of Logan, 435/245-6866, has 31 tent sites and 10 RV sites without hookups.

Private campgrounds include: **Riverside**, 447 West 1700 South, off Highway 91, 435/245-4469, with 15 sites with full hookups and a handful of tent sites; **Traveland RV Park** behind the Travelodge Motel, 435/787-2020, with 45 full hookup sites; and **Phillips 66**, 1936 N. Main Street, 35/753-1025, with 13 sites with full hookups.

NIGHTLIFE
Popular taverns include **Berdues**, 22 West Center, Logan, 435/753-9943, and the **White Owl**, 36 West Center, Logan, 435/753-9165. Both taverns occasionally have live bands, as does **Café Habanero**, 600 West Center, 435/753-8880.

PERFORMING ARTS
The **Ellen Eccles Theatre and Bullen Center**, 43 South Main, Logan, 435/752-0026, has a variety of events, from operas and Broadway musicals to country-and-western concerts and orchestral recitals. The **Old Lyric Theatre**, 28 West Center, Logan, 435/797-0305, hosts summer musical dramas.

FESTIVALS
Nearly every city in Cache Valley has some kind of annual celebration, from **Trout and Berry Days** in Paradise, which features the fish and luscious fruits that are raised locally, to **Black & White Days** in Richmond, one of the oldest holstein shows in the country. Call 800/882-4433 for information about dates of each celebration. Around the Fourth of July, Logan hosts the **Cache Valley Cruise-In**, one of the largest vintage hot rod and collectible car shows in the West. The show concludes with a parade down the city's Main Street, 435/258-5493. The **Utah Festival Opera Company** brings renowned performers and musicians to Cache Valley each year for a series of summer operas in the Ellen Eccles Theatre, 435/750-0300 or 435/752-0026.

Scenic Route: Logan to Bear Lake

Named by Audubon Magazine *as one of the best scenic byways in the country,*
U.S. Highway 89 *through* **Logan Canyon** *is a 41-mile winding drive through the*
Bear River Mountains *from Logan to Garden City and Bear Lake. This scenic
drive takes motorists beneath breathtaking cliffs, alongside a rushing river, and
through forested canopies. Picnic spots and camping facilities are located throughout the canyon, as are numerous hiking and biking trailheads and several good fishing spots. The byway is a welcome feature on the drive between Salt Lake City and
Yellowstone National Park.*

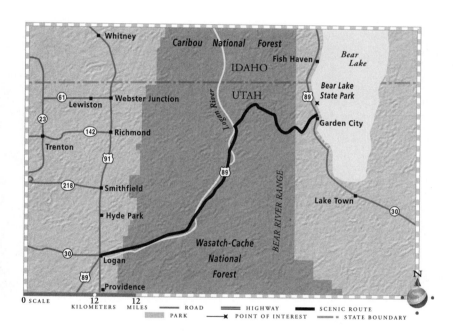

5
BEAR LAKE

The spectacular turquoise waters of Bear Lake attract thousands of people each summer to its 48 miles of shoreline in the northeastern-most part of Utah. The unique color of the lake, which straddles the Utah-Idaho border, is caused by limestone particles suspended in the water. The color also gives the lake the moniker Caribbean of the Rockies.

Scottish fur trapper Donald MacKenzie is credited with naming the lake in 1819. He called it Black Bears Lake. The second largest natural freshwater lake in the state is fed by the Bear River, which starts in Utah's Uinta Mountains and runs through parts of Wyoming, Utah, Idaho, and Utah again before it ends at the Great Salt Lake. The river and the lake were joined in 1918 by an inlet so river water could be stored in the lake for downstream agricultural and hydro-electric uses.

Fur trappers, as well as Native Americans, gathered at the south end of the lake two consecutive summers in the late 1820s for a rendezvous. They gathered to trade, renew acquaintances, party, and catch up on news from the East. A little more than 20 years later, immigrants traveling along the Oregon Trail may have stopped in Montpelier, Idaho, north of the lake after crossing the Rocky Mountains. Wagon ruts are still visible there today. Bear Lake remains an important crossroads. It's the halfway point between Salt Lake City and Jackson, Wyoming—a gateway to the Grand Tetons and Yellowstone National Park. After driving through Logan Canyon, motorists often stop at Garden City for a burger and a shake—raspberry (locally grown) is the flavor of choice.

The lake itself is popular for waterskiing, Jet skiing, boating, sailing, and fishing. Swimming and sunbathing are also quite popular on the fine sandy beaches. But be wary—rumor has it that the Bear Lake monster still lives in the lake.

A PERFECT DAY AT BEAR LAKE

Drive to the Bear Lake Overlook at the top of Logan Canyon for a panoramic view of Bear Lake's turquoise waters some 1,500 feet below. After stopping in Garden City for a raspberry shake, you have to make a choice: frolic in the water or bask in the rich history of the area. If you want to play, drive south to Rendezvous Beach State Park, where you can rent boats and jet skis. There's plenty of room for camping, picnicking, and relaxing in the sand. If history is your choice, drive north along the shoreline into Idaho through the historic towns of St. Charles and Paris. Paris has more registered historic homes than any other city in Idaho. Finish your day at the combined National Oregon/California Trail Center and Rails and Trails Museum in Montpelier.

SIGHTSEEING HIGHLIGHTS

★★★★ **NATIONAL OREGON/CALIFORNIA TRAIL CENTER AND RAILS AND TRAILS MUSEUM**
At the junction of U.S. Hwy. 89 and U.S. Hwy. 30
Montpelier, Idaho, 800/448-BEAR
Located in Montpelier, Idaho, this relatively new museum depicts the life of those who traveled across the plains and over the mountains, and settled in the West. Visitors to the museum will chat with Peg Leg Smith at his trading post, hear tales from early pioneers as they rest their livestock at a grazing area along the Bear Lake Valley's Clover Creek, and see a full-size wagon train encampment. The Rails and Trails Museum is in the basement. It houses a collection of pioneer artifacts, historic photographs, and other items from the early settlers and Native Americans of Bear Lake Valley. The Oregon Trail itself runs through the northeast section of Bear Lake County and follows the Bear River and Highway 30 north, through Montpelier.

Details: Expected to be open Mon–Sat 10–9. $6–$7. (3–4 hours)

★★★ MINNETONKA CAVE
North of St. Charles, Idaho, 208/945-2407

You don't have to be a spelunker to enjoy the nine rooms of stalactites and stalagmites in Minnetonka Cave, east of St. Charles, Idaho. Guided tours are available during the summer. Those touring the cave should be prepared for more than 400 steps going up and down. Jackets are recommended because the cave is quite cool—between 35 and 40 degrees. The entrance is reached by a foot trail leading from the parking lot. The half-mile walk into the cave takes visitors back more than 340 million years, when the limestone cavern first started to form. "Minnetonka," a Native American word for "falling waters," is an appropriate name for the abundance of water that drips in the cave, creating the various formations.

Details: Head 9 miles west up St. Charles Canyon from U.S. 89. Tours run during the summer Mon–Thu 10–5:30, Fri and Sat 10–5:30. $4 ages 16 and up, $3 ages 6–15, free under age 6. Discount passes may be available for families and large groups. (2 hours)

★★★ PARIS HISTORICAL MUSEUM AND HOME TOUR
On U.S. Hwy. 89 northwest of Bear Lake in Paris, Idaho
800/448-BEAR

This very small museum displays artifacts and old photographs from one of the oldest settlements in the region. Here you'll find a list and descriptions of the historic Paris homes. The homes are numbered and decorated with white picket fences during the summer. The museum is located across the street and a quarter of a block north of the **Paris LDS Tabernacle**. The tabernacle was completed by Mormon pioneers in 1889, using red sandstone quarried in the Indian Creek area on the east side of Bear Lake. The **Charles C. Rich Memorial** is on the tabernacle grounds. It describes how the early Mormon apostle was sent by Brigham Young to settle in the Bear Lake Valley. The county on the Utah side of the border was named after Rich.

Details: Open Memorial Day–Labor Day. Tours of the tabernacle available during the summer. Donations accepted. (2–3 hours)

★★ BEAR LAKE NATIONAL WILDLIFE REFUGE
Access from Paris or from U.S. Hwy. 89 between Ovid and Montpelier, 208/847-1757

BEAR LAKE

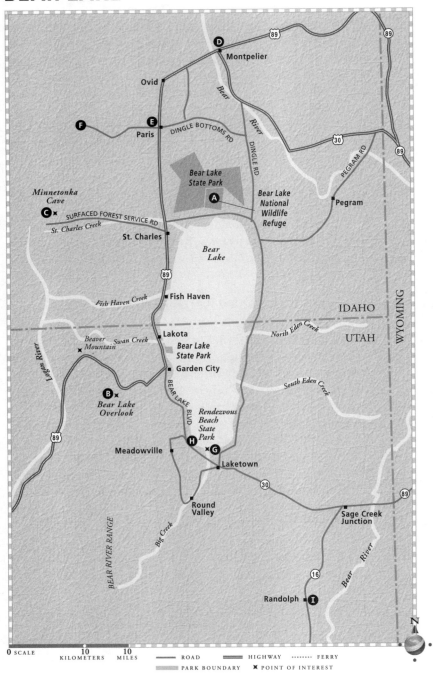

Montpelier

Ovid

Bear River

D

89

89

89

30

PEGRAM RD

Paris

F

E

DINGLE BOTTOMS RD

DINGLE RD

Bear Lake
State Park

Bear Lake
National
Wildlife
Refuge

A

Pegram

Minnetonka
Cave

C ✗

SURFACED FOREST SERVICE RD

St. Charles Creek

St. Charles

Bear
Lake

Fish Haven Creek

Fish Haven

North Eden Creek

IDAHO

WYOMING

Lakota

Beaver
Mountain ✗

Swan Creek

UTAH

Logan River

Bear Lake
State Park

Garden City

South Eden Creek

B ✗
Bear Lake
Overlook

BEAR LAKE BLVD

Rendezvous
Beach
State
Park

89

Meadowville

H
✗ **G**

Laketown

30

89

16

Sage Creek
Junction

BEAR RIVER RANGE

Big Creek

Round
Valley

Bear River

Randolph ■ **I**

N

0 SCALE   10   10
KILOMETERS   MILES   ▬▬ ROAD   ▬▬ HIGHWAY   ···· FERRY

▦ PARK BOUNDARY   ✗ POINT OF INTEREST

More than 17,600 acres of marsh, flooded meadows, open water, and grasslands have been dedicated to preserving bird and wildlife habitats on the north shore of Bear Lake. Many ducks and unique birds such as sandhill cranes, herons, egrets, and white pelicans have been spotted at the refuge. It is also a seasonal home for a large number of Canada geese, for which the refuge was first established in 1968. It is located seven miles southwest of Montpelier, Idaho. Observation sites are located along a motor tour route. Walking trails are also available.

Details: (1 hour–full day)

★★ PARIS ICE CAVE
In Paris Canyon, west of Paris, Idaho

This is where early pioneers collected ice—all year long! Accessible generally by the middle of July, the main cavern is open to the sky with cracks and crevasses. The temperature remains around a chilly 30 degrees. There are also several smaller caves and tunnels around the area.

Details: Explore it on your own, since there are no formal tours. (30 minutes–1 hour)

★ BEAR LAKE OVERLOOK
On U.S. Hwy. 89, West of Garden City

Enjoy the view of Bear Lake's turquoise waters from the overlook, just east and downhill from the summit of Logan Canyon. It's not much more than a pullout along the highway above Garden City, but there are interpretive displays and a spectacular view.

Details: (30 minutes)

SIGHTS
A Bear Lake National Wildlife Refuge
B Bear Lake Overlook
C Minnetonka Cave
D National Oregon/California Trail Center and Rails and Trails Museum
E Paris Historical Museum and Home Tour
F Paris Ice Cave
G Rendezvous Beach State Park
H Rendezvous Rest Stop
I Wilford Woodruff Home

★ RENDEZVOUS REST STOP AND RENDEZVOUS BEACH STATE PARK

On the south shore of the lake near Laketown on Hwy. 30, 435/946-3343

A highway rest stop marks the location of the two summer rendezvous that took place along the south shore of Bear Lake during the late 1820s. That was when fur trappers and Native Americans gathered to trade, learn about the rest of the world, and have fun. Farther southeast around the lake is the state park that was named after the gatherings. Camping, picnicking, swimming, and boating are popular here.

Details: *$5 day-use fee at the park. (10 minutes–full day)*

★ WILFORD WOODRUFF HOME

85 South Main St., Randolph, for info. call 435/752-2161

This home was built in 1872 for Woodruff, who became the fourth president of the LDS Church five years later. The log cabin was an early duplex, with one side for one of Woodruff's (polygamist) wives and the other side for his eldest son and his family.

Details: *Late May–mid-Sep, 10–5. Free. (1 hour)*

FITNESS AND RECREATION

Boating, windsurfing, Jet skiing, sunbathing, swimming, and other water activities can be enjoyed at **Rendezvous Beach State Park**. Slips are available to moor your own boat at **Bear Lake State Park Marina**, 435/946-3343, where there's also a visitors center and a picnic area. Watercraft rentals are available at both parks, as well as at **Blue Water Beach**, 435/946-3333, and **Ideal Beach**, 435/946-3364. Scuba diving is popular on the east shore, where it drops off to 208 feet. Fishing is also popular on the lake, both during the summer and through the ice during the winter.

The **Bear Lake Bicycle/Pedestrian Path** is a 4.2-mile paved trail that runs adjacent to the highway from the marina south to Ideal Beach, providing an excellent view of the lake for walkers, runners, and cyclists.

There are two nine-hole golf courses on the west side of the lake: **Bear Lake Golf Course**, south of Garden City, 435/946-8742, and **Bear Lake West**, just north across the Utah-Idaho border, with nice views overlooking the lake and valley, 208/945-2744. **Montpelier Municipal Golf Course** in Montpelier also offers nine holes, 208/847-1981.

Just 15 miles west of Garden City is **Beaver Mountain Ski Resort**,

435/753-0921, providing top-notch downhill skiing at a small, family-owned-and-operated resort in Logan Canyon. You can find hundreds of groomed snowmobile trails in Logan Canyon, as well as several cross-country skiing and summer hiking, mountain biking, and horseback-riding trails in the **Wasatch-Cache National Forest**, 435/755-3620. A segment of the **Great Western Trail**, which stretches from Arizona to the Canadian border, travels through these mountains. Rock climbing is also popular in the canyon on outcroppings just off the highway.

FOOD

Many people stop in Garden City just to get a raspberry shake while they're passing through the area. Some will even make a special trip from Logan just to indulge their taste buds. The sumptuous fruits are harvested in nearby fields each fall and used to make shakes at several small roadside burger stands around the south and west sides of Bear Lake, particularly at the intersection of U.S. Highway 89 and Utah Highway 30 in Garden City. If you don't like raspberries, several other flavors are also offered at places like **La Beau's Drive In**, 69 North Bear Lake Boulevard (Highway 89), 435/946-8821, and at **Quick 'N' Tasty Drive-Inn**, 28 North Bear Lake Boulevard, 435/946-3489.

Most restaurants around the lake offer simple food for a simple price. Some of the Garden City eateries include: **Bear Lake Motor Lodge**, 50 South Bear Lake Boulevard, 435/946-8892; **Bear Lake Pizza Co.**, 240 South Bear Lake Boulevard, 435/946-3600; **Cactus Cafe**, 205 North Bear Lake Boulevard, 435/946-3233; **Grandma's Pantry**, 80 West Logan Road, 435/946-8865; and **Hometown Drive In**, 105 North Bear Lake Boulevard, 435/946-2727. The fanciest and priciest restaurant in the area is **Harbor Village Resort**, 785 North Bear Lake Boulevard, 800/324-6840. Here, in addition to a burger and fries, you can get filet minon, pasta, and prime rib—the large cut is the highest priced item on the menu at $16.95.

For a quick bite in Laketown, there's the **Lakeshore Drive In**, 435/946-8673.

In Idaho, try **Bear Lake West**, just north across the Utah-Idaho border, 208/945-2646. Its food concession has changed owners a few times, but the restaurant is likely to serve something a little upscale, even if it's just sandwiches. The **Bear Cave Drive Inn** is a quick place to stop in St. Charles, 208/945-2444, and the **Paris Cafe** in Paris, 208/945-9900, offers simple homecooked meals.

Many of the restaurants around the lake are open only during the summer season.

BEAR LAKE

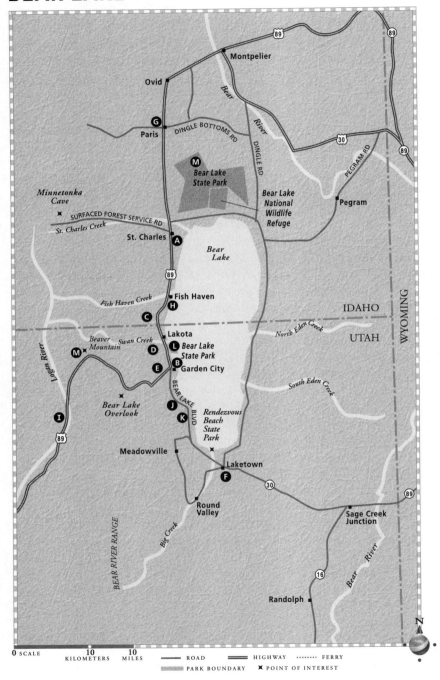

LODGING

Rentals in the area include beachfront condominiums at the somewhat pricey **Blue Water Beach**, 2126 South Bear Lake Boulevard, 435/946-3333. Handicap facilities are available. **Harbor Village Resort**, the newest and perhaps nicest accommodations around the lake, at 785 North Bear Lake Boulevard, 435/946-3448, has several condominiums and townhomes for rent in an upscale resort atmosphere overlooking the lake. Surprisingly, the prices here tend to be a little lower than at Blue Water; handicap facilities are available. It's easy to find, just look for the lighthouse as you drive north of the Garden City intersection.

Most accommodations around Bear Lake are located along the beachfront. Very reasonably priced accommodations here include the simple **Bear Lake Motor Lodge**, 50 South Bear Lake Boulevard, Garden City, 435/946-3271, which has 19 rooms; the **Ideal Beach Resort**, 2176 South Bear Lake Boulevard, 435/946-3364, which has 55 rooms along the south shore and offers several beachfront amenities; handicap facilities are available. And for those looking for bed-and-breakfast accommodations, **Eagle Feather Inn**, 135 South Bear Lake Boulevard, in Garden City, 435/946-2846, has two rooms in a cozy prairie-style house one block from the lake. **Bear Lake B&B**, 500 Loveland Lane, in Fish Haven, Idaho, 208/945-2688, has four rooms in a small mountain lodge overlooking the water. **Beaver Creek Lodge**, 12 miles west of Garden City on U.S. Highway 89 in Logan Canyon, 435/753-1076, has 11 rooms tucked away

FOOD

- Ⓐ Bear Cave Drive Inn
- Ⓑ Bear Lake Motor Lodge
- Ⓑ Bear Lake Pizza Co.
- Ⓒ Bear Lake West
- Ⓑ Cactus Cafe
- Ⓑ Grandma's Pantry
- Ⓓ Harbor Village Resort
- Ⓑ Hometown Drive In
- Ⓔ La Beau's Drive In
- Ⓕ Lakeshore Drive In
- Ⓖ Paris Cafe
- Ⓔ Quick 'N' Tasty Drive-In

LODGING

- Ⓗ Bear Lake B&B
- Ⓑ Bear Lake Motor Lodge
- Ⓘ Beaver Creek Lodge
- Ⓙ Blue Water Beach
- Ⓑ Eagle Feather Inn
- Ⓓ Harbor Village Resort
- Ⓚ Ideal Beach Resort

CAMPING

- Ⓑ Bear Lake KOA
- Ⓛ Bear Lake State Parks
- Ⓚ Sweetwater RV Park & Marina
- Ⓐ Minnetonka RV & Campground
- Ⓐ St. Charles Canyon Campground
- Ⓜ Beaver Mountain Ski Resort

Note: Items with the same letter are located in the same place.

in a remote forest setting across the highway from Beaver Mountain Ski Resort; handicap facilities are available.

CAMPING

Bear Lake KOA, 485 North Bear Lake Boulevard, in Garden City, 435/946-3454, has 140 sites for RVs and tents, as well as five cabins. A variety of campsites for tents and RVs is also available at the **Bear Lake State Parks**, (Eastside, Marina, and Rendezvous Beach), 800/322-3770. **Sweetwater RV Park & Marina**, at Ideal Beach, 435/946-8735, has 19 sites with full hookups along the south shore. To the north there's **Minnetonka RV & Campground**, 220 North Main, St. Charles, 208/945-2941, and **St. Charles Canyon Campground**, 208/945-2407. Hookups and tent sites are also available at **Beaver Mountain Ski Resort**, in Logan Canyon west of Garden City, 435/753-0921.

PERFORMING ARTS

The **Pickleville Playhouse**, at the south end of Garden City along Utah Highway 30, 435/946-2919 or 435/753-1944, features a Western cookout and old-fashioned musical melodrama at its summer theater. Open late June through Labor Day.

6
UTAH VALLEY

To many Utahns the words "Provo" and "Brigham Young University" are synonymous. Founded as the Brigham Young Academy in 1875, BYU has since grown into the largest church-affiliated university in the United States. Today, with its fine museums, theaters, and athletic events, it is the centerpiece of Utah Valley.

Provo is bounded on the west by Utah Lake, the largest natural freshwater lake in the state, and on the east by the towering Wasatch Mountains—the most prominent of which is 11,957-foot Mount Timpanogos. Dominguez and Escalante visited the Ute Indians in this valley while attempting to find an overland route from New Mexico to California in 1776. Fifty years later, fur trapper Étienne Provost came and left his name. Shortly thereafter, Mormons moved into the Salt Lake Valley in 1847, and a group of them settled in Provo in 1849, establishing the first Mormon colony in Utah outside the Salt Lake Valley. When President James Buchanan sent troops to Salt Lake City to put down the Mormon insurrection in 1858, thousands of Mormons—including Brigham Young—moved to Provo.

Industries such as Geneva Steel have made a home in the Provo area. In the mountains above the city, at the base of Mount Timpanogos, is the world-renowned Sundance Resort, which is owned by actor/director Robert Redford. This ski resort, artist retreat, and conference center is home to the famous Sundance Institute and Sundance Film Festival.

A PERFECT DAY IN THE UTAH VALLEY

Provo's museums are enough to keep you busy for several days. Start at the BYU Earth Science Museum. If you're lucky, you might get a peek at work-in-progress on fossils being added to the museum's extensive collection. The BYU Museum of Peoples and Cultures is also worth a visit. Then drive out to see the 13 nationally recognized galleries in Springville's Museum of Art. If art's not your favorite subject, try the McCurdy Historical Doll Museum before driving up Provo Canyon to Sundance to catch the latest film in the Institute's screening room or a production at the summer theater.

SIGHTSEEING HIGHLIGHTS

★★★★ TIMPANOGOS CAVE NATIONAL MONUMENT

About 20 miles from Provo in American Fork Canyon, on Hwy. 92, 801/756-5239

Man-made tunnels connect three limestone caverns—**Hansen**, **Middle**, and **Timpanogos**—that are full of fascinating geologic creations. The first cavern was discovered in 1887 by a man cutting timber. The remaining two were discovered in the early 1920s. The one-and-a-half-mile steep hike to the cave offers outstanding views of the Wasatch Mountains and Utah Valley. A trail guide is available at the visitors center to point out the kinds of plants and wildlife you're likely to see on the way to the cave. Rangers lead small groups through the caverns, where the temperature is about 45 degrees Fahrenheit.

Details: Reservations are recommended because tours are limited in size. Mid-May–Oct 7–5:30. $6 adults, $5 ages 6–15, $3 ages 5 and under. (3–4 hours)

★★★ HISTORIC LEHI TOUR

55 North Center St., Lehi, 801/768-4578

Shop at 110-year-old **Broadbents Family Department Store**. See Butch Cassidy's sawed-off shotgun and the extensive mineral collection at the **John Hutchings Museum of Natural History**. Follow the original Pony Express and Overland Stage Coach routes to **Camp Floyd**, the largest military outpost in the United States in 1858. Walk through the 135-year-old **Carson Stagecoach Inn**. And, visit the sites of Indian massacres, a stagecoach ambush, and a gunfight with Porter Rockwell, Brigham Young's less-than-wholesome bodyguard. All this and more is wrapped up into one tour, including lunch, bus fare, and entrance fees.

Details: *Tours leave from the Hutchings Museum. $30 adults, $20 children. (6–7 hours)*

★★★ SUNDANCE
Hwy. 92, which branches off Hwy. 189, in Provo Canyon
800/892-1600

In 1969 actor/director Robert Redford bought a small, single-lift ski resort at the foot of Mount Timpanogos. Today, Sundance is a unique village for filmmakers, playwrights, artists, and craftspeople— and skiers, too. The village has a gift shop, country store, several restaurants, and a bar.

In 1981 Redford established the Sundance Institute to support independent filmmaking, and the annual Sundance Film Festival serves as an international showcase for those films. Foreign films, independent films, classics, and documentaries are shown in Sundance's screening room. The Institute also supports a theater program dedicated to commissioning, developing, and producing new stage and screen plays—some of which can be seen at the resort's Summer Theatre, set in a natural amphitheater surrounded by old-growth firs. A variety of workshops are offered throughout the year.

Details: *(2 hours minimum)*

★★ BRIDAL VEIL FALLS
Hwy. 189 in Provo Canyon, between Orem and Hwy. 92
turnoff for Sundance

If you're looking for a nice backdrop for a photo to send home, this is the place. This double-cataract waterfall drops more than 600 feet and can be seen from a highway pullout four miles up Highway 189 in Provo Canyon.

Details: *(30 minutes)*

★★ GENEVA STEEL TOUR
10 South Geneva Rd., Orem, 801/227-9420

Visit the only integrated steel mill west of the Mississippi. Here, near Utah Lake, the metal that continues to build this nation, and others throughout the world, is forged. This is the largest industrial complex in the region.

Details: *Tours Mon, Wed, Fri. Call one week in advance to schedule a tour. Visitors must be at least age 8. Free. (1–2 hours)*

UTAH VALLEY

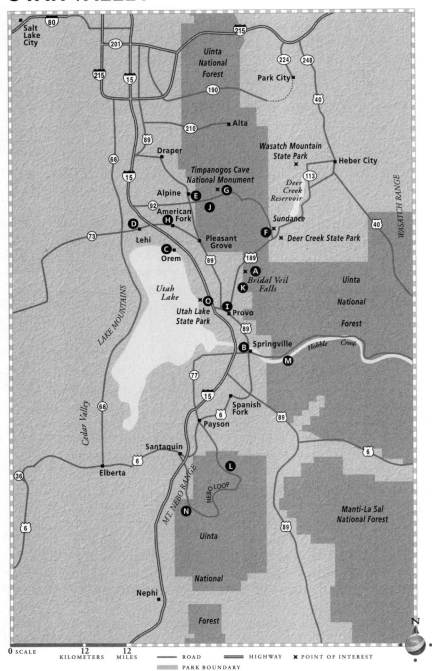

Salt Lake City

80

201

215

15

215

Uinta National Forest

215

224 248

Park City

190

40

89

68

Draper

210

Alta

Wasatch Mountain State Park

Heber City

15

Timpanogos Cave National Monument

113

92

Alpine

E

G

Deer Creek Reservoir

American Fork

H

J

D

73

Lehi

Pleasant Grove

Sundance

F

Deer Creek State Park

WASATCH RANGE

40

Orem

C

89

189

A

LAKE MOUNTAINS

Utah Lake

Bridal Veil Falls

K

Uinta

National

Forest

O

I

Utah Lake State Park

Provo

89

B

Springville

Hobble Creek

M

77

15

Spanish Fork

6

89

68

Payson

Santaquin

6

36

Elberta

MT. NEBO RANGE

NEBO LOOP

L

N

6

6

Manti-La Sal National Forest

89

Uinta

Nephi

National

Cedar Valley

Forest

N

0 SCALE 12 KILOMETERS 12 MILES ROAD HIGHWAY ✕ POINT OF INTEREST PARK BOUNDARY

★★ McCURDY HISTORICAL DOLL MUSEUM

246 North 100 East, Provo, 801/377-9935

This museum houses more than 4,000 dolls. Costume themes include folk dresses of the world, women of the bible, Native Americans, and first ladies of the White House. A collection of antique toys and games is also featured in the museum, which is in a restored carriage house.

Details: *Tue–Sat 1–5. $2 adults, $1 ages 12 and under. (1–2 hours)*

★★ PEPPERMINT PLACE

155 East 200 North, Alpine, 801/756-7400

This candy factory features more than 500 kinds of candies, and there are gift items as well. Take in the tour and taste the free candy samples.

Details: *Tours Mon–Fri 10–2, production stops noon–12:30 p.m. Free. (1 hour)*

★★ PROVO'S HISTORIC BUILDINGS

51 S. University Ave., 801/370-8393

A brochure outlining a self-guided tour shows you the exteriors of Provo's historic buildings. The tour includes **Academy Square** (site of the original Brigham Young Academy), the **Utah County**

SIGHTS
- **A** Bridal Veil Falls
- **B** Daughters of Utah Pioneers Museum
- **C** Geneva Steel
- **D** Historic Lehi
- **E** Moyle's Home and Indian Tower
- **G** Orem Heritage Museum
- **E** Peppermint Place
- **B** Springville Museum of Art
- **F** Sundance
- **G** Timpanogos Cave

FOOD
- **C** Carvers
- **F** Foundry Grill
- **B** La Casita
- **F** Sundance Tree Room

LODGING
- **H** American Fork B&B
- **F** Sundance
- **B** Victorian Inn B&B

CAMPING
- **I** American Campground
- **H** American Fork
- **J** American Fork Canyon Campgrounds

CAMPING
(continued)
- **K** Deer Creek Park
- **K** Frazier RV Park
- **M** Hobble Creek Canyon Campgrounds
- **I** Lakeside RV Campground
- **L** Payson Canyon Campgrounds
- **K** Provo Canyon Campgrounds
- **I** Provo KOA
- **N** Santaquin Canyon Camgrounds
- **O** Utah Lake State Park

Note: Items with the same letter are located in the same place.

Courthouse, and **North Park**, the place where original Mormon settlers moved to after Fort Utah became too swampy.

Details: Brochure is available at the Utah County Visitors Center. (2–4 hours)

★★ SPRINGVILLE MUSEUM OF ART
126 East 400 South, Springville, 801/489-2727

Nine of the museum's 13 galleries are dedicated to Utah artworks, and they're arranged chronologically to show the development of art in the state. The four other galleries are used for rotating exhibits from around the world. Guided tours are offered during the week.

Details: Tue–Sat 10–5, Wed 10–9, Sun 3–6. Donations encouraged. (2 hours)

★ CRANDALL HISTORICAL PRINTING MUSEUM
275 East Center St., Provo, 801/377-7777

This is a unique museum featuring various print shops. See the 1450 Gutenberg print shop, the 1830 Benjamin Franklin shop, and the 1850 *Deseret News* print shop, among others.

Details: Tours by appointment. (2 hours)

★ DAUGHTERS OF UTAH PIONEERS MUSEUM
175 South Main St., Springville, 801/489-7525

Features items, including furniture and musical instruments, used by the area's pioneers.

Details: Tue–Sat 1–5, Wed 2–5. Free. (30 minutes–1 hour)

★ MOYLE'S HOME AND INDIAN TOWER
606 East 770 North, Alpine, 801/756-1194

Instead of living in a protective fort, John Moyle built a tower next to his home to shelter his family during the Black Hawk War in the mid-1860s. A tunnel was to connect the home to the tower, but the Ute Indians moved east to the Uintah Reservation before it was completed. The city of Alpine now maintains the buildings and surrounding land as a park. A video presentation and tour are available by appointment.

Details: May–Sep Sat 9–1. Free. (1 hour)

★ OREM HERITAGE MUSEUM
745 South State St., Orem, 801/225-2569

This museum houses a 30,000-piece collection of items that together depict Orem's history. It includes one of the largest arrowhead collections in the country and a video interview with descendants of Orem's first family.

Details: *Mon–Fri 1–4. Tours can be scheduled in advance. Free. (1–2 hours)*

BRIGHAM YOUNG UNIVERSITY SIGHTSEEING HIGHLIGHTS

The flagship educational institution of the LDS Church, BYU attracts Mormons and non-Mormons from all over the world. Tours of campus are offered through the Hosting Center, 801/378-4678, at 11 a.m. and 2 p.m. Monday to Friday. The university has nationally recognized sports teams and several renowned museums. You can get information about sporting events by calling 801/378-TEAM. BYU Theater, 801/378-4322, has four facilities offering a variety of productions throughout the year. The university's Harold B. Lee Library, 801/378-2926, is the largest library in the state and includes an extensive genealogical library. The campus is located east of U.S. Highway 89, roughly between 800 and 1700 North.

★★★ MUSEUM OF ART
492 East Campus Dr., 801/378-2787

This museum is one of the largest art museums in the West. The museum tries to host at least one special exhibit each year. Recent exhibits have included Rodin's sculptures and Andy Warhol's *Marilyn Monroe* series.

Details: *Tue, Wed, Fri 10–6, Mon and Thu 10–9, Sat noon–5. Free. (1–2 hours)*

★★★ MUSEUM OF PEOPLES AND CULTURES
700 North 100 East, 801/378-2787

This museum features anthropological artifacts from cultures around the world—primarily from the Western Hemisphere—including numerous items from the Native Americans who once inhabited the land that is now Utah.

Details: *Mon–Fri 9–5. Free. (1–2 hours)*

★★ B.F. LARSON GALLERY AND GALLERY 303
In the Harris Fine Arts Center on campus, 801/378-2881

These galleries house contemporary works, primarily by BYU students and faculty. Call to see if there's a traveling exhibition on display.

Details: *Daily 9–5. Free. (1 hour)*

★★ EARTH SCIENCE MUSEUM
1683 North Canyon Rd., 801/378-3680

This museum houses one of the nation's most extensive collections of fossils. Regular exhibits include a Jurassic dinosaur egg and two mounted, life-size dinosaur skeletons.

Details: *Mon 9–9, Tue–Fri 9–5, Sat noon–4. Donations encouraged. (1–2 hours)*

★★ MONTE L. BEAN LIFE SCIENCE MUSEUM
1430 North Campus Dr., 801/378-5051

Numerous plants, shells, and animals from Utah and from all over the world are on exhibit in this museum. Ask about the live reptile, insect, and animal shows.

Details: *Mon–Fri 10–9, Sat 10–5. Free. (2 hours)*

PROVO

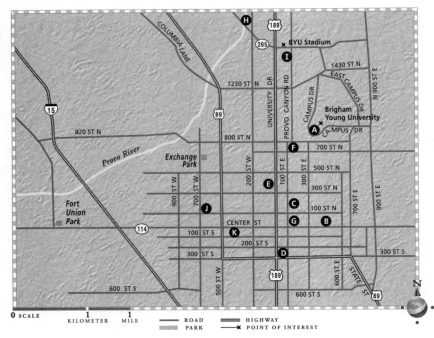

FITNESS AND RECREATION

Mount Timpanogos, which towers over Provo, attracts many hikers each year. The 9.4-mile (one-way) trail from the **Aspen Grove** trailhead climbs almost 5,000 feet to the peak. Less challenging hiking can be found on the eight-mile **Provo River Parkway**, which follows the Provo River from Utah Lake through town and up Provo Canyon to Vivian Park. It is popular with hikers, bikers, and joggers. The **Provo River** and **American Fork Creek** are top-notch destinations for fly fishing. Lake fishing is popular on the 150-square-mile **Utah Lake**, as well as on the seven-mile-long **Deer Creek Reservoir**. Boating and waterskiing are common on these lakes, too.

Sundance is the local ski resort, with four lifts serving 41 runs. The Rock Garden indoor climbing gym keeps climbers in shape throughout the year.

For more traditional activities, the **Provo Recreation Center**, 1155 North University Avenue, 801/379-6610, has a swimming pool, racquetball courts, and a weight room. The Provo area is also home to eight golf courses. **East Bay Golf Course**, 801/373-6262, has an executive nine-hole course and a championship 18-hole course. The greens are quite challenging at **Spanish Oaks Golf Course**, 801/798-9816, in nearby Spanish Fork. Elevated tees and lush fairways highlight **Seven Peaks Golf Course**, 801/375-5155, in Provo.

FOOD

Provo's eclectic population is reflected in the variety of restaurants in the city. If it's pizza, pasta, and calzones you're looking for, try **La Dolce Vita**, 61 North 100 East, Provo, 801/373-8482, or the **Brick Oven**, 111 East 800 North, Provo, 801/374-8800, where students and families have been going to get pizza

---

SIGHTS

- Ⓐ Brigham Young University
- Ⓑ Crandall Historical Printing Museum
- Ⓒ McCurdy Historical Doll Museum
- Ⓓ Provo's Historic District

FOOD

- Ⓔ Bombay house
- Ⓕ Brick Oven
- Ⓖ La Dolce Vita
- Ⓗ Mangleby's

LODGING

- Ⓘ Comfort Inn University
- Ⓙ Provo Park Hotel
- Ⓚ R. Spencer Hines Mansion B&B

---

for more than 40 years. If you're looking for something exotic, there's the **Bombay House**, 463 North University Avenue, Provo, 801/373-6677, which serves up fine Indian cuisine at a good price. The **Sundance Tree Room**, at the resort, 801/223-4200, offers elegant candlelight dinners in a dining room decorated with Native American memorabilia from Robert Redford's personal collection. But if you're not quite ready for its prices, try Sundance's **Foundry Grill** instead. Open for lunch and dinner, the grill features items grown in the resort's gardens. A woodburning grill and rotisserie are highlights of the open "foundry" kitchen, where windows provide fantastic views of Mount Timpanogos. **Carver's**, 672 South State Street, Orem, 801/235-9422, can be a bit pricey, but you can get good poultry, seafood, and pasta here. It can be quite intimate if you find a seat in the garden areas away from the main seating. Located in a Provo office complex, **Mangleby's**, 1875 North 200 West, 801/374-6249, is in an unlikely location for a fine restaurant, but it's the top choice for semi-casual special events and business dinners. For a real treat, head out to Springville and look for the brightly colored pueblo. **La Casita**, 333 North Main Street, Springville, is known to draw crowds on the weekends for its Mexican dinner specials.

LODGING

If you want to get a little closer to nature, try one of the cottages at **Sundance**, 801/225-4107. The rustic accommodations are built with hand-hewn posts and rough-sawed beams, and decorated with Native American arts and crafts, stone fireplaces, and wood stoves. Prices for accommodations range from moderate to very expensive.

The moderately priced **Victorian Inn B&B**, 94 West 200 South, Springville, 801/489-0737, has eight beautiful rooms in the old Kearns Hotel. By contrast, the luxurious **Provo Park Hotel** is a full-service, modern high-rise hotel, but it is also moderately priced. Located at 101 West 100 North, Provo, 801/377-4700, it offers nice views of the Utah Valley from its towering location. Again in the moderate price range, the **R. Spencer Hines Mansion B&B**, 383 West 100 South, Provo, has nine rooms in a home that was built in 1895. The exterior may be old, but the Jacuzzi shows that some improvements have been made inside during the last 100 years.

For budget travelers, there's the **American Fork B&B**, 1021 North 150 West, American Fork, 801/756-9459. It may not be in an old building, but the friendly hostess works hard to ensure you have a pleasant stay. BYU fans will like the **Comfort Inn University**, 1555 Canyon Road, Provo, 801/374-6020. Located just down the street from the stadium, this inexpensive hotel has nice

MOUNT TIMPANOGOS

Steve Mulligan

rooms, and the hallways are decorated with historic photographs of the university and the Provo community.

CAMPING

There are numerous National Forest campgrounds in the adjacent Wasatch Mountains. Most have running water, toilets, and some RV hookups. **Diamond, Whiting, Balsam,** and **Cherry** campgrounds are located in Hobble Creek Canyon. **Blackhawk, Maple Bench,** and **Payson Lakes** campgrounds are along the Nebo Loop Road in Payson Canyon. **Hope, Mount Timpanogos,** and **Rock Canyon** campgrounds are in Provo Canyon. **Tinney Flat** campground is up Santaquin Canyon. American Fork Canyon is home to **Echo, Roadhouse, Martin, Warnick, Mile Rock, Granite Flat, Timpooneke,** and **North Mill** campgrounds. To get information about reservations for these and other Forest Service campgrounds, call 800/280-CAMP.

The state oversees camping at **Utah Lake State Park,** 4400 West Center Street, 801/375-0731.

There are several private RV parks and campgrounds in the Provo area, including: **Deer Creek Park,** 620 Provo Canyon, 801/225-9783; **Frazier RV Park,** 3362 East Provo Canyon, 801/225-5346; **Lakeside RV Campground,** 4000 West Center Street, Provo, 801/373-5267; **American Campground,**

418 East 620 South, **American Fork**, 801/756-5502; and **Provo KOA**, 320 North 2050 West, Provo, 801/375-2994.

NIGHTLIFE
Some popular nighttime activities include watching live comedy acts at **Johnny B's Comedy Club**, 177 West 300 South, Provo, 801/377-6910; listening to live relaxing music at **Mama's Cafe**, 840 North 700 East, Provo, 801/373-1525; and dancing at one of Utah's largest dance clubs, **Club Omni**, 153 West Center Street, Provo, 801/375-0011.

PERFORMING ARTS
BYU's Theater Department, 801/378-4322, has productions throughout the year. **Utah Valley State College**, 800 West 1200 South, Orem, 801/222-8000, also has theater productions. The **Hale Center Theater**, 225 West 400 North, Orem, 801/226-8600, features family-oriented theater productions. Broadway musicals and concerts are held under the stars at the **SCERA Summer Shell**, 699 South State Street, Orem, 801/225-2569. And, as mentioned above, **Sundance** is home to summer theater productions of broadway musicals (also under the stars), and childrens theater, 801/225-4100. The **Valley Center Playhouse** has a long history in nearby Lindon, 780 North 200 East, 801/785-1186. You also might catch a production by the **Provo Theatre Company**, 105 North 100 East, Provo, 801/379-0600, or at the **Villa Playhouse**, 254 South State Street, Springville, 801/489-3088.

FAMILY FUN
The **Seven Peaks Resort Water Park**, 1330 East 300 North, Provo, 801/373-8777, features more than 25 heated water attractions, including pools and water slides to please young and old alike. It's open during the summer when weather permits. The **Trafalga Family Fun Center**, 168 South 1200 West, Orem, 801/225-0195, has miniature golf, an arcade center, bumper boats, batting cages, and more.

7
WEST-CENTRAL
REGION

If you look at a map of Utah, there really isn't much to see on the west side of the state south of the Great Salt Lake. The eastern portion of the Great Basin was settled primarily by farmers and ranchers and communities are spread far apart across the western desert. Industries have come and gone, but agriculture has always been an important industry in Utah's west-central communities, in spite of the scarcity of water. Even the young territory's leaders gave up, abandoning their idea of Fillmore as a capital.

A grand design for Utah's first territorial capitol was drafted by Truman Angell, architect of the Salt Lake City LDS Temple. The first of four wings, using local red sandstone and native timber, were completed for the legislature to meet there in December 1855. Lawmakers met again the following year, but the isolation and lack of accommodations in this central Utah community prompted the legislature to move the seat of government to Salt Lake City. The rest of the territorial capitol was never completed.

With the help of Utah Surveyor General George Snow and capitalists like Chicago's W. J. Moody, the Delta Land and Management Company succeeded in providing a reliable source of water for crop production where several others had failed. By the 1920s the Delta region was producing more than one-fourth of the total alfalfa seeds harvested in the nation.

The relocation of Japanese Americans here during World War II is remembered as a shameful episode in the nation's history.

Today, Delta is the seat of power—electrical power—in west-central Utah. The coal-burning Intermountain Power Project was built in the early 1980s to produce electricity for Utah and California. Delta also serves as the gateway to Great Basin National Park, just across the Nevada border.

A PERFECT DAY IN THE WEST-CENTRAL REGION

Start where Utah's government started—in Fillmore—and tour the first territorial capitol. Then drive out to Delta and visit the Great Basin Museum, paying close attention to its artifacts from the Topaz Japanese Relocation Camp. Afterward, drive out to the camp just northwest of Delta. From there you could head out to a trilobite quarry and dig up your own fossil, or drive to Eureka and visit one of Utah's historic mining districts.

SIGHTSEEING HIGHLIGHTS

★★★★ TERRITORIAL STATEHOUSE
50 West Capitol Ave., Fillmore, 435/743-5316
This is Utah's oldest existing government building. Today it is a museum and a state park. Brigham Young directed construction of the building as a capitol, anticipating Utah's eventual statehood. The first of four proposed wings was completed in time for the 1855 meeting of the territorial legislature, but accommodations in Fillmore were inadequate and too far from the activities in Salt Lake City. So, the seat of the state government was then moved to Salt Lake City. The Daughters of Utah Pioneers restored the territorial statehouse and reopened it as a museum in 1930. The museum houses a variety of items from the late nineteenth and early twentieth centuries, most of which were donated by local residents. The museum also displays pioneer relics, Native American artifacts, and early documents. A rose garden and picnic area are adjacent to the building.
   Details: *Open summer Mon–Sat 8–8, Sun 9–6; the rest of the year Mon–Sat 9–6. $2/person or $5/car. (1 hour)*

★★★ GREAT BASIN MUSEUM
328 West 100 North, Delta, 435/864-5013
You'll find exhibits of pioneer memorabilia, early Western farm equipment, and the history of western Utah's mining methods and tools on

display in this museum in Delta—gateway to Great Basin National Park. Also on display is a collection of various rocks, minerals, gems, as well as beryllium—an ore mined and processed locally that is used in the aerospace industry. At the time of this writing, the museum also housed an exhibit on the Topaz Relocation Camp, but work was under way to develop a separate museum devoted to the Japanese-American internment camp. A restored barrack from the site is next to the museum.

Details: *Open Mon 1–4, Tue–Sat 10–4. Staffed by volunteers so the hours may not be exact. Donations encouraged. (1 hour)*

★★★ TOPAZ RELOCATION CAMP
Northwest of Delta, 435/864-2098

Shortly after the Japanese attack on Pearl Harbor in World War II, the U.S. government started relocating Americans of Japanese descent from the West Coast to 10 internment camps across the country. One of these camps was near Delta. At one time it housed 9,000 people in large barracks. A plaque in Delta's city park says the prisoners were "victims of wartime hysteria, racial animosity, and economic opportunism." It also notes that they not only "endured the bitter physical discomforts of the desert heat and cold, but sustained a shocking affront to their sense of justice and fair play and human dignity." Little remains at the site today except foundations and a marker. There are some private homes near the camp site, but visitors can walk around the remaining foundations and steps that once led to the barracks. Several artifacts remain on the site, and visitors are encouraged to leave items where they rest—take pictures instead. At the time of this writing, a local history group had purchased a piece of the property at the site and work was under way to build a museum in Delta featuring the relocation camp.

Details: *Get directions from the Great Basin Museum. Call after 5 p.m. (1 hour)*

★★ COVE FORT AND FORT DESERET
435/438-5547

During the Black Hawk Indian War, two forts were built under directions from Brigham Young to protect travelers as well as mail carriers, telegraph agents, and freighters. Cove Fort was built in 1867 using black volcanic rock and dark limestone. It served as a way station between Fillmore and Beaver. A number of families lived in the fort

WEST-CENTRAL REGION

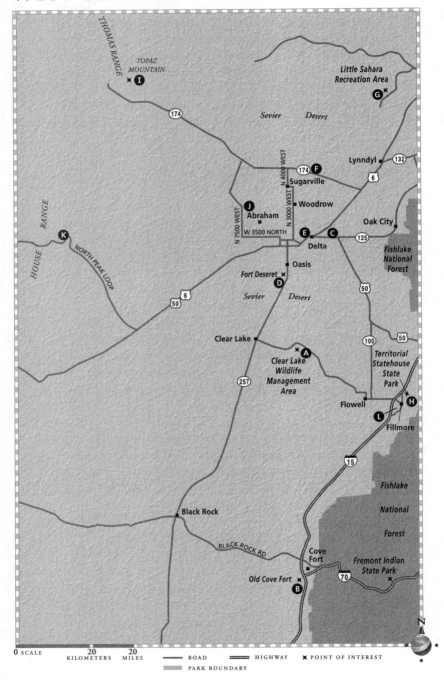

THOMAS RANGE

TOPAZ
MOUNTAIN

Little Sahara
Recreation Area

G

174

Sevier   Desert

HOUSE RANGE

NORTH PEAK LOOP

K

N 4000 WEST

174 **F**

Lynndyl   132

6

Sugarville

N 3000 WEST   ■ Woodrow

N 7500 WEST

J

Abraham
■

Oak City ■

W 3500 NORTH

E   **C**

125

Delta

*Fishlake
National
Forest*

■ Oasis

Fort Deseret ✗
D

50

6
50

Sevier   Desert

Clear Lake ■

100
50   50

A ✗

*Clear Lake
Wildlife
Management
Area*

*Territorial
Statehouse
State
Park*

257

✗ **H**

Flowell

L

Fillmore

15

Fishlake

National

Black Rock ■

Forest

BLACK ROCK RD

Cove
Fort

*Fremont Indian
State Park* ✗

Old Cove Fort ✗
B

70

N

0 SCALE   20   20
        KILOMETERS   MILES   ━━━ ROAD   ▭▭▭ HIGHWAY   ✗ POINT OF INTEREST
                              ▭▭▭ PARK BOUNDARY

over the years and, in 1988, it was donated back to the LDS Church and restored. Fort Deseret was built about the same time as Cove Fort, but it took only nine and a half days instead of seven months to build. What's left of the adobe walls can still be seen about two miles south of Deseret, just southwest of Delta.

Details: *Cove Fort is located near the intersection of I-70 and I-15, 1 mile north of I-70, exit 1 or 2 miles south of I-15 exit 135. Open daily 8–dusk. Free. (30 minutes–1 hour)*

★★ INTERMOUNTAIN POWER PROJECT
850 W. Brushwellman, Delta, 435/864-4414

This is one of the largest coal-burning power plants in the world. It was built after power companies in Utah and southern California realized that there was not enough energy available from the hydroelectric power plants in the Colorado River Storage Project. You can't miss the 710-foot chimney just north of Delta.

Details: *Guided tours of the plant can be arranged by calling the public relations department. Free. (2 hours)*

★★ U-DIG FOSSILS TRILOBITE QUARRY
435/864-3638

Grab a hammer (provided by the quarry) and start cracking at the limestone shale for pieces of ancient marine life—trilobites—that may

---

SIGHTS

- **A** Clear Lake State Waterfowl Management Area
- **B** Cove Fort
- **C** Delta Valley Farms Cheese Factory
- **D** Fort Deseret
- **E** Great Basin Museum
- **F** Intermountain Power Project
- **G** Little Sahara Recreation Area
- **H** Territorial Statehouse
- **I** Topaz Mountain

SIGHTS (continued)

- **J** Topaz Relocation Camp
- **K** U-Dig Fossils Trilobite Quarry

FOOD

- **D** Deano's Pizza
- **L** Garden of Eat'N
- **E** Jade Garden
- **E** Leo's Delta Freeze/The Loft
- **E** Rancher Cafe

LODGING

- **D** Best Western Motor Inn
- **E** Best Western Paradise Inn
- **D** Country Garden Inn
- **D** Roadway Inn
- **D** Suite Dreams

CAMPING

- **E** Antelope Valley RV Park
- **E** Kitten Klean
- **D** Fillmore KOA
- **L** Wagons West

Note: Items with the same letter are located in the same place.

FREMONT INDIAN STATE PARK

This park was established to protect and preserve **Clear Creek Canyon***'s treasury of rock art and Native American archeological sites. At the visitors center, you can look at artifacts and watch a video about the evolution of the Fremont culture. The park is located in Sevier, about 40 minutes south of Fillmore, at 11550 Clear Creek Canyon Road, 435/527-4631. It is open from 9 a.m. to 6 p.m. daily during the summer, and from 9 a.m. to 5 p.m. the rest of the year. Admission is $5 per car, $2 for those walking or riding bikes and motorcycles.*

be 550 million years old. This region is considered one of the best trilobite collecting areas in the world.

Details: Drive 32 miles west of Delta on U.S. Hwys. 6 and 50, turn right at the Long Ridge Reservoir sign between mile markers 56 and 57, continue 20 miles down a gravel road to the quarry. Open Apr 1–Oct 15 Mon–Sat 9–6. Unlimited trilobites can be collected for a per-hour fee. $6/hour adults, $4/hour ages 8–16, free kids 7 and under. (2 hours)

★ **CLEAR LAKE STATE WATERFOWL MANAGEMENT AREA**
East of Hwy. 257, south of Delta
Bird watchers find this marsh an exceptional place to view a wide variety of birds. Numerous species live or stop here, including egrets, Canada geese, cranes, and avocets. There are generally over 100 species of birds in the area, as well as coyotes, bobcats, skunks, and badgers. An underground spring keeps the marsh from freezing during the winter. There are several trails into the marshes.

Details: (half day)

★ **DELTA VALLEY FARMS CHEESE FACTORY**
2 miles north of Delta on U.S. Hwy. 6, 435/864-3566
This factory north of Delta makes 15 varieties of cheese. You can buy cheese here, watch it being made, or sit down for lunch in the factory's restaurant.

Details: Open summer 8–7; winter 8–6. (45 minutes)

★ **LITTLE SAHARA RECREATION AREA**
34 miles north of Delta on U.S. Hwy. 6
Known as the "nation's sandbox," the dunes at Little Sahara Recreation Area attract thousands of off-highway–vehicle enthusiasts each year. The area is divided by fences and includes a protected natural area and sand dunes for people to play, sunbathe, and build castles on without fear of being run over.
Details: *(half day)*

★ **TOPAZ MOUNTAIN**
On Topaz Rd., 42 miles northwest of Delta on Hwy. 174
This mountain is a terrific source of topaz crystals, which sparkle in the sun, making them easy to find. The mountain is mined commercially, but a section has been reserved for amateur collectors. No special tools are necessary, but a hammer and chisel can come in handy to carefully crack open the white rocks.
Details: *(half day)*

FITNESS AND RECREATION

The north face of **Notch Peak**, 43 miles west of Delta, is a 3,000-foot sheer limestone cliff—just a few feet lower than the mighty walls in Yosemite. The cliff attracts a handful of rock climbers each year, but the hike around the other side of the mountain offers an easier way to the top. **Tabernacle Hill**, southwest of Fillmore, is a lava hill said to resemble the Mormon Tabernacle in Salt Lake City. Volcanic activity formed it and the lava tubes, or caves, around it. Bring a flashlight to peek in the caves on this hike. There are also lots of hiking and mountain bike trails in the **Pavant Mountains** east of Fillmore.

Rock hounding is popular in west-central Utah. Check with the local Bureau of Land Management officials, 435/743-6811, or local rock shops for good places to hunt rocks and gems.

Off-highway–vehicle enthusiasts flock to **Little Sahara Recreation Area**. They also like the 200-mile-long **Piute ATV Trail**, 435/896-9233. Local boaters and anglers brag about **Yuba Lake** and **Gunnison Bend Reservoir**.

Golfers will like the links at **Sunset View Golf Course**, north of Delta, 435/864-2508. It's one of the least expensive public courses in the state. And if it gets too hot, you can jump in one of Millard County's two pools—one's in Fillmore, 435/743-4602, the other's in Delta, 435/864-3133.

EUREKA AND THE TINTIC MINING DISTRICT

Eureka, about a 45-minute drive north of Delta on U.S. Highway 6, was the financial center of the Tintic Mining District, a wealthy gold and silver mining area. The district was organized in 1869 and became one of the top mineral producing areas in Utah by 1899. The big mines were the Bullion Beck and Champion, the Centennial Eureka, Eureka Hill, the Gemini, and the Chief Consolidated. Today, Eureka is almost a ghost town. Small-scale mining operations continue, but most of the town's few residents now work elsewhere. The **Tintic Mining Museum**, *435/433-6842, in the historic* **Eureka City Hall**, *has artifacts, newspapers, and displays about Eureka and the community's mining history. It is open 10 a.m. to 6 p.m. Monday to Saturday, and 1:30 p.m. to 6 p.m. on Sunday, between May and October. Admission is free.*

FOOD
One stop in Delta can get you the best of two restaurants. **Leo's Delta Freeze**, 411 East Main Street, 435/864-4790, serves up old-fashioned burgers and shakes. Upstairs, at the same address, you might want to make reservations for **The Loft**, 435/864-4223, which specializes in steaks, prime rib, and seafood. If that's a bit too much, stop at the **Rancher Cafe**, 171 West Main Street, Delta, 435/864-2741, for a good hot roast beef sandwich. The **Jade Garden**, 540 East Topaz, Delta, 435/864-2947, is a simple coffee shop with a popular and affordable luncheon buffet. In Fillmore, the **Garden of Eat'N**, 1035 North Main Street, 435/743-5414, is worth a stop—at least for the name. If you've got the kids along, you might want to try **Deano's Pizza**, 90 South Main Street, Fillmore, 435/743-6169, because it has a miniature golf course and an arcade.

LODGING
There are two moderately priced bed-and-breakfast inns in Fillmore that I would recommend. **Suite Dreams**, 172 North Main Street, 435/743-6622, has two rooms, each with its own private entrance, in a modern home deco-

rated in a Victorian style. The rooms have fireplaces and Jacuzzi tubs, and the hosts will make whatever you want for breakfast. The **Country Garden Inn**, 190 South Main Street, 435/743-7608, is a real Victorian home with beautiful gardens around it.

Otherwise, you could stay at any one of the few clean, economical, and simple motels like the **Best Western Paradise Inn**, 1025 North Main Street, Fillmore, 435/743-6895, which has 80 rooms and an indoor pool next to the Garden of Eat'N restaurant. The **Roadway Inn**, 1060 South Utah Highway 99, Fillmore, 435/743-4334, also has an indoor pool and is quite similar to many of the motels in the nationwide chain. In Delta, the **Best Western Motor Inn,** 527 East Topaz Boulevard, 435/864-3882, is an attractive, two-story, 82-room motel with an outdoor pool.

CAMPING

There's only a handful of RV parks in the Delta-Fillmore area: **Antelope Valley RV Park**, 776 West Main Street, Delta, 435/864-1813, has 96 tent and RV sites on five acres with coin-operated showers. **B Kitten Klean**, 181 East Main Street, is located in the middle of Delta, 435/864-2614. The **Fillmore KOA**, 800 South 270 West (Interstate 15 exit 163), 435/743-4420, has the most amenities of any campground in the region. It has 60 sites, a pool, and five cabins on 13 acres. Closer to the heart of town, **Wagons West**, 545 North Main Street, Fillmore, 435/743-6188, has 50 sites on four acres.

8
CEDAR CITY AND BRYCE CANYON

Cedar City is a thriving town—nearby Bryce Canyon and Zion National Parks, Cedar Breaks National Monument, Brian Head Ski Resort, and the city's annual Utah Shakespearean Festival draw crowds year-round. But long before *Romeo and Juliet* or *The Taming of the Shrew* attracted tourists to Cedar City, people came to the area looking for iron. In 1851, 35 men from nearby Parowan settled in the area, established a town they called "Fort Cedar," and began work on an iron foundry. The town site moved several times during the next few years, then Mormon Church leader Brigham Young selected a place in 1855 that was closer to the blast furnace and out of the Coal Creek flood plain. The original ironworks never got beyond the initial stages, and Young eventually shut the project down.

The town's economy turned to agriculture, although iron mining remained an important industry for several decades. The coming of the railroad in 1923 signaled the beginning of Cedar City's tourism industry, as people from all over the world came to see Utah's national parks. Nearby Bryce Canyon, for example, became a national monument that year. Articles about the park in Union Pacific and Rio Grande tourist magazines helped put Bryce Canyon and Cedar City on the map.

Southern Utah University, founded in 1897, has been instrumental in the region's tourism development. It sponsors the annual Shakespearean Festival, the Utah Summer Games, numerous cultural events, concerts, and sporting events.

A PERFECT DAY IN CEDAR CITY AND BRYCE CANYON

You could spend the day at Bryce Canyon National Park, about an hour's drive east of Cedar City, enjoying the colorful "hoodoos" and the giant natural amphitheaters where Ebenezer Bryce once said it's "a hell of a place to lose a cow." Or, if you're a history buff, check out the world-renowned petroglyphs at Parowan Gap, tour the museum at Iron Mission State Park, see the old Union Pacific Depot, and head out to the ruins at Old Iron Town. Come back to Cedar City for pizza and breadsticks at the Pizza Factory.

SIGHTSEEING HIGHLIGHTS

★★★★ BRYCE CANYON NATIONAL PARK
Hwy. 63, south of Hwy. 12, southeast of Panguitch
435/834-5322

Native American lore says an ancient people were turned to stone by a powerful coyote. Modern science says erosion sculpted the many colorful rocks and pillars into fantastic forms called "hoodoos." Oxides have provided the unusual limestone formations with a wide array of colorful red, yellow, brown, and purple hues. Technically, Bryce is not a canyon but a series of natural amphitheaters carved by the Paria River.

Ebenezer Bryce moved from Pine Valley to the mouth of Bryce Canyon in 1875, where he grazed cattle. He and his wife stayed only a few years before moving to Arizona, but his name remained.

Descriptions of the park's features in survey reports and magazine articles prompted its establishment as a national monument in 1923. By the end of that decade, it was designated a national park. Today, the park is one of the most popular tourist attractions in the state. An 18-mile paved road with numerous viewpoints—including **Inspiration Point**, **Sunrise Point**, **Natural Bridge**, and **Rainbow Point**—runs south through the length of the park to a dead end. Several hiking trails provide a closer look at the park's many formations. The visitors center has exhibits and a slide presentation on the history and geology of the park.

Details: *$10/car, $5 for people walking or riding bikes and motorcycles. (4–8 hours)*

★★★ BRIAN HEAD
12 miles east of I-15 on Hwy. 143, south of Parowan
435/677-2035

This is Utah's highest city, at 9,600 feet, and the state's southernmost ski resort. Brian Head was likely named for William Jennings Bryan, even though the name is spelled differently now. He was a former presidential candidate and one of the lawyers in the famous "Scopes monkey trial." The resort has a peak elevation of 10,920 feet, with snowcat service to 11,307 feet. There are five triple lifts, one double lift, and several surface lifts providing access to the resort's 53 trails. Night skiing, ice-skating, and a snowboard park are also featured at Brian Head, as well as cross-country skiing, snowshoeing, tubing, and snowmobiling.

During the summer, the lifts are used to carry hikers and mountain bikers to the top of the mountain, where more than 100 miles of trails lead through aspen groves and alpine meadows.

Details: *(4–8 hours)*

★★★ CEDAR BREAKS NATIONAL MONUMENT
Along Hwy. 48 between Hwys. 14 and 143, south of Brian Head Ski Resort, 435/586-9451

This natural amphitheater is nearly four miles long and contains numerous ridges, cliffs, and spires among the broken and deeply eroded canyon walls. With colors similar to those of the hoodoos in Bryce Canyon National Park, Cedar Breaks has tremendous scenery, and much of it can be seen from several vantage points along the five-mile paved road through the monument. President Franklin Roosevelt declared it a national monument in 1933, and the log-cabin visitors center was built by the Civilian Conservation Corps in 1937. Ranger-guided nature and geology walks are offered during the summer. The park is noted for its wildflowers, which bloom in late summer.

Details: *$4/car, $2 for people walking or riding bikes or motorcycles. (2–3 hours)*

★★★ IRON MISSION STATE PARK
585 North Main St., Cedar City, 435/586-9290

This park is on the site of the original iron foundry started by Mormon missionaries sent by Brigham Young in 1851. A diorama depicts this foundry. The ironworks never progressed beyond the initial stages, and the project was shut down in 1858. Today, the park features the Gronway Parry collection of horse-drawn vehicles, which date from 1870 to 1930. Native American and pioneer artifacts are also on exhibit.

CEDAR CITY AND BRYCE CANYON

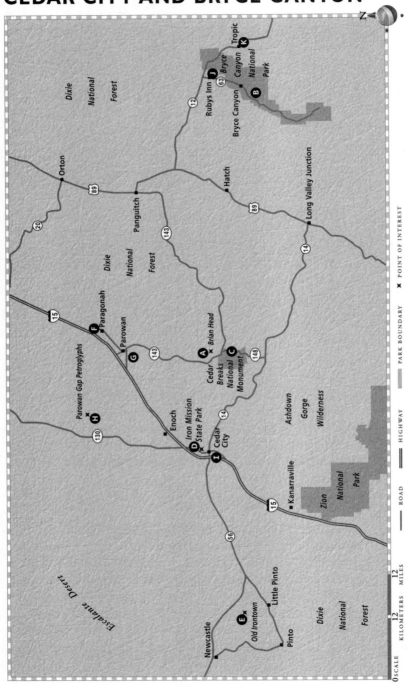

Details: Open summer 9–7; rest of the year 9–5. $1.50 adults, $1 ages 6–16, $6 for families. (1 hour)

★★ SOUTHERN UTAH UNIVERSITY
351 West Center St., Cedar City, 435/586-7701

This university was established in 1897 with a little help from an old sorrel horse that pulled timber through the snow from a mill close to Brian Head Peak. It was originally a branch of the state school (University of Utah), and then became a branch of Utah's agricultural college (Utah State University) in 1913. It eventually gained university status in 1991. In addition to hosting the annual Utah Shakespearean Festival in a replica of the open-air Globe Theatre, SUU is home to the **Braithwaite Fine Arts Gallery**. The gallery's permanent collection includes nineteenth-century and contemporary paintings. Exhibits by Utah and national artists are rotated in the gallery, which also features pottery and textiles. SUU also hosts the Utah Summer Games and is headquarters for Burch Mann's American Folk Ballet.

> *Details:* (half day)

★★ PAROWAN GAP PETROGLYPHS

The gap is a 600-foot-deep notch carved by an ancient river through the Red Hills. The rock art etched into the gap's stone walls by early

---

SIGHTS
- Ⓐ Brian Head
- Ⓑ Bryce Canyon National Park
- Ⓒ Cedar Breaks National Monument
- Ⓓ Iron Mission State Park
- Ⓔ Old Iron Town
- Ⓕ Paragonah
- Ⓖ Parowan
- Ⓗ Parowan Gap Petroglyphs
- Ⓘ Southern Utah University
- Ⓘ Union Pacific Depot

FOOD
- Ⓘ Adriana's
- Ⓑ Bryce Canyon Lodge
- Ⓘ Escobar's
- Ⓘ Milt's Stage Stop
- Ⓘ Pizza Factory
- Ⓙ Ruby's Inn

LODGING
- Ⓖ Adam's Historic Home B&B
- Ⓘ Bard's Bed-and-Breakfast
- Ⓙ Best Western Ruby's Inn

LODGING (continued)
- Ⓐ Brian Head Ski Resort
- Ⓑ Bryce Canyon Lodge
- Ⓚ Bryce Point B&B

CAMPING
- Ⓚ Bryce Pioneer Village
- Ⓛ Cedar City KOA
- Ⓚ Kings Creek
- Ⓒ North
- Ⓒ Point Supreme Campground
- Ⓙ Ruby's Inn
- Ⓒ Sunset

Note: Items with the same letter are located in the same place.

THE HOODOOS IN BRYCE CANYON

Steve Mulligan

Native Americans is nationally renowned. Some of the panels have been fenced off to prevent vandalism, but there are several more to see throughout the gap.

Details: *13.5 miles north of Cedar City on Hwy. 130, then east for 2.5 miles on a gravel road. (1–3 hours)*

★ OLD IRON TOWN

There's not much left here at the site of the second major attempt to mine and process iron ore near Cedar City. The original Mormon pioneers called it quits in 1858, but larger ore deposits were located on Iron Mountain in 1870. This prompted a second, more successful operation that continued through the 1880s. A lack of coke and the availability of cheaper iron from elsewhere led to the project's abandonment. Ruins of old buildings, foundation stones, and a well-preserved coke oven are all that remain today.

Details: *Drive west of Cedar City on Hwy. 56 for about 19 miles, turn south and drive for 4–5 miles. (1 hour)*

★ PAROWAN AND PARAGONAH

Parowan, which was founded in 1851, was southern Utah's first settlement. It has been called the "mother town of the Southwest," because it was from here that many Mormon pioneers were sent to colonize southern Utah and parts of the adjoining states. Their home church is now a landmark. Built between 1862 and 1866, the **Parowan Rock Church** had separate entrances for men and women. Today, it houses a museum operated by the Daughters of Utah Pioneers. Pioneer homes in nearby Paragonah display unique styles of construction. The **Edwards House**, 19 South 200 East, was built in the 1880s with poured adobe walls covered with plaster. The **Robb House**, 128 North Main Street, was one of the most elaborate pioneer-era Paragonah homes. The **Ensign/Smith House**, 96 North Main Street, was built around 1862 with red-clay adobe.

Details: *(half day)*

★ UNION PACIFIC DEPOT

In 1923 President Warren Harding dedicated the new Cedar City railroad line and depot. This, is where thousands of tourists arrived to tour the nearby national parks. Today, the depot has been restored and houses a restaurant with a pictorial history of the railroad's influence in southern Utah.

Details: At the corner of Main St. and 200 North, Cedar City. (30 minutes)

FITNESS AND RECREATION

There's a lot to do in the outdoors around Cedar City. Hiking is said to be the best way to see Bryce Canyon National Park. Popular hikes there include the **Fairyland Loop, Queen's Garden Trail, Navajo Trail, Rim Trail**, and **Hat Shop Trail**. Mountain biking is not allowed on the trails or cross-country in Bryce, but you can ride on **Dave's Hollow Trail**, which starts at the park boundary on Highway 63 and connects with several Forest Service roads outside the park. Bikers might also be interested in the trails around Brian Head Ski Resort. Other popular bike trails in the region are **Red Mountain Trail** and **New Harmony Trail**. Check with local bike stores for more details. Cedar Breaks National Monument has two popular hiking trails: the two-mile **Alpine Pond Trail** and the four-mile **Spectra Point Trail**, which follows precariously along the cliff edge.

Anglers might want to try their luck at **Tropic** or **Enterprise Reservoirs**, or **Navajo Lake**. Fly-fishing is supposed to be good along **Parowan Creek**.

Alpine skiers might want to make the trip farther north to **Elk Meadows Ski Resort** near Beaver, 888/881-SNOW, which has five lifts and 35 runs. There are also numerous places for cross-country skiing, snowshoeing, and snowmobiling throughout the region.

For more traditional activities, try tennis at **SUU** or golf at **Cedar Ridge Golf Course**, 435/586-2970.

FOOD

There are several good family restaurants in Cedar City. The **Pizza Factory**, 124 South Main Street, 435/586-3900, is popular among SUU students and young families. Try their unique breadsticks. For a good bite to eat from south of the border, try **Escobar's**, 155 North Main Street, 435/865-0155. **Adriana's**, 161 South 100 West, 435/865-1234, is a fancier place featuring healthy and hearty meals in a house resembling an English inn. For special occasions calling for steaks and prime rib, head out to **Milt's Stage Stop**, five miles east of Cedar City on Highway 14, 435/586-9344. You may want to make reservations for Adriana's and Milt's.

STATELINE AND GOLD SPRINGS GHOST TOWNS

About an hour's drive west of Cedar City, on Highway 56, there are remnants of two mining towns that prospered briefly during the gold and silver booms. Gold Springs (the turnoff is between mile markers six and seven on the highway) and Stateline (north of Modena and west of the Hamlin Valley junction) still have several remnants of mining buildings and the mines themselves. Be extremely careful around the shafts, many of which remain open today.

If Bryce Canyon is part of your itinerary, you might want to try **Bryce Canyon Lodge** in the park, 435/834-5361. It features prime rib, chicken breasts, and vegetarian meals, too. Reservations are required for dinner. The lodge also offers packed lunches for hikers. **Ruby's Inn**, just north of the park's entrance on Highway 63, 435/834-5341, is known for its very popular breakfast, lunch, and dinner buffets featuring country-style home cooking. The desserts change daily and, if you're lucky, you'll get a piece of Ruby's cobbler.

LODGING

For the name alone, the **Bard's Bed-and-Breakfast**, 150 South 100 West, Cedar City, 435/586-6612, is a good place to stay during the Utah Shakespearean Festival. It has seven moderately priced rooms, including two minisuites, in a historic 1908 home. For a taste of pioneer Utah, try **Adam's Historic Home B&B**, 94 North 100 East, Parowan, 435/477-8295. It offers three reasonably priced rooms in an 1870 home and a former granary.

Additional accommodations that fall within the moderate price range include the **Bryce Canyon Lodge**, in the park, 435/834-5361, which has motel rooms and cabins. **Bryce Point B&B**, 61 North 400 West, Tropic, 435/679-8629, has five rooms and a cottage just outside the park. But **Best Western Ruby's Inn**, at the entrance to the park, 435/834-5341, has history. Reuben "Ruby" Syrett built a ranch here in 1916. He built a lodge near the mouth of Bryce Canyon in 1923, called "Tourist Rest." When Bryce was designated a national monument, Ruby moved his inn to a spot near his ranch. Today, it is a large complex with a restaurant, stores, an art gallery, and tour desks where all sorts of excursions—from helicopter to four-wheel-drive tours—can be arranged.

A little more expensive is **Brian Head Ski Resort**, 800/272-7426, is a little pricier. It has numerous accommodations that range in price.

CAMPING

Since **Ruby's Inn** has everything, it shouldn't be surprising that it has a campground with 127 RV sites and 100 tent sites. Inside Bryce there are two campgrounds: **North** and **Sunset**. North has 105 sites and it's open year-round. Sunset has 111 sites, but it's only open during the summer. **Bryce Pioneer Village**, 80 South Main Street, Tropic, has 10 to 15 RV and tent sites east of the park. The Forest Service, 435/865-3700, also operates a campground, **Kings Creek**, in the Dixie National Forest just above Tropic. Closer to Cedar City, there are 30 summer sites in **Point Supreme Campground** in Cedar Breaks National Monument, 435/586-9451. In and around the city itself, there are several RV parks and campgrounds, including **Cedar City KOA**, 1121 North Main Street, 435/586-9872, which has 100 sites, some of which have RV hookups.

PERFORMING ARTS

Cedar City is about as far from England as one can imagine. But the Renaissance has come alive in the small southern Utah community every summer since 1962 at the **Utah Shakespearean Festival**. Professionally staged plays are performed in an open-air replica of the old Globe Theatre. In addition, "Royal Feastes" are served in the evening, backstage tours are given, and literary workshops are conducted. It is hosted by SUU. For tickets and information, call 800/PLAYTIX.

9
ST. GEORGE AND
UTAH'S DIXIE

Brigham Young had the right idea when he built a winter home in St. George. The Mormon Church leader helped establish the community, and a decade or so later, he bought and renovated a second home there so he could live out his last winters in comfort. Today, St. George is often rated in national publications as one of the best communities to retire to. Early Chamber of Commerce promoters said St. George is "where the summer sun spends the winter," and many people flock to southeastern Utah in the winter because temperatures are warmer there than in other parts of the state.

In 1861, 309 families were sent by the Mormon Church to settle in what is now St. George—which was likely named after George Smith, who personally selected many of the families who went on that mission. Those families were encouraged to grow cotton because of the Civil War. Many of those families were from the South, and they coined the term "Utah's Dixie" for the state's southern region.

Those early pioneers also experimented with producing molasses, dried fruit, wine, and silk—some of the mulberry trees that were planted to feed the silkworms continue to provide shade today.

Tourism is one of St. George's leading industries. It's not difficult to sell tourism with jewels like Zion National Park, Snow Canyon State Park, and, only a few miles away, the Pine Valley Mountains.

The relatively mild climate also makes St. George the only year-round golfing destination in Utah. The area boasts nine championship golf courses, which look like oases growing in the red-and-white southern Utah desert.

The city serves at Utah's southern gateway, greeting travelers heading north into the state on Interstate 15. It also serves as a staging area for people bit by the gambling bug; about 30 minutes south of the city is Mesquite, Nevada.

A PERFECT DAY IN ST. GEORGE AND UTAH'S DIXIE

Frankly, one day just isn't enough to spend in Zion National Park. But, if your time is limited, you can do it. Start at Zion Lodge and catch the tram that runs up to the Temple of Sinawava, which was named for a Piute spirit who is said to live in the natural amphitheater formed near the gateway to the Narrows. Hike along the paved one-mile Riverside Walk. At the end of the trail, jump in the water and continue for another mile or so into the Narrows—most of the other people on the trail won't follow you here. After turning around and catching another tram back to your car, head into St. George for dinner or out to Pah Tempe Hot Springs for a relaxing dip.

SIGHTSEEING HIGHLIGHTS

★★★★ ZION NATIONAL PARK

Main entrance is on Hwy. 9, near Springdale, 435/772-3256

A trip to Utah's Dixie wouldn't be complete without a stop at Utah's oldest national park. Its prominent features are canyon walls that have been carved by the Virgin River and its tributaries, and the giant monoliths that tower over the valleys.

Isaac Behunin built a one-room log cabin near today's Zion Lodge. He named the area "Zion," after the Mormon homeland. But John Wesley Powell recorded the canyon's Indian name, Mukuntuweap, after surveying the area in 1872. That was still the name of the area when President William Howard Taft declared it a national monument in 1909. It was renamed Zion in 1918 and was then designated a national park.

Popular features in the park include the 2,200-foot **Great White Throne**, the **Court of the Patriarchs**, the **Sentinel**, the **Watchman**, **Kolob Arch**, and the **Narrows**—where you can walk upstream between steep, narrow, 1,000-foot canyon walls. Don't miss the 1.1-mile tunnel that was cut into the sandstone between 1927 and 1930. (Vehicles wider than 7 feet 10 inches, including mirrors, must pay to be escorted through the tunnel.) Many of the trails in the park were created by Civilian Conservation Corps crews during the 1930s. The **Kolob Canyons** region was set aside as a national monument in 1937 and was later incorporated into Zion National Park in 1956.

A tram runs from **Zion Lodge** to the **Temple of Sinawava**. Eventually, shuttles like the tram will replace private cars in the main section of **Zion Canyon** because of increased traffic congestion, noise, pollution, and a lack of parking. There are two visitors centers; one at the main (south) entrance near Springdale and another at the north end of the park off Interstate 15 near Kolab Canyons. The visitors center at the south entrance includes a museum with a variety of exhibits and video presentations on the geology and history of the park.

Details: *Visitors center open summers daily 8–7; rest of the year 9–5. Visitors center is free. Park $10/car, $5 for people walking or riding bikes or motorcycles. (4–8 hours minimum)*

★★★ SNOW CANYON STATE PARK
Off Hwy. 18 or Hwy. 300, northwest of St. George, 435/628-2255

Red-and-white sandstone juxtaposed against ancient black lava beds and the bright blue sky make photography, hiking, horseback riding, and camping in this park a special treat. Sand dunes, lava caves, volcanic cones, and Native American petroglyphs are highlights here. Easy hikes lead to **Johnson Arch** and **Lava Caves**.

Details: *$4/car, $1.50 for people walking or riding bikes or motorcycles. (3–6 hours)*

★★ HAMBLIN HOUSE
On Santa Clara Dr. in Santa Clara, northwest of St. George, 435/673-2161

Jacob Hamblin was a noted missionary, Indian agent, colonizer, and peacemaker. He worked out treaties with the sometimes-hostile Indians and was asked to negotiate whenever trouble arose. His home in Santa Clara, west of St. George, became headquarters for his work. It was built in 1862 with red sandstone and ponderosa pine from the nearby Pine Valley. It is one of five historic buildings maintained by the LDS Church in the area. The others include the **St. George Temple** and **Tabernacle**, **Brigham Young's winter home**, and the **Pine**

UTAH'S DIXIE

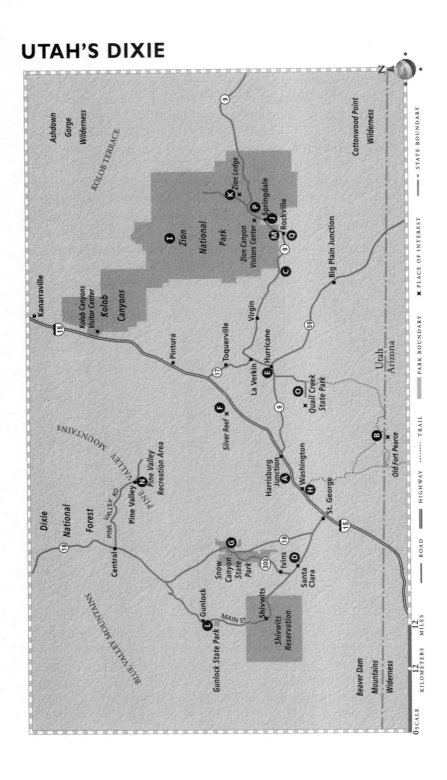

N

Ashdown Gorge Wilderness

KOLOB TERRACE

Cottonwood Point Wilderness

Kanarraville

Kolob Canyons Visitor Center ✕ Kolob Canyons

I Zion National Park

K Zion Lodge ✕

P Springdale

J Rockville

Zion Canyon Visitors Center ✕ **M** **Q**

C 9

Big Plain Junction

Pintura

17 Toquerville

Virgin

59

La Verkin

Hurricane

E

9

Quail Creek State Park ✕ **O**

Silver Reef ✕ **F**

PINE VALLEY MOUNTAINS

Pine Valley Recreation Area **N**

Harrisburg Junction **A**

Washington **H**

St. George

Old Fort Pearce ✕ **B**

Utah
Arizona

Dixie National Forest

PINE VALLEY RD

Pine Valley

Central

18

Gunlock **L**

MAIN ST

Snow Canyon State Park **G**

Ivins **18**

D **300**

Santa Clara

Shivwits

Gunlock State Park

Shivwits Reservation

BLUE VALLEY MOUNTAINS

Beaver Dam Mountains Wilderness

15

STATE BOUNDARY

✕ PLACE OF INTEREST

PARK BOUNDARY

········ TRAIL

HIGHWAY

ROAD

0 SCALE 12 KILOMETERS

12 MILES

Valley Chapel, on the north side of the nearby **Pine Valley Mountains**.

Details: Open summers daily 9–8; rest of the year 9–5. Free tours. (30 minutes–1 hour)

★ DAUGHTERS OF UTAH PIONEERS MUSEUM
145 North 100 East, 435/628-7274

A variety of pioneer artifacts are on display in this museum, housed in the **McQuarrie Memorial Hall**, which was built in 1938 to store and display such relics.

Details: Open Mon–Sat 10–5. Guided tours given by DUP volunteers. Donations encouraged. (1 hour)

★ DIXIE COLLEGE
255 South 700 East, 435/673-3704

The Mormon Church opened Dixie College in 1911, and the state took it over in 1933. Both Dixie High School and Dixie College were housed at the college until the early 1960s, when the campus was moved from downtown St. George to accommodate the college's growth. The old building now serves as the St. George Art Center. In addition to its original liberal arts curriculum, the college offers associate degrees in science and vocational fields. It also offers superb golf and tennis programs as well as one of the most active and sought-after Elderhostel programs in the country for seniors.

Details: (half day)

SIGHTS
- **A** Civilian Conservation Corps Camp
- **B** Fort Pearce
- **C** Grafton
- **D** Hamblin House
- **E** Hurricane Valley Heritage Park
- **F** Silver Reef
- **G** Snow Canyon State Park
- **H** Washington Cotton Mill
- **I** Zion National Park

FOOD
- **J** Bit and Spur Restaurant
- **J** Flanigan's Inn
- **K** Zion Lodge

LODGING
- **J** Harvest House B&B
- **E** Pah Tempe Hot Springs
- **K** Zion Lodge

CAMPING
- **E** Brentwood RV Resort
- **L** Gunlock State Park
- **M** Kolab Terrace
- **N** Pine Valley
- **O** Quail Creek State Park
- **H** Redlands RV Park
- **G** Snow Canyon State Park
- **P** South Campground
- **P** Watchman Campground
- **Q** Zion Canyon Campground

Note: Items with the same letter are located in the same place.

★ FORT PEARCE
For info. call 435/673-4654
Navajo unrest and the threat of raids prompted early settlers in this area to build a stone fort with eight-foot-high walls in 1866 to protect livestock and a nearby spring. But the fort never saw any action. It has been preserved by the Bureau of Land Management.

Details: *Drive south from Washington on 400 South for 12 miles. Tour of the fort's ruins is free. (30 minutes–1 hour)*

★ HURRICANE VALLEY HERITAGE PARK
35 W. State St., 435/635-3245
Located in the center of town (pronounced by locals as HER-i-ken), this park and museum serve as a testament to the determination of the community's early pioneers, who, against all odds, built a canal to deliver water.

Details: *Northeast of St. George on Hwy. 9, Mon–Fri 9:30–5:30, Sat 10–5.(1 hour)*

★ WASHINGTON COTTON MILL
On the west side of Washington, northeast of St. George
Mormon settlers were sent to St. George to grow cotton. This mill is practically all that is left from that pioneer venture. It was built of sandstone in 1866. It was restored in 1986 and is privately owned today. It is used for parties, receptions, reunions, and other gatherings.

Details: *(30 minutes)*

DOWNTOWN ST. GEORGE SIGHTSEEING HIGHLIGHTS

St. George has more historic pioneer buildings than any other Utah city, except Salt Lake City. The city's Chamber of Commerce produces a business directory and visitors guide every couple of years that describes a self-guided historical buildings tour. Several of the buildings are private homes, several are bed-and-breakfast inns. But several others are open to the public, and a few even offer guided tours. Copies of the Chamber of Commerce Business Directory and Visitors Guide are free and can be picked up at the old Washington County Courthouse, 435/628-1658.

Living History Tours are offered in downtown St. George during the summer. For $1 per person, a guide will introduce you to characters like Brigham Young, Erastus Snow, and Orson Pratt in their original homes and settings.

★★★ BRIGHAM YOUNG'S WINTER HOME
200 North 200 West, 435/673-2517

This home was built between 1869 and 1871; a front addition was completed in 1873. The Mormon Church leader became the city's first "snowbird" when he spent winters in St. George supervising the construction of the St. George Temple.

Details: *(45 minutes)*

★★ HARDY HOUSE
46 West St. George Blvd., 435/628-5989

Sheriff Augustus Hardy built this house in 1871. It is still scarred by a bullet hole that, according to local lore, was made when a vigilante group broke into the house and stole the keys to the nearby jail so they could hang one of its prisoners. Today, the house is Los Hermanos Restaurant.

Details: *(30 minutes)*

★★ MORMON TABERNACLE
Main and Tabernacle Sts., 435/628-4072

The tabernacle was completed in 1876 after 13 years of work. Stone for the three-foot-thick basement walls was hand-quarried from the local foothills. The 56-foot trusses were cut 32 miles away and hand-hewn with a broad axe. Take note of the individual chisel marks on the sandstone blocks.

Details: *(30 minutes)*

★★ WASHINGTON COUNTY COURTHOUSE
97 East St. George Blvd., 435/628-1658

This building, completed in 1876, is made of local bricks. Interior features include the original chandeliers and old paintings of Zion National Park and the Grand Canyon. The building has a full basement which originally served as a jail. Today, it houses the St. George Area Chamber of Commerce.

Details: *(30 minutes)*

★ MORMON TEMPLE
440 South 300 East, 435/673-5181

Another historic St. George building is the Mormon Temple. Completed in 1877, it was the first Mormon temple finished west of the Mississippi and it is the oldest Mormon temple in use today. Only church members with proper credentials are allowed into the temple, but there is a visitors center on the grounds that is open to the public.

Details: *Daily 9–9. Special programs are offered evenings, call for more information. (15 minutes)*

GHOST TOWN SIGHTSEEING HIGHLIGHTS

There are remnants of several communities in Utah's Dixie that, for one reason or another, haven't survived. Two of the best-preserved ghost towns are Grafton and Silver Reef.

★★★ SILVER REEF

Located in the only place where silver was discovered in sandstone, Silver Reef was once a prospering mining community. The boom lasted from 1870 to 1881. Today, the old Wells Fargo building serves as the Silver Reef Museum. There are numerous ruins throughout the area, reminders of the rip-roaring mining operations that used to be here.

ST. GEORGE

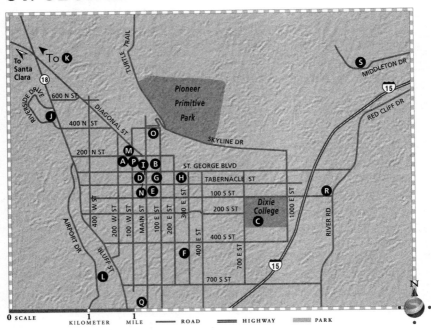

Details: *From the north end of Leeds, which is adjacent to I-15, follow the signs west about 2 miles to Silver Reef. (30 minutes)*

★★ GRAFTON

Floods and Indian unrest are to blame for the demise of Grafton. A church and a few homes are all that is left of this pioneer community. The town site became a popular tourist attraction after the movie *Butch Cassidy and the Sundance Kid* was filmed here.

Details: *Drive south of Rockville across the Virgin River Bridge; once across the bridge, turn west and follow the dirt road for about 2.5 miles. (half day)*

★ CIVILIAN CONSERVATION CORPS CAMP
Off I-15, 14 miles northeast of St. George

While passing through Leeds, you might want to stop at the old Civilian Conservation Corps camp. The camp, which is being restored, was used to house CCC workers during the 1930s, when many of the guard buildings, bridges, roads, and trails were built in Zion National Park.

Details: *(2 hours)*

FITNESS AND RECREATION

The St. George area proudly promotes itself as Utah's only all-season golf destination. The nine courses in the region are open year-round. Tee times for the

SIGHTS

- Ⓐ Brigham Young's Winter Home
- Ⓑ Daughters of Utah Pioneers Museum
- Ⓒ Dixie College
- Ⓓ Hardy House
- Ⓔ Mormon Tabernacle
- Ⓕ Mormon Temple
- Ⓖ Washington County Courthouse

FOOD

- Ⓗ Andelin's Gable House
- Ⓘ Basila's
- Ⓙ McGuire's
- Ⓚ Scaldoni's Gourmet Grocer & Grill
- Ⓛ Sullivan's Rococo Steakhouse

LODGING

- Ⓜ An Olde Penny Farthing Inn
- Ⓝ Greene Gate Village
- Ⓞ Quicksand and Cactus Bed-and-Breakfast
- Ⓟ Seven Wives Inn

CAMPING

- Ⓠ McArthur's Temple View RV Resort
- Ⓡ Settlers RV Park
- Ⓢ St. George Campground and RV Park

courses operated by the city's Leisure Services Department (**Red Hills, Southgate, St. George Golf Club**, and **Sunbrook**) can be reserved through the Golf Automated Tee Time System. You need to first register at one of the courses or at the Leisure Services Office, 86 South Main Street.

Entrada, in St. George, 435/674-7500, and **Sky Mountain Golf Course**, in Hurricane, 435/635-7888, are the region's two newest golf courses. Entrada is known for its rolling dunes, ancient black lava beds, and winding arroyos, which are intertwined with the fairways and greens. But it's expensive, with greens fees around $40 to $60 for non-Washington County residents. Sky Mountain is similarly set around lava beds, but with $16 to $27 greens fees, it's cheaper to play. **Sunbrook**, in St. George, 435/634-5866, was rated a few years ago by *Golf Digest* as the best golf course in Utah. The course winds through humps and hollows above the picturesque Santa Clara River. It's challenging because the fairways are dotted with lakes, waterfalls, and rock walls. **Dixie Red Hills**, in St. George, 435/634-5852, offers nine holes nestled in pockets of red sandstone cliffs. Groves of mature trees accent the course.

Southgate Golf Club, in St. George, 435/628-0000, also operates an indoor **Family Golf Center** with computerized golf-swing analysis, photo and computer graphic displays, and video analysis systems, 435/674-7728.

But there's more to do in Utah's Dixie than golf. The nearby **Pine Valley Mountains** and **Snow Canyon State Park** offer numerous hiking adventures. **Zion National Park** is filled with unique hiking trails, including the very popular **Riverside Walk**, which runs from the Temple of Sinawava to the Narrows entrance. The trail is paved and runs along the Virgin River. Don't be discouraged if you're sharing the trail with thousands of people. At the end of the one-mile hike, jump in the water and keep going into the Narrows. Permits aren't required to simply venture a mile or two up the narrow, steep-walled canyons. But if you're planning to spend the night in the Narrows or hike the full 17.5-mile length of this section of the canyon, you'll have to get a permit. DO NOT GO INTO THE NARROWS IF THERE'S A CHANCE OF RAIN OR FLASH FLOODS! Other popular hikes in the park include **Emerald Pools, Angels Landing Trail**, and the **Canyon Overlook Trail**. With the exception of the **Pa'rus Trail**, mountain bikes are restricted from trails and cross-country use in Zion National Park.

Boating and fishing fans will like the reservoirs at **Gunlock State Park**, northwest of St. George on U.S. Highway 191, 435/628-2255, and **Quail Creek State Park**, between Washington and Hurricane off Highway 9, 435/879-2378.

Steve Mulligan

FOOD

There are several good restaurants in St. George. Some local favorites include **Andelin's Gable House**, 290 East St. George Boulevard, 435/673-6796, which offers old English charm with a casual, family-oriented dining experience. Reservations may be necessary for the restaurant's special three- and five-course prix fixe dinners ($22 to $26). **Basila's**, 2 West St. George Boulevard, 435/673-7671, offers sumptuous Greek and Italian specialties. **Scaldoni's Gourmet Grocer & Grill**, 929 West Sunset Boulevard, 435/674-1300, provides a unique selection of gourmet dishes in a casual setting. **McGuire's**, 531 North Bluff Street, 435/628-4066, looks and sounds Irish. But it serves good Italian pasta dinners as well as steaks and seafood. **Sullivan's Rococo Steakhouse**, 511 Airport Road, 435/628-3671, is the place to go for beef and a good view of the city. Dinners range from $9 to $36.

Visitors to Zion National Park might want to eat in Springdale, near the park's main entrance. The **Bit & Spur Restaurant**, 1212 Zion Park Boulevard, 435/772-3498, looks like an Old West saloon and serves top-notch southwestern fare. **Flanigan's Inn**, 428 Zion Park Boulevard, 435/772-3244, offers food direct from its own garden, as well as burgers, chicken, and salmon. **Zion Lodge** in the park, 435/772-3213, provides what you'd expect from a mountain lodge, including the spectacular view. Hikers can even get packed lunches to go. Reservations should be made for any restaurant in or near the park.

LODGING

There are a number of reasonably priced accommodations in the area. The **Greene Gate Village**, 76 West Tabernacle Street, 800/350-6999, is one of the most unique bed-and-breakfast complexes in the state. Nine pioneer homes—some of which were once slated for demolition and moved here from their original locations—have been restored to provide 19 guest rooms in the middle of St. George's historical district. Breakfast is served in the historic Orson Pratt home. (Pratt was one of the Mormon colony's leaders.) Just down the street, four other historic buildings have been converted into bed-and-breakfast inns. **Seven Wives Inn**, 217 North 100 West, 800/600-3737, has 13 rooms located in two historic homes: the George Whitehead home and the Woolley-Foster home. The attic of the Woolley home is known to have hidden Mormon polygamists from the law. Across the street, **An Olde Penny Farthing Inn** is located in the Erastus Whitehead home, 278 North 100 West, 435/673-7755. There are five guest rooms in the "painted lady" that was built upon a lava rock foundation. The **Quicksand and Cactus**

Bed-and-Breakfast, 346 North Main Street, 435/674-1739, has three rooms in the historic Juanita Brooks home, which was built in the late 1870s with stone chips and irregular rocks from the cleanup of the Mormon Tabernacle and Temple yards.

Also in the moderate price range is the **Harvest House B&B**, 29 Canyon View Drive, near Zion National Park, 435/772-3213. It has four rooms in a modern stucco home. Or, you can stay at the only lodging accommodations in the park, **Zion Lodge**, 435/772-3213, which has motel rooms, suites, and cabins. The first lodge was built in 1925, but it burned down in 1966. A new building was constructed the same year, but it didn't have any of the historic, rustic appearance of the original building. Renovation in the early 1990s made the building's exterior fit into the park setting better.

Pah Tempe Hot Springs is a relaxing treat near Hurricane, 435/635-2879, and is priced right. It is a hot springs, resort, spa, and bed-and-breakfast inn all rolled into one. There are six to 16 guest rooms, as well as camping sites, which include use of the hot springs. Massages are also available. Day use of the hot springs by guests who aren't staying overnight is between 9 a.m. and 10 p.m., and costs $10 for adults and $5 for kids ages two to 12.

CAMPING

The Forest Service maintains several developed campgrounds in **Pine Valley**, on the north side of the nearby Pine Valley Mountains, 800/280-2267. The local state parks also have campgrounds. **Snow Canyon State Park**, 435/628-2255, has 36 sites, some with RV hookups. **Quail Creek State Park**, 435/879-2378, has 23 sites. **Gunlock State Park**, 435/628-2255, has a primitive campground.

There are two developed campgrounds just inside the main (south) entrance to Zion National Park, 435/772-3256. **South Campground** has 126 sites and is open March to October; **Watchman Campground** is open year-round with 231 sites, some with RV hookups. Lava Point has six sites at **Kolab Terrace** that are open May to October. There are toilets there, but no water.

Just south of the park is the private **Zion Canyon Campground**, 479 Zion Park Boulevard, 435/772-3237. It has 150 sites and is open year-round.

There are several RV parks in the St. George area, including: **McArthur's Temple View RV Resort**, 975 South Main Street, 435/673-6400, which is the largest RV park in St. George. It has 266 sites with shade, a pool and Jacuzzi, laundry and showers, a putting green, shuffleboard, and horseshoes and billiards; **Redlands RV Park**, 650 West Telegraph Street,

Washington, 435/673-9700, which ranks up there with 200 sites, shade trees, a laundry, and a Jacuzzi; **Settlers RV Park**, 1333 East 100 South, St. George, 435/628-1624, which has 155 sites, a pool, and a Jacuzzi, as well as many other amenities; and **St. George Campground and RV Park**, 2100 East Middleton Drive, St. George, 435/673-2970, which has 100 RV sites and a few tent sites.

Brentwood RV Resort, 150 North 3700 West Utah Highway 9, Hurricane, 435/635-2320, is one of the most luxurious RV parks in the region. It has 187 RV sites and a few tent sites, with a golf course, tennis courts, an indoor pool, a waterslide park, bowling, and miniature golf.

THEATERS

You can see Zion National Park without even entering it. Near the park's main entrance, in Springdale, *Zion Canyon—Treasure of the Gods* is shown on a movie screen six stories tall. Other IMAX-format films are also shown at the **Zion Canyon Cinemax Theatre**, 145 Zion Park Boulevard, 435/772-2400. The theater is open from 9 a.m. to 9 p.m. daily throughout the summer, and from 11 a.m. to 7 p.m. during the winter.

The Grand Circle—A National Park Odyssey features the parks and monuments in southern Utah and northern Arizona. It is shown daily during the summer on a 24-by-40-foot screen at the outdoor **O. C. Tanner Amphitheater**, near the park's south entrance. Concerts are also held in the amphitheater. Call 435/652-7994 for information.

Utah! is a musical that depicts the state's early explorers and pioneers in an elaborate outdoor production beneath majestic red sandstone cliffs deep in a canyon near Snow Canyon State Park. Built in 1995, the **Tuacahn Amphitheater** features special effects on a grand scale. Performances are held Monday to Saturday evenings between June and September. It is located 10 miles west of Ivins, off Highway 91, 435/652-3200.

A variety of programs and events are held throughout the year at the **Dixie Center** at **Dixie College**, 435/628-7003.

10
LAKE POWELL AND THE GRAND STAIRCASE REGION

Construction of Glen Canyon Dam started in 1956. It was completed in 1963, and it took 17 years for the waters of the Colorado River to fill what is now Lake Powell, the second largest man-made lake in the United States. Today the 186-mile-long lake is a paradise for boaters, fishers, and water-skiers.

The lake was named for famous explorer John Wesley Powell, who mapped the region while following the Colorado River into Glen Canyon in 1869. Creation of the lake provided access to what was once remote and inaccessible land. Now, Rainbow Bridge, the world's largest natural bridge and a sacred monument for Native Americans, can be visited. However, the dam tamed a once mighty free-flowing river, and the lake covered up numerous desert canyons that were once home to an ancient people. Many environmentalists consider Glen Canyon Dam their greatest defeat.

In 1996, while environmentalists were fighting to get 5.7 million acres of southern Utah declared wilderness, President Bill Clinton used the 1906 Antiquities Act to set aside 1.7 million acres as the Grand Staircase-Escalante National Monument. The monument worked like a puzzle piece, filling the spot between Glen Canyon National Recreation Area, Bryce Canyon National Park, Capitol Reef National Park, and the Dixie National Forest. The new monument is a remnant of a park proposed in 1937—Escalante National Park—that would have also included today's Glen Canyon National Recreation Area and Canyonlands National Park.

Development of Grand Staircase-Escalante National Monument was just getting underway in 1998. It encompasses three distinct regions: a series of cliffs and plateaus in the south and southwest portion of the monument called the Grand Staircase; the Kaiparowits Plateau; and the canyons of the Escalante River. It is also adjacent to Kodachrome Basin State Park, Escalante Petrified Forest State Park, and Anasazi Indian Village State Park.

A PERFECT DAY AT LAKE POWELL AND THE GRAND STAIRCASE REGION

This could be as simple as tootling around the many canyons of Lake Powell in a houseboat, including a stop at Rainbow Bridge, or it could be driving through Cottonwood Canyon in the Grand Staircase-Escalante National Monument past Grosvenor Arch and into Kodachrome Basin—a great place to shoot a roll or two of film. Then, take a scenic drive along Highway 12 through Escalante and into the town of Boulder, where you could put your feet up next to a large sandstone fireplace and relax for the evening—perhaps contemplating your next day on the Burr Trail.

SIGHTSEEING HIGHLIGHTS

★★★★ LAKE POWELL AND GLEN CANYON DAM

Off U.S. Hwy. 89, 2 miles north of Page, Arizona
520/608-6404

Concrete for the dam and power plant was poured around-the-clock for more than three years. The dam is 1,560 feet long and rises 710 feet above bedrock at the bottom of the river channel. Its lake, with nearly 2,000 miles of coastline, provides water storage for agriculture and powers eight turbine hydroelectric generators. In addition, it supplies endless recreational opportunities for boating, water-skiing, fishing, swimming, and just plain lounging. The project—including dam, power plant, access roads, bridge, and facilities in Page, Arizona—cost about $272 million. Guided tours inside the dam and generating room are offered daily in the summer. Self-guided tours can be taken throughout the year. The tours start at the visitors center.

Details: Open Memorial Day–Labor Day daily 7–7; the rest of the year daily 8–5. $5/vehicle, $3 for people walking or biking to enter Glen Canyon National Recreation Area. Additional fee for motorized boats. (1–2 hours for the tour)

★★★★ RAINBOW BRIDGE

The world's largest natural bridge was in one of the most remote and inaccessible regions in the Lower 48. But, with the creation of **Lake Powell**, the 275-foot span of Rainbow Bridge, which towers 290 feet high, can now be reached by boat and a half-mile hike. It is located within the **Glen Canyon National Recreation Area**. The nearly symmetrical shape of the formation resembles a rainbow. It was declared a national monument in 1910, long before Lake Powell was created.

Native Americans consider the natural bridge a sacred place. In 1995 Navajos blocked the route to the bridge to protest commercialization of the site and to perform a cleansing ceremony.

Two trails through Navajo land offer hiking access to Rainbow Bridge. One trail is 13 miles long, the other is 14 miles long. Necessary permits and detailed information about the routes can be obtained from the Navajo Nation, Recreational Resources Department, Box 308, Window Rock, Arizona 86515, 602/871-6647 or 602/871-4941.

Details: Boat tours are offered from Bullfrog Marina, Hall's Crossing, and Wahweap Marina. Call 800/528-6154 for details. (2 hours)

★★★ CARL HAYDEN VISITORS CENTER
Located next to the dam off U.S. Hwy. 89, 2 miles north of Page, Arizona, 520/608-6404

This center was named after the U.S. senator from Arizona. It houses photographs, paintings, movies, and slide presentations about the dam, Lake Powell, and the surrounding recreation area. A large relief map provides visitors with a three-dimensional view of the region. Exhibits also include Native American rugs, weaving, and art. Free evening programs are given occasionally at **Wahweap Campground**, north of the visitors center. Check at the center for a list of dates and times.

Details: Memorial Day–Labor Day daily 7–7; the rest of the year daily 8–5. Visitors center is free. $5/vehicle, $3 for people walking or biking to enter Glen Canyon National Recreation Area. An additional fee is charged for motorized boats. (1–3 hours for the visitors center and dam tour)

★★★ DEFIANCE HOUSE
For info. call 435/684-3000

In 1959, before Lake Powell was created, University of Utah archeologists followed a tricky trail up a sandstone cliff, where they

LAKE POWELL REGION

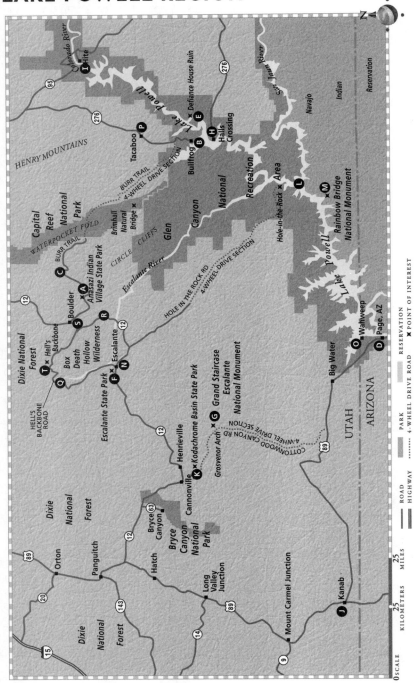

found an ancient Anasazi home and other buildings. Most of the roofs were still intact and the scientists found two bowls with scraps of food still in them. The ruin was named after the large pictograph of three warriers carrying clubs and shields painted on a nearby cliff wall. The site is believed to have been used between A.D. 1250 and 1285. No large communities were built by the Anasazi in this area. A few small cliff dwellings and other archeological sites have been found, and Defiance House is one of the best-preserved Anasazi dwellings in Glen Canyon National Recreation Area.

The National Park Service points out that the structures and rock art are very old and fragile. Do not sit, lean, or stand on the walls. Enter buildings only through doorways or by a ladder into the kiva. Do not touch or deface rock art. And don't add graffiti to the cliff walls.

Details: 3 miles up the middle fork of Forgotten Canyon, on the east side of Lake Powell, northeast of Bullfrog and Hall's Crossing. It can only

SIGHTS

🄰 Anasazi Indian Village State Park
🄱 Bullfrog Visitors Center at Bullfrog Marina
🄲 Burr Trail
🄳 Carl Hayden Visitors Center
🄴 Defiance House
🄵 Escalante State Park
🄶 Glen Canyon Dam
🄶 Grosvenor Arch
🄷 Hall's Crossing
🄸 Hite
🄳 John Wesley Powell Museum
🄹 Kanab Area Movie Sets
🄺 Kodachrome Basin State Park
🄻 Lake Powell
🄱 Lee's Ferry
🄼 Rainbow Bridge

FOOD

🄱 Anasazi Restaurant
🄽 Circle D
🄽 Cowboy Blues Diner
🄹 Houston's Trail's End
🄹 Parry Lodge
🄳 Rainbow Room
🄹 Wildflower

LODGING

🄰 Boulder Mountain Lodge
🄱 Defiance House Lodge
🄾 Lake Powell Motel
🄹 Nine Gables Inn
🄹 Parry Lodge
🄽 Rainbow Country Bed-and-Breakfast
🄿 Tacaboo Lodge
🄾 Wahweap Lodge

CAMPING

🄌 Blue Spruce
🄱 Bullfrog
🄡 Calf Creek Recreation Area
🄹 Crazy Horse Campground
🄢 Deer Creek Campground
🄵 Escalante State Park
🄷 Hall's Crossing
🄺 Kodachrome Basin State Park
🄱 Lee's Ferry
🄣 Posy Lake
🄽 Triple S RV Park
🄞 Wahweap

Note: Items with the same letter are located in the same place.

be reached by boat. Check with officials at either marina for specific directions to the site. (1 hour)

★★★ JOHN WESLEY POWELL MUSEUM
Lake Powell Blvd. and N. Navajo Dr., Page, Arizona
520/645-9496 or 520/645-5258.
This museum presents Native American cultures from the region, geology, the Colorado River, and of course John Wesley Powell. Powell led the first expedition down the Colorado River, in 1869, and repeated the trip in 1871. Drawings and photographs illustrate Powell's life and explorations.

   Details: May–Sep Mon–Sat 8–6, Sun 10–6; Apr–Oct Mon–Sat 8–5; mid-Feb–Mar and Nov–mid-Dec Mon–Fri 9–5; closed mid-Dec–mid-Feb. Free. (1 hour minimum)

★★★ LEE'S FERRY
For info. call the Carl Hayden Visitors Center, 520/608-6404
In the early 1870s, John D. Lee became the first permanent resident of the area that is now 15 miles downriver from Glen Canyon Dam. He was sent by the Mormon Church to build and operate a ferry on the Colorado River. His 17th wife, Emma Lee, first saw the area and declared it a "lonely dell," which later became the name of the ranch John Lee built for her. Ferry operations started in 1873.

Lee was executed in 1877 for his part in the Mountain Meadows Massacre, an attack by Mormons and Paiutes on California-bound settlers. He has since been labeled a scapegoat for that 1857 tragedy. The church bought the ferry operation, and service continued until 1928, when **Navajo Bridge** was being built across the river, about five miles downstream.

Today, Lee's Ferry is the starting point for numerous rafting trips through the Grand Canyon. Remains of the community's post office, which operated for residents and gold miners until 1923, can still be seen. Lee's Ferry Fort, which was built to protect Mormons from the Navajo uprising in 1874 and later served as a Navajo trading post, can also be seen just upstream from the modern boat launch ramp on the Colorado River. A little farther upriver, a large boiler and other remains from a sunken steamboat, the **Charles H. Spencer**, can be seen when the water is low. The boat was used briefly to haul coal for an unsuccessful gold-dredging operation nearby.

CALF CREEK FALL IN GRAND STAIRCASE/
ESCALANTE NATIONAL MONUMENT

Steve Mulligan

The actual ferry crossing was about one mile upriver from the historic district.

Lonely Dell Ranch is a short distance up the Paria River from the Lee's Ferry historic district. A log cabin, believed to have been built by Lee in the early 1870s, is there. So is an old blacksmith's shop, an orchard, and a cemetery.

A brochure detailing a self-guided tour of the historic buildings at Lee's Ferry and Lonely Dell Ranch can be purchased at the sites or at the Carl Hayden Visitors Center.

Details: A paved road leads north to Lee's Ferry just west of Navajo Bridge off U.S. 89A. (2–3 hours)

★★ ANASAZI INDIAN VILLAGE STATE PARK
North of Boulder on Utah Hwy. 12, 435/335-7308

Located near Boulder, just outside Grand Staircase-Escalante National Monument, are the remnants of one of the largest Anasazi communities west of the Colorado River. The village was excavated in 1958 and 1959 by archeologists from the University of Utah. At that time, 87 rooms were uncovered. The site was then re-covered with plastic and dirt until 1978, when it was re-excavated.

The site is believed to have been inhabited between A.D. 1050 and 1200. It is unclear why the residents left their village. It was burned, possibly by the inhabitants shortly before they abandoned it.

A trail leads through the site. There is also a life-size, six-room replica of an Anasazi dwelling and many artifacts from the site on display.

Details: Open mid-May–mid-Sep 8–6; the rest of the year 9–5. $2/person, $5/car. (2 hours)

★★ ESCALANTE STATE PARK
1 mile west of Escalante on Hwy. 12, 435/826-4466

This park is well known for its petrified wood and fossilized dinosaur bones. Two established trails take visitors through vast deposits of the mineralized wood. You will also see an abundance of plants and wildlife in the park, which borders on the 30-acre **Wide Hollow Reservoir**. The park is one of the few wetland bird viewing sites in southern Utah. The park has a visitors center and campground.

Details: $4/car. (1–5 days)

★★ HALL'S CROSSING
435/684-7000

Mormon settlers sent to colonize the San Juan Valley established a river crossing in 1879 at **Hole-In-The-Rock**, just below the confluence of the Colorado and Escalante Rivers. Charles Hall, one of the settlers, operated a ferry there with his two sons. In 1880 he found an easier crossing and moved his ferry operation 35 miles upstream to what is now Hall's Crossing.

Hall's boat was built with materials hauled 50 miles from Escalante. Cross planks about 10 feet long were nailed to two 30-foot-long pine logs. The crude boat was tapered at each end and sealed with pitch. There was no cable or rope to guide the craft, and it was steered using only oars and the river's current. Ferry charges were about $5 per wagon and 75¢ for each horse.

Cass Hite developed a more accessible crossing farther upstream. It remained in operation until it was flooded by the creation of Lake Powell.

The State of Utah maintains a regularly scheduled ferry, capable of carrying cars, trucks, RVs, and trailers, between Hall's Crossing and Bullfrog. Arrival and departure times are usually two hours apart. The **John Atlantic Burr** ferry is occasionally out of service for repairs. Call ahead to verify that it's operating.

Details: One-way pedestrian fees $2 ages 12–64, $1 ages 5–11; $2 bike riders, $3 motorcycle riders. One-way fees $9–$50 for passengers in cars, trucks, and RVs (based on vehicle size). (1–2 hours)

★★ HITE
At the northern end of Lake Powell, off Hwy. 195
435/684-2278

Above Lee's Ferry, Cass Hite developed the best ford in the Colorado River. Originally called "Dandy Crossing," it was located near the place where the Dirty Devil and Colorado Rivers meet. The ford was used by prehistoric peoples, whose structures can still be seen nearby. In the 1880s and 1890s, gold miners congregated at Hite because it had the only post office in Glen Canyon at that time. A ferry operated at the crossing until the creation of Lake Powell flooded the original Hite settlement. Today, Hite's name is given to the nearby marina. The region around Hite is considered by many to be the most scenic in **Glen Canyon National Recreation Area**.

Details: (2 hours)

★★ KANAB AREA MOVIE SETS
Johnson Canyon and Old Paria are off U.S. Hwy. 89 east of Kanab

John Wayne, Clint Eastwood, Gregory Peck, and numerous other Hollywood actors were not uncommon sights in and around Kanab, where Westerns have been shot for nearly nine decades. *Deadwood Coach*, starring Tom Mix, was shot here in 1922. Since then, many movies and television shows have been shot on location here, including: *Gunsmoke*, *The Lone Ranger*, *Death Valley Days*, *F Troop*, *She Wore a Yellow Ribbon*, *Sergeants Three*, *How the West Was Won*, *Bandolero*, and *The Outlaw Josie Wales*. Kane County earned the nickname "Little Hollywood." Movie sets still stand in nearby **Johnson Canyon** and at **Old Paria**.

Details: (2 hours)

★★ KODACHROME BASIN STATE PARK
From Hwy. 12 in Cannonville, drive south 7 miles
435/679-8562

The National Geographic Society named this region—with permission from Kodak—during its 1949 expedition into the area. There are numerous giant sandstone chimneys in the park, which geologists believe are the result of solidified sediment that filled ancient springs or geysers. There are also numerous multicolored rock formations throughout the park. And, there are numerous short hikes within the park, including **Panorama Trail** and **Shakespeare Arch**—which was named after the park ranger who discovered it.

Details: Guided horseback and stagecoach tours can be arranged at the park's Trail Head Station, 435/679-8536. $3/car, $1 pedestrians and bicyclists. (half–full day)

★ BULLFROG VISITORS CENTER AT BULLFROG MARINA
435/684-3000

Bullfrog Marina offers the widest variety of services on Lake Powell outside of Wahweap. The National Park Service operates a visitors center there with exhibits relating to the geological and human history of Glen Canyon.

Details: Open early Mar–Oct daily 8–5; Nov Fri, Sat, Sun; closed Dec–Feb. (30 minutes–1 hour)

GRAND STAIRCASE-ESCALANTE NATIONAL MONUMENT SIGHTSEEING HIGHLIGHTS

At the time this book was written, there were no official visitors centers in the national monument, but it was announced that the monument's headquarters would be in Kanab. Until a visitors center is built, answers to questions about weather and road conditions, as well as directions to specific sights, can be obtained at the Escalante Interagency Visitors Center, 755 West Main Street, Escalante, 435/826-5499, between 7:30 a.m. and 5:30 p.m. daily. The monument encompasses one of the most remote regions in the country. People venturing into the area should be prepared for every contingency, including bad weather and flash floods. Additional information may be available at the Bureau of Land Management's Escalante field office, 435/826-4291. There are no stores or museums within the monument. Accessibility to many of the monument's natural features is limited to those on foot and in four-wheel-drive vehicles.

★★★ BURR TRAIL

This 66-mile road cuts across the northern part of Grand Staircase-Escalante National Monument and the southern tip of Capitol Reef National Park, and connects with the northern end of Glen Canyon National Recreation Area. It provides some of the most spectacular views of southern Utah's rich and colorful scenery.

The trail was named after John Burr, who established the town of Burrville in 1876, northeast of Loa. He developed the trail to move cattle back and forth between winter and summer ranges and to market. Originally, only the switchbacks that cut a notch through the Waterpocket Fold—which is now the centerpiece of Capitol Reef National Park—were called the Burr Trail. Eventually, however, the name was given to the entire road between Boulder and Bullfrog.

The trail was embroiled in controversy in the 1980s, when Garfield County officials wanted to see it paved to help attract tourists to Bullfrog Resort on Lake Powell. Environmentalists feared that a paved road would only lead to more abuse of adjacent wilderness study areas by people driving off-road vehicles. The environmentalists lost, and most of the road had been paved by the end of the 1990s.

The Burr Trail offers wonderful views of **Long Canyon**, the **Circle Cliffs**, **Muley Twist Canyon**, the **Waterpocket Fold**, and the **Henry Mountains**. Several rock formations can also be seen, including **Brimhall Natural Bridge** and **Peek-a-Boo Arch**.

Details: *The Burr Trails starts/ends on Utah Hwy. 12 in Boulder and on Utah Hwy. 276 just north of Bullfrog. The road can generally be driven*

NATURAL BRIDGES AND MONUMENT VALLEY

If you've ever seen a John Wayne Western, you've probably seen Monument Valley, in the far southeast corner of Utah. The valley straddles the Utah-Arizona border in the **Navajo Reservation**. The **Monument Valley Tribal Park** is just off U.S. Highway 163, south of Mexican Hat. Some of the natural monuments are visible from the highway, others are best seen from the 14-mile graded loop road within the tribal park. The buttes, mesas, canyons, and freestanding rock formations are best seen at sunrise and sunset.

Natural Bridges National Monument is about 40 miles north of **Mexican Hat**. A monument since 1908, it features three natural bridges: **Sipapu**, **Kachina**, and **Owachomo**. The names are Hopi, and trails lead to each of the bridges. East of Mexican Hat, on the Utah-Colorado border, is **Hovenweep National Monument**. It features six groups of ancient pueblo ruins. Square Tower and Cajon Groups are in Utah. The others are spread out across the Colorado border. **Goosenecks State Park** is located just outside Mexican Hat and features a 1,000-foot chasm carved by the meandering **San Juan River**.

in a passenger car, but storms can make the road and its sideroads impassible even to four-wheel-drive vehicles. RVs are not recommended. Take plenty of water. (5 hours minimum)

★★ GROSVENOR ARCH

This cluster of white-and-gold arches was named after Gilbert Grosvenor, who was president of the National Geographic Society, after the society's 1947 expedition into the area.

The road to the arch, **Cottonwood Canyon Rd.**, cuts through the heart of Grand Staircase-Escalante National Monument. The southern end of the road runs along a prominent hogback formation known as the "Cockscomb." This road can generally be driven in a passenger car during the summer, but it may be like a washboard in places. It should be avoided during storms.

Details: *Can be reached by taking Cottonwood Canyon Rd., a 46-mile-long unpaved road between Utah Hwy. 12 near Kodachrome Basin State Park, and U.S. Hwy. 89 west of Big Water and Lake Powell. (3 hours)*

FITNESS AND RECREATION

Glen Canyon National Recreation Area is becoming more and more crowded each year as recreational use on Lake Powell continues to grow. On the other hand, **Grand Staircase-Escalante National Monument**—at least for the time being—remains one of the most remote regions in the country. The new monument offers numerous opportunities to hike, bike, and travel in solitude while enjoying the fantastic natural scenery. You may have to travel to the far reaches of Glen Canyon to find solitude there—especially during the peak summer season on Lake Powell.

One of the only maintained hiking trails in the monument at the time it was established was the 5.5-mile round-trip hike to **Lower Calf Creek Falls**, about 15 miles northeast of Escalante, off Highway 12, in the **Calf Creek Recreation Area**. The trail passes two panels of Fremont petroglyphs, and an interpretive brochure is available at the trailhead.

The **Burr Trail** cuts across the northern section of the monument. It is mostly paved, but there are numerous trails that branch off the main road for hikers, bikers, horseback riders, or four-wheel-drives. Routes off the Burr Trail, which are mostly rough dirt roads, include **Pedestal Alley**, a three-mile round-trip hike that leads to some interesting pedestal rocks. There is no shade on this hike. **Brimhall Natural Bridge**, named for Dean Brimhall, an authority on prehistoric Indian rock art in Utah's rugged canyon country, can be seen from Burr Trail. A very difficult two-mile trail that should be attempted only by experienced hikers descends cliffs and crosses streams on its way to the bridge. You can hike into **Lower Muley Twist Canyon**, which was so named because it is so narrow and twisty that it would twist a mule to get through it, or you can explore the **Wolverine Loop Road**, a side road that leads to an area with petrified wood.

There are also several trails off **Hell's Backbone Road** and the **Hole-In-The Rock Trail**. Hell's Backbone is the old road between Boulder and Escalante. One popular trailhead that starts from Hell's Backbone is the **Box and Death Hollow**. The 57-mile-long Hole-In-The-Rock Trail runs from Utah Highway 12, about five miles east of Escalante, to the Colorado River, 30 miles downstream from Bullfrog and Hall's Crossing. It runs through the "hole" Mormon pioneers carved in the canyon rim to serve as a pass to a ford on the Colorado River. Much of their original trail can be seen today. Trailheads along the road include **Davis Gulch, Fifty-Mile Creek, Harris Wash, Coyote Gulch**, and **Fence Canyon**.

Of course, boating, fishing, water-skiing, and Jet skiing are popular activities on **Lake Powell**. ARAMARK, 800/528-6154, operates marinas at Bullfrog, Hall's Crossing, Hite, and Wahweap. It also operates a floating marina, the Dangling Rope. Arrangements can be made to rent houseboats, ski boats, and Jet skis at these marinas.

There are also hiking trails in **Glen Canyon National Recreation Area**, including **Horseshoe Bend View** and **Wiregrass Canyon**. Trails to **Rainbow Bridge** cross Navajo property; permits can be acquired by contacting the Navajo Nation, Recreational Resources Department, Box 308, Window Rock, Arizona 86515, 602/871-6647 or 602/871-4941. A brochure covering Glen Canyon's bike trails is available at local visitors centers. Biking is allowed only on established roads—dirt or paved.

River rafting and kayaking are also popular along the Escalante and Colorado Rivers, as well as on other rivers running through the monument and Glen Canyon.

There are several hiking, biking, and boating guidebooks available. You should pick up the appropriate books and be prepared for all types of weather conditions and terrain. Take plenty of water wherever you go, and check with local officials about necessary permits and regulations.

FOOD

Restaurants tend to have an Old West or Southwestern flare to them in southern Utah. You can generally get a good burger, steak, or trout filet at most eateries around Grand Staircase-Escalante National Monument and Glen Canyon National Recreation Area.

In Escalante try **Circle D**, 475 West Main Street, 435/826-4550, a Southwestern café that serves burgers and steaks as well as tacos and burritos. **Cowboy Blues Diner**, 530 West Main Street, 435/826-4251, is recommended by locals for its Mexican food.

The restaurant at **Parry Lodge**, 89 East Center Street, Kanab, 435/644-2601, is adorned with photographs of movie stars who once stayed in the hotel while filming Westerns in the nearby deserts. Typical American fare is on the menu, and portions are large. But be prepared to shell out nearly $20 for a big piece of prime rib. Waitresses across the street at **Houston's Trail's End** restaurant, 32 East Center Street, 435/644-2488, are packing six-shooters on their hips while they serve you. Chicken-fried steak is popular at this family restaurant. Vegetarians, however, might want to stop in at the **Wildflower** health food store, 18 East Center Street, 435/644-3200. In addition to selling health food, they operate a deli where you can get nutritious meat-free sandwiches.

There are several restaurants in Page, Arizona, catering to people who are playing at nearby Lake Powell. ARAMARK manages all of the lodging and dining facilities in Glen Canyon National Recreation Area, including the **Rainbow Room** at Wahweap Marina, 520/645-2433, and **Anasazi Restaurant** at Bullfrog Marina, 435/684-3000. Remember, the facilities at these marinas cater to tourists and you're likely to pay more for a meal here than you would elsewhere.

LODGING

When I asked friends to recommend a place to stay near Grand Staircase-Escalante National Monument, they all said **Boulder Mountain Lodge**, at the corner of Utah Highway 12 and the Burr Trail, near Boulder, 435/335-7460. The reasonably priced lodge features five buildings around a private lake and bird sanctuary. There's also a common room with a large sandstone fireplace and a restaurant featuring organic beef raised in nearby Boulder.

Budget accommodations include the **Rainbow Country Bed-and-Breakfast**, 585 East 300 South, Escalante, 435/826-4567, which has four guest rooms in a modern home atop a small hill on the east end of town. A hot tub overlooks the pastoral valley. And, in Kanab, **Parry Lodge**, 89 East Center Street, 435/644-2601, was home to stars like John Wayne, Frank Sinatra, Dean Martin, and James Garner while they were making movies and television shows in the nearby desert canyons. (The Duke, by the way, stayed in room 192.) Built in 1929, it is Kanab's oldest motel.

More moderately priced accommodations include the **Nine Gables Inn**, 106 West 100 North, a small bed-and-breakfast a couple of blocks away from Parry Lodge, 435/644-5079. It was built in 1872, and, because there were no hotels at the time, it was used to accommodate visitors while it was still a private home—novelist Zane Grey and Western showman Buffalo Bill Cody were among its guests. The **Ticaboo Lodge**, a renovated modular motel probably built in the 1970s and later left vacant for a decade, is located on Highway 276 about 12 miles north of Bullfrog, 435/788-2110.

ARAMARK (Lake Powell Resorts and Marinas), 800/528-6154, operates all of the lodging facilities in Glen Canyon National Recreation Area. The **Wahweap Lodge**, 520/645-2433, is priced moderately and is probably the largest and fanciest of the hotels. The **Lake Powell Motel**, 520/645-2477, offers rooms at the same marina that are significantly less expensive than those at the Wahweap Lodge. The hotel at Bullfrog Marina, the **Defiance House Lodge**, 435/684-3000, offers luxurious lakeside accommodations at moderate rates. Trailer homes, called "housekeeping units," are available at Bullfrog, Hall's Crossing, and Hite Marinas. They sleep about six people and cost $150 a night in the summer.

Perhaps the favorite lodging at Lake Powell is on Lake Powell. **Houseboats** of various sizes and offering various amenities are available through Lake Powell Resorts and Marinas/ARAMARK, 800/528-6154.

CAMPING

Backcountry camping is available throughout Grand Staircase-Escalante National Monument. Check with the Interagency Visitors Center, 435/826-5499, for regulations and to see if permits are necessary.

There are four campgrounds in the monument. **Posy Lake** and **Blue Spruce** campgrounds, on Hell's Backbone Road, are operated by the Forest Service, 435/826-5499. **Calf Creek Recreation Area**, about 15 miles northeast of Escalante, off Highway 12, and **Deer Creek Campground**, near Boulder on the Burr Trail, are managed by the Bureau of Land Management. Check with the Interagency Visitor Center for information. Campgrounds are also located at **Kodachrome Basin State Park** and **Escalante State Park**.

There are also some private campgrounds, including **Crazy Horse Campground**, 625 East 300 South, Kanab, 435/644-2782, and **Triple S RV Park**, 495 West Main, Escalante, 435/826-4959.

The National Park Service operates a campground at Lee's Ferry. ARAMARK operates campgrounds at **Wahweap**, **Bullfrog**, and **Hall's Crossing** on a first-come, first-served basis. Primitive camping without facilities is possible at Wahweap, Bullfrog, and Hite. Shoreline camping is also allowed outside developed areas around the lake. But anyone camping within one mile of the lake is required to have portable toilets or self-contained toilets in his or her camper.

Scenic Route: Utah Highway 12

This road, from U.S. Highway 89 south of Panguitch to Torrey, runs though some of the most remote land in the country. In fact, the section between Boulder and Torrey wasn't paved until the late 1980s. The 122-mile scenic byway cuts across the northern portion of **Bryce Canyon National Park** *and stretches across the top of* **Grand Staircase-Escalante National Monument** *before ending on the western flank of* **Capitol Reef National Park**. *Along the way it passes by* **Kodachrome Basin State Park, Escalante State Park,** *and* **Anasazi Indian Village State Park.** *It climbs along cliffs overlooking Boulder Valley before reaching the 9,400-foot mark on the* **Aquarius Plateau** *in the* **Dixie National Forest.** *There are numerous viewpoints along the road, including one near the end offering a spectacular look at the* **Waterpocket Fold** *and the* **Henry Mountains**.

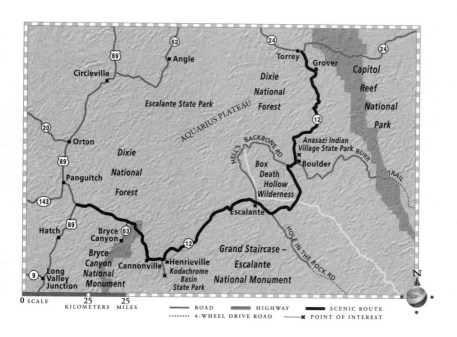

11
CAPITOL REEF
NATIONAL PARK

It may not be as popular as Utah's other national parks (e.g., Bryce Canyon, Zion, and Arches), but Capitol Reef National Park is certainly just as spectacular. Unusual sandstone formations splash color across Utah's south-central desert. The vibrant colors inspired the Native Americans who once lived here to call it the "land of the sleeping rainbow."

The park got its name from the reef-like cliffs that served as a natural barrier to travelers. The cliffs are capped by white sandstone formations resembling the U.S. Capitol. The Waterpocket Fold, a 100-mile-long bulge in the earth's crust, is the most prominent feature in the park. It has been shaped and eroded into a variety of deep, narrow, twisting canyons, massive domes, sandstone monoliths, and spires. The fold got its name in the 1870s for the numerous waterpockets that were created in the eroded sandstone.

In the midst of Capitol Reef's sensational desert scenery is an oasis of sorts in the verdant Fremont River Valley, where you can see rock art from the Fremont people who once inhabited much of southern Utah. (Their culture was named after research was done along this river.) The oasis includes fruit orchards that date back to the area's pioneer settlement. Today, the little town of Fruita serves as park headquarters.

Capitol Reef was set aside as a national monument in the 1930s. A road was paved through the area in 1962. The monument's boundaries were enlarged nine years later and the area was designated a national park.

The park is rich with history as well as beauty. Activities can be as simple as touring the old Fruita schoolhouse or taking a scenic drive to see the impressive sandstone formations, including Capitol Dome. More adventurous activities include hiking to Hickman Bridge or driving into the remote Cathedral Valley.

A PERFECT DAY IN CAPITOL REEF NATIONAL PARK

Start at the visitor center in Fruita, where you can see a short slide show about the geology and history of the park. Grab a copy of the brochure that gives details about the 25-mile round-trip scenic drive that leads south from the visitors center. Remember to bring a lunch so you don't have to leave the park until the end of the day. Take the side trips leading to Cassidy Arch and Capitol Gorge Trail. After returning to Fruita, check out the orchards and schoolhouse before venturing farther into the park. Drive along Utah Highway 24 a ways, perhaps to Behunin Cabin, before turning around to feast in Torrey at the Capitol Reef Inn or Cafe Diablo.

SIGHTSEEING HIGHLIGHTS

★★★ FREMONT PETROGLYPHS

Off the northside of Hwy. 24, one mile east of Fruita visitor center, 435/425-3791

The Fremont people who lived and farmed in this region left their mark east of the Fruita schoolhouse, just off the north side of Highway 24. A trail runs along the base of the cliffs where the petroglyphs were etched in the sandstone.

An archeologist working in the late 1920s along the Fremont River (which was named for explorer John C. Fremont, who had been in this area in the 1850s) was the first to identify the Fremonts as a separate and distinct culture from the Anasazis. He named the culture after the nearby river.

Details: (1 hour)

★★★ FRUITA

11 miles east of Torrey on Hwy. 24, 435/425-3791

The Fremont people were using irrigation along the banks of the Fremont River more than 700 years ago. Mormon pioneers in the late 1870s planted a variety of fruit trees in the fertile soil of the river

GOBLIN VALLEY STATE PARK

*Who said there are no such things as goblins? Located in the southern part of the **San Rafael Swell**, Goblin Valley State Park is filled with numerous rock formations that seem to come to life from a world of fantasy. The park includes picnic areas and a campground among the squat, mushroom-like formations. Located 17 miles north of Hanksville, west of Highway 24; 435/564-3633. Fee is $3 per car.*

valley, using irrigation techniques similar to their predecessors'. At the time, the small settlement was called "Junction," but the post office wouldn't open under that name—there were already too many Junctions. So residents chose "Fruita" for the numerous orchards that filled their community.

Today, there are more than 2,500 fruit trees in Fruita, including cherries, apricots, peaches, pears, apples, and a few plums and mulberries. Since Capitol Reef was designated a national monument in 1937, the federal government has purchased all of the buildings and land in Fruita—including the orchards. People are welcome to stroll through any unlocked orchard and eat fresh fruit right off the trees. Larger quantities of fruit can be picked and purchased during designated harvests (see page 155).

Details: *(2–4 hours)*

★★★ HICKMAN BRIDGE
On Hwy. 24

Arches National Park isn't the only park in Utah that has spectacular rock spans. Capitol Reef's Hickman Bridge is an impressive sight. The natural bridge, originally called Broad Arch due to its size, is 133 feet wide and stands 125 feet tall. It was named after local teacher Joseph Hickman, an early advocate for the preservation of Capitol Reef as a park.

A ring of black boulders to the right of the arch once formed the foundation of a pit house used by Fremonts. The rocks came from a nearby lava flow. If you look up along the cliff, you can see a small granary that was used by Fremonts to store food.

CAPITOL REEF NATIONAL PARK

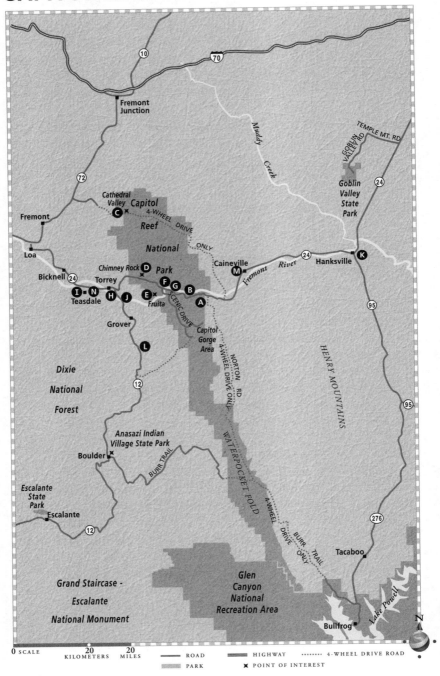

0 SCALE   20 KILOMETERS   20 MILES   ROAD   HIGHWAY   4-WHEEL DRIVE ROAD

PARK   POINT OF INTEREST

The trail to the bridge provides spectacular views of Capitol Dome, Fruita, and the Fremont River Gorge.

Details: *The trailhead is 2 miles east of the visitors center on Hwy. 24; a gradual 1-mile hike leads to Hickman Bridge. (1–2 hours)*

★★ CAPITOL DOME
On Hwy. 24

There are several viewpoints on Highway 24, which bisects Capitol Reef National Park east to west. One viewpoint, located between the visitors center and the park's eastern boundary, provides a view of the monumental Capitol Dome. The formation of a white sandstone outcropping resembles the Capitol and the park was named, in part, after it.

Details: *(30 minutes)*

★★ CATHEDRAL VALLEY
Off Hwy. 24, east of visitors center

This is a remote part of the park that is accessible only by four-wheel-drives and other high-clearance vehicles—or by people on horseback and by those who like really long hikes. This northern region of the park got its name from the huge sandstone monoliths

---

SIGHTS
- **A** Behunin Cabin
- **B** Capitol Dome
- **C** Cathedral Valley
- **D** Chimney Rock
- **E** Fruita
- **F** Fremont Petroglyphs
- **G** Hickman Bridge

FOOD
- **H** Brink's Burgers
- **H** Cafe Diablo
- **H** Capitol Reef Inn and Cafe
- **H** Wonderland Inn Restaurant

LODGING
- **I** Cactus Hill Ranch Motel
- **H** Capitol Reef Inn and Cafe
- **I** Cockscomb Inn
- **I** Lodge at Red River Ranch
- **I** Pine Shadows
- **I** Skyridge Bed-and-Breakfast Inn

CAMPING
- **J** Boulder Mountain RV Park
- **C** Cathedral Valley
- **E** Fruita Campground
- **K** Redrock Campground
- **H** Sand Creek RV Park
- **L** Singletree Campground
- **M** Sleepy Hollow Campground
- **N** Thousand Lakes RV Park

Note: Items with the same letter are located in the same place.

---

that resemble desert cathedrals. A 60-mile loop drive takes adventurous drivers into the heart of Cathedral Valley. You even get to cross the Fremont River. But don't worry; the river is less than two feet deep at the crossing.

Details: *Starts about 11.5 miles east of visitors center off Hwy. 24 at Fremont River Ford; ends outside the park at Cainsville, just less than 19 miles east of the visitors center. (4–8 hours)*

★ BEHUNIN CABIN
Off Hwy. 24
Near the eastern boundary of Capitol Reef National Park is a remnant of pioneer life. Elijah Behunin built this cabin in 1882, using red sandstone like that which forms the cliffs and rock formations throughout Capitol Reef.

Details: *(30 minutes)*

★ CHIMNEY ROCK
Off Hwy. 24, west of visitors center
The multilayered, 400-foot-tall Chimney Rock can be seen from Highway 24 about three miles west of the visitors center. There's a 3.5-mile loop trail that starts here and winds around the rock to a mesa overlooking the **Henry Mountains**. It provides a striking panoramic view of Capitol Reef.

Details: *(30 minutes–3 hours)*

FITNESS AND RECREATION
There are numerous options for hiking and horseback riding in the park. There are also plenty of places for mountain bikes and four-wheel-drive vehicles, but they must remain on established roads—even though some roads may not be much more than a trail.

Hikers should be well aware that it gets dangerously hot in Capitol Reef National Park in the summer. Bringing extra water is not an option—it's a must. Guidebooks at the visitors center give details of many hikes in the park, including long and difficult ones.

As mentioned earlier there are relatively easy hikes to **Chimney Rock**, **Hickman Bridge**, and **Pioneer Register**. Other short hikes include three-and-a-half-mile round trip **Cassidy Arch Trail**, which climbs nearly 1,000 feet in less than two miles, and the gentle one-mile-long **Fremont River Trail**.

FRUITA ORCHARD BLOOM AND HARVEST SEASONS

The Fruita orchards come alive when the trees begin blooming, and again later in the year when the fruit is ripe for harvest.

Bloom

Cherries	March 31–April 19
Apricots	February 27–March 20 (early)
Apricots	March 7–April 13 (regular)
Peaches	March 26–April 23
Pears	March 31–May 3
Apples	April 10–May 6

Harvest

Cherries	June 11–July 7
Apricots	June 27–July 22 (early)
Apricots	June 28–July 18 (regular)
Peaches	August 4–September 6
Pears	August 6–September 8
Apples	September 4–October 17

FOOD

The nearby town of Torrey is home to some of the finest restaurants in the state. The **Capitol Reef Inn & Cafe**, 360 West Main Street, 435/425-3271, offers fresh and healthy food including trout, 10-vegetable salad, pasta, steaks, and homemade desserts. A 1997 survey of Rocky Mountain restaurants called it the best food in the state south of Salt Lake City. It is closed between November and March. The café also has a bookstore inside the restaurant featuring works on the local area. Across the street, **Cafe Diablo** tantalizes taste-buds with fiery Southwestern cuisine, 599 West Main Street, 435/425-3070. Specialties include chipotle-fried ribs, three-pepper sauce shrimp, and home-made desserts. It is also closed during the winter, from mid-October to April. Both will cost a bit more than most restaurants, but the food, the view, and the atmosphere are well worth it.

If you're looking for a steak, stop down the street at the **Wonderland Inn Restaurant**, part of the motel at the junction of Highways 12 and 24 in Torrey, 435/425-3775. The Wonderland also specializes in full, hearty breakfasts. Or, if you're just looking for a good meat or veggie burger, try **Brink's Burgers**, 165 East Main Street, Torrey, 435/425-3710. The Wonderland is open year-round, but Brink's closes during the winter.

LODGING

For those on a budget, you can stop to eat and spend the night at **Capitol Reef Inn & Cafe**, 360 West Main Street, Torrey, 435/425-3271. The rooms are neat and cozy, and the inn has a hot tub and a trampoline. But there are more unique overnight accommodations in the region. **Cockscomb Inn**, 97 South State Street, Teasdale, 435/425-3511, is a small, economical, intimate bed-and-breakfast in a 100-year-old farmhouse. **Pine Shadows**, 125 South 200 West, Teasdale, 800/708-1223, is reasonably priced and offers Western cabins. Guests don't quite rough it like Utah's pioneers because the buildings are equipped with stoves, microwaves, refrigerators, and private baths.

 Skyridge Bed-and-Breakfast Inn, 950 East Highway 24, Torrey, 435/425-3222, has six moderately priced rooms in a modern building influenced by the territorial-style homes found in Colorado and New Mexico. The inn provides views of Capitol Reef National Park and nearby Boulder Mountain. The **Cactus Hill Ranch Motel**, just outside Teasdale, 800/50-RANCH, is an economical choice. The motel has five rooms located on a 100-acre working cattle ranch. The **Lodge at Red River Ranch**, also just outside Teasdale, 800/20-LODGE, is more moderately priced and is a rustic 15-room log lodge by a river. Each room has a fireplace, private bath, and a balcony.

CAMPING

There's only one developed campground in Capitol Reef National Park. The **Fruita Campground** has 63 RV sites and seven tent sites. There are also five tent sites in a primitive campground in **Cathedral Valley**. The campground can be reached only by four-wheel-drives and other vehicles with high clearance. It's about 30 miles down the Cathedral Valley loop drive from the Fremont River Ford.

 The Forest Service operates **Singletree Campground** in the Dixie National Forest, 435/425-3702, west of the national park. It has 31 RV and tent sites and is about 17 miles south of Torrey on Highway 12.

 There are several private campgrounds in the Torrey/Teasdale area,

HANKSVILLE AND
THE HENRY MOUNTAINS

*Hanksville is in the valley just below the **Henry Mountains**, which rise above the desert east of **Capitol Reef National Park**. They were the last mountain range in the Lower 48 to be named and put on a map. On his second expedition, John Wesley Powell named the mountains after the secretary of the Smithsonian Institution, Joseph Henry. The highest peak in the range, Mt. Ellen, was named after Powell's sister. Climbing to more than 11,000 feet above sea level, these mountains tower above the surrounding desert floor. One of America's few free-ranging herds of buffalo inhabit the area. A mill was built on **Mount Pennell** in the Henry Mountains in 1921 by Edwin Wolverton, who thought he had found Spanish gold mines in the mountains. The mill processed some ore, but not much. It was abandoned in 1929. **Wolverton Mill** was restored and moved to a site behind the Bureau of Land Management offices in Hanksville, 435/542-3461. A self-guided tour explains the mill's history and how it operated.*

including **Boulder Mountain RV Park**, four miles south of Torrey on Highway 12, 435/425-3374; **Sand Creek RV Park**, 540 Highway 24, Torrey, 435/425-3577; and **Thousand Lakes RV Park**, one mile west of Torrey on Highway 24, 435/425-3500. Thousand Lakes offers Western barbecue dinners Tuesday through Saturday.

Sleepy Hollow Campground has 36 sites and is located 15 miles east of Capitol Reef National Park, 435/456-9130. **Redrock Campground** in Hanksville, 435/542-3235, has 45 RV sites and 15 tent sites.

NIGHTLIFE AND THE ARTS

Pine Shadows Singers and Horse Show, 200 West 125 South, Teasdale, 435/425-3362, features Western musicals Tuesday, Wednesday, Friday, and Saturday.

The **Entrada Institute and Roost Bookstore**, 85 West Main Street, Torrey, 435/425-3265, offers arts and environmental workshops and weekend cultural events.

Believe it or not, that's what they call it—Scenic Drive. Some people refer to it by its old name, the **Blue Dugway Wagon Road**. *Whatever you want to call it, an illustrated brochure is available at the visitors center for this 25-mile round-trip scenic drive. If you can do only one thing at the park, take this drive. The brochure offers details about the plants, geology, formations, and history at 11 points along the road. Follow the road to Grand Wash and Capitol Gorge. Both spur roads should be avoided in stormy weather because dangerous flash floods are not uncommon. The one-mile* **Grand Wash** *drive leads past* **Cassidy Arch**, *which was named after outlaw Butch Cassidy, who was believed to have used the area as an occasional hideout. The abandoned* **Oyler Uranium Mine** *is located near the junction of Grand Wash spur road and the Scenic Drive. The holes at the base of a layer of yellowish-grey rock date back to 1904. Farther down the Scenic Drive is another spur that leads to* **Capitol Gorge**. *At the end of the two-and-a-half-mile spur road, a relatively easy two-mile round-trip hiking trail leads to the* **Pioneer Register**, *where early travelers recorded their passage. The earliest inscriptions were made in 1871, a few years before Mormon pioneers built this road. The road was used through Capitol Gorge until 1962, when Highway 24 was opened.*

The drive starts near the visitors center off Highway 24 and continues south into the park; 435/425-3791. There is an entrance fee of $4 per vehicle.

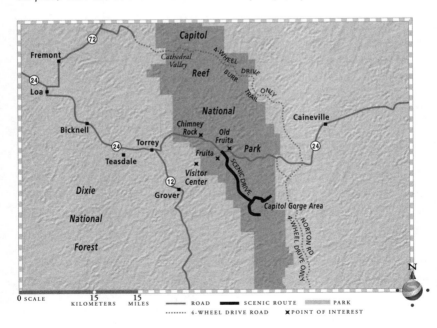

12
RED ROCK COUNTRY

Moab is smack in the middle of Utah's red rock wonderland. It's adjacent to Arches National Park and the Colorado River, a few miles north of the Needles district of Canyonlands National Park and Dead Horse Point State Park, and in the shadow of the often-snowcovered peaks of the La Sal Mountains. Its proximity to these natural playgrounds has fed the small city's thriving tourist industry.

Moab is a party town. Many people work just enough in the restaurants and shops to pay their bills. The rest of their time is spent playing in the nearby mountains, rivers, and deserts.

River running began sometime in the 1950s, gained popularity in the 1960s, and was well-rooted in Moab by the 1970s. Mountain bikers turned their attention on Moab in the 1980s, making the nearby slickrock trails famous throughout the world. Today, Moab also hosts an annual Jeep safari, a film festival, a music festival, a car show, and bike races, among other community festivals and events.

But tourism wasn't always the foundation of Moab's economy. There are thousands of reminders of the region's early residents, which included the Anasazi and Fremont peoples. Explorer Juan Rivera reached the area in 1765. A Colorado River crossing was established there in 1830 on the Spanish Trail, which ran from Santa Fe, New Mexico, to Los Angeles, California. Mormon leaders tried to establish a settlement here in 1855 but were driven out by

Indians. Permanent settlement came in 1878, and the biblical name "Moab" was chosen for the area in 1880, when a mail route was established. The city's economy was based on agriculture—farming, ranching, and fruit—until the 1950s, when uranium brought hundreds of prospectors, miners, and others to the quiet community. The nation's second largest uranium processing mill was built just outside Moab in 1956.

An oil boom replaced uranium for a short time, but that too gave way to something else—potash in the 1960s. Now, tourism is the largest industry in Moab. Each year Moab welcomes thousands of visitors with its unofficial mascot—Kokopelli.

A PERFECT DAY IN RED ROCK COUNTRY

In most parts of the state, you might try to cram a lot of sights and activities into one day. Moab is a place to relax and take your time. Spend the day in Arches National Park. Start with a ranger-guided tour of the Fiery Furnace followed by a drive to each of the park's designated viewpoints. Bring a lunch and plenty of water. Save the hike to Delicate Arch for last—preferably at sunset, when the vibrant colors radiate off the beautiful sandstone. If you can peel yourself away from the arch before it gets too dark, return to Moab for dinner and fun at Eddie McStiff's or dancing at the Rio.

SIGHTSEEING HIGHLIGHTS
★★★★ ARCHES NATIONAL PARK
Main entrance is north of Moab and the Colorado River on U.S. Hwy. 191, 435/259-8161

This is the world's largest concentration of natural stone arches. More than 1,500 of these "miracles of nature" formed by wind and frost erosion of the red sandstone, are found within the park's 114 square miles. The park's first white resident—who lived there long before it was a park—was Civil War veteran John Wesley Wolfe, who settled on Salt Creek in 1898. His homestead was located near Delicate Arch, which today is one of the state's most famous symbols. It even adorns Utah's centennial license plates. Other residents were gradually drawn to the natural wonders in the area. It wasn't, however, until the 1920s that the arches were considered a potential tourist attraction. In 1929 President Herbert Hoover established Arches National Monument, and President Richard Nixon made it a national park in 1971. Newspaper editor Frank Beckwith led an expedition through the new monument in 1933 and 1934. He is responsible for naming many of the arches and spires in the park.

A road stretching about 18 miles from the visitors center to **Landscape Arch**, one of the longest natural rock spans in the world, is lined with numerous viewpoints and trailheads. Most of the major arches can be seen from the roadway or from the park's well-maintained trails. The road passes by **Courthouse Towers**, the often photographed **Balanced Rock**, and the **Fiery Furnace**, a region of maze-like sandstone fins that requires a special permit to enter. Ranger-guided tours of the Fiery Furnace are offered twice a day during the summer. Branching off the main road are spurs to **The Windows** section of the park and Delicate Arch. A three-mile round-trip trail to **Delicate Arch** starts at the cabin Wolfe built for his daughter in 1907 and passes by some petroglyphs left by the park's earlier inhabitants. People who don't want to make the moderately difficult hike to the arch can catch a good glimpse of it from the Delicate Arch Viewpoint, farther down the road.

Details: *The visitors center is open Mar–Oct daily 7:30–6:30; the rest of the year 8–4. $10/vehicle, $5 for people hiking, biking, or on motorcycles; fees good for 7 consecutive days' park admission. Ranger-guided walks through the Fiery Furnace cost $6/adult, $3/child. (4–8 hours)*

★★★★ CANYONLANDS NATIONAL PARK
435/259-7164

Declared a national park in 1964 by President Lyndon Johnson, Canyonlands—with 337,258 acres—is the largest of Utah's five national parks. The confluence of the Green and Colorado Rivers is in the center of the park, and the "Y" formed by the rivers divides Canyonlands into three separate and distinctly different districts: **Island in the Sky**, the **Needles**, and the **Maze**. These districts are not connected by inner roads, and visitors must leave the park to get to another district. Canyonlands is primarily a backcountry destination. Most of the sites within the park can be seen only by hikers or those in four-wheel-drive vehicles.

Island in the Sky is the most accessible district. It is at the north end of the park on a high and extensive mesa between the two rivers. One of its most popular features is **Grand View Point**, which offers spectacular panoramic views 2,000 feet above the surrounding terrain. It's the easiest district to visit in a short period of time. The Needles

RED ROCK COUNTRY

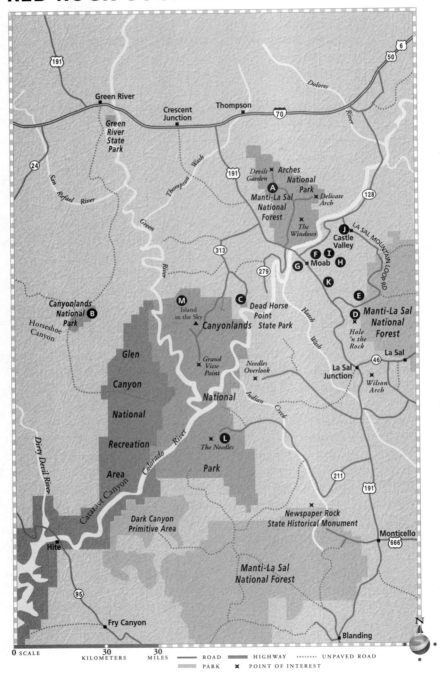

Green River

191

6
50

Dolores River

Green River

Crescent Junction

Thompson

70

24

San Rafael River

Green River State Park

Thompson Wash

191

Devils Garden ✕ Arches National Park

Manti-La Sal National Forest

✕ Delicate Arch

128

313

✕ The Windows

J Castle Valley

LA SAL MOUNTAIN LOOP RD

F I

G ● Moab H

279

K

E

Green River

Canyonlands National Park B

Horseshoe Canyon

M Island in the Sky ▲

Canyonlands

C Dead Horse Point State Park

Hatch Wash

D Manti-La Sal National Forest

Hole 'n the Rock

La Sal

✕ Grand View Point

✕ Needles Overlook

La Sal Junction

46

✕ Wilson Arch

Glen

Canyon

National

Recreation

Area

Colorado River

Indian Creek

National

Park

Cataract Canyon

✕ The Needles L

Dirty Devil River

Dark Canyon Primitive Area

211

191

✕ Newspaper Rock State Historical Monument

Monticello
666

Hite

95

Manti-La Sal National Forest

N

Fry Canyon

Blanding

0 SCALE

30 KILOMETERS

30 MILES

ROAD   HIGHWAY   .... UNPAVED ROAD

PARK   ✕ POINT OF INTEREST

offers more of a backcountry experience, requiring some hiking or four-wheeling to see the area's attractions. It was named for the colorful spires of sandstone in the park's southeast corner. The Maze is an intricate network of steep-walled canyons. It is the least accessible district in the park. Because of its remoteness, you will need more time and a greater degree of self-sufficiency to see and enjoy its features.

Horseshoe Canyon is a detached unit of Canyonlands National Park. Located west of Island in the Sky off Highway 24, it was made part of the park in 1971 to help protect significant rock art made by the Fremont and Anasazi peoples. The **Great Gallery** is the most popular panel in the canyon.

The rivers are quite calm above the confluence, but the combined flow of the two rivers spills down **Cataract Canyon** with remarkable speed and power, making 14 miles of world-class rapids.

Details: Island in the Sky is best reached on Hwy. 313, west of Moab; the Needles can be reached by Hwy. 211, off of Hwy. 191 and south of Moab; the Maze can be reached from Hwy. 24. $10/vehicle, $5 for people hiking, biking, or on motorcycles; fees good for 7 consecutive days' park admission. (2 hours minimum)

★★★ DEAD HORSE POINT STATE PARK
On Hwy. 313, 435/259-2614

Adjacent to the Island in the Sky district of Canyonlands National Park, Dead Horse Point State Park is often described as Utah's most spectacular state park. The mesa towers 2,000 feet above the

SIGHTS

- Ⓐ Arches National Park
- Ⓑ Canyonlands National Park
- Ⓒ Dead Horse Point State Park
- Ⓓ Hole 'n the Rock
- Ⓔ Mill Canyon Dinosaur Trail
- Ⓕ Petroglyph Driving Tour
- Ⓖ Scott M. Matheson Wetlands Preserve
- Ⓗ The Slickrock Bike Trail

FOOD

- Ⓘ Slickrock Cafe

LODGING

- Ⓙ Castle Valley Inn
- Ⓚ Lazy Lizard International Hostel

CAMPING

- Ⓒ Dead Horse Point State Park
- Ⓐ Devils Garden
- Ⓛ Squaw Flat
- Ⓜ Willow Flat

Note: Items with the same letter are located in the same place.

surrounding canyons and provides colorful panoramic views of the neighboring national park. A strip of land only 30 feet wide connects the mesa with a point at the end. The point, according to local lore, was used by cowboys who drove wild horses over the narrow strip and corralled them on the point. It got its name after some horses, for one reason or another, were left on the point and died.

Details: *At the end of Hwy. 313, west of Moab; continue on to Dead Horse Point rather than turning off to Canyonlands/Island in the Sky. $4/car, $1.50 for people hiking, biking, or on motorcycles. (1–2 hours)*

★★★ MILL CANYON DINOSAUR TRAIL
Off Hwy. 191, for info. call 435/259-8825

This is a self-guided walking tour through an outdoor museum. Dinosaur bones and other fossils are found partially exposed in the rocks along Mill Canyon, about 15 miles north of Moab. The trail is relatively short and easy. In addition to fossils, the trail provides a view of an old copper mill that was used when ore was mined and processed here in the late 1800s. The **Halfway Stage Station** is nearby. It served the traveling public between Moab and the railroad, which was 35 miles away in Thompson. The trip from Moab to the

CATARACT CANYON IN CANYONLANDS NATIONAL PARK

Steve Mulligan

train took eight hours, so passengers stopped at the station for lunch. Pick up a trail guide at the visitors center in Moab.

Details: 15 miles north of Moab off of U.S. Hwy. 191; turn left at the intersection just north of mile marker 141, cross the railroad tracks, and continue 2 miles on a dirt road to the trailhead (dirt road is impassable in wet weather). (full day)

★★★ THE SLICKROCK BIKE TRAIL
The trailhead is 2.3 miles east of the intersection of Sand Flats Rd. and Millcreek Dr., Moab, for info. call 435/259-8825

This is the most famous mountain bike trail in Utah. People from all over the world come to Moab just to ride on this 9.6-mile trail that was originally laid out by motorcyclists in 1969. Today, it is used by motorized and pedal-powered bikes. It is marked with white dashes painted on the slickrock. Intersections, points of interest, and caution zones are marked with yellow paint. Don't underestimate the difficulty of this trail. It is very difficult and demanding, but it's not without rewards. The course runs across the cliffs overlooking canyons and the Colorado River, with panoramic views of the nearby national parks and the La Sal Mountains. Novice riders can test their skills and stamina on a 2.2-mile practice loop.

Details: Brochures on this trail and other mountain bike trails in the area are available at the visitors center in Moab. (4–6 hours)

★★★ PETROGLYPH DRIVING TOUR
For info. call 435/259-8825

There are numerous places throughout Moab where ancient Native Americans, including the Fremont and Anasazi peoples, left their marks on rocks and cliff faces. Most of the sites are along frontage roads that parallel the Colorado River. Sites that can be reached in passenger cars, include Golf Course, Kane Creek Boulevard, Courthouse Wash, Potash Road (Highway 279), and Wolfe Ranch. Dinosaur tracks are visible along Potash Road.

Details: Brochures and guidebooks are available at the visitors center in Moab. (3–4 hours)

★★ DAN O'LAURIE MUSEUM
118 East Center St., 435/259-7985

Moab's history, from dinosaurs and early Native Americans to the old Spanish Trail and uranium mining, is featured in this small museum. The museum also features changing art exhibits by local artists. And before you pick up the free brochure at the museum that gives details about a walking tour of several historic homes and buildings in Moab, check out the player piano.

Details: Open summer Mon–Sat 1–8; winter Mon–Thu 3–7, Fri–Sat 1–7. Donations encouraged. (2 hours)

★★ MOAB TO MONUMENT VALLEY FILM COMMISSION AND MUSEUM
50 East Center St., Number 1, 435/259-6388

Numerous movies and television commercials have been filmed in southeastern Utah. The film commission helps promote the region as a location for such shoots and works directly with the film companies when they are on location. A collection of photographs, posters, and other movie memorabilia is on display in the commission's office.

Details: Open Mon–Fri 8–noon and 1–5. Free. (2 hours)

★ ARCHES WINERY
420 Kane Creek Blvd., 435/259-5397

Wine in the middle of this desert? Yes. The University of Arizona and Schick International studied the southeastern Utah region beginning in 1973. Seven years later they determined it was an excellent grape-growing area for varieties that can take cold winters. Area vineyards were expanded in the early 1980s, and Arches Vineyards, Utah's first winery, opened in 1989. Tours and tasting are available.

Details: Open Mon–Sat 11–7. Free. (1–2 hours)

★ **HOLE 'N THE ROCK**
15 miles south of Moab on U.S. Hwy. 191, 435/686-2250

Imagine telling your spouse that you're planning to build a cave instead of a house. That's what Albert and Gladys Christensen did south of Moab. They removed 50,000 cubic feet of sandstone to make their 14-room home.

Details: Open daily 9–5. $2.50 adults, $1.50 children. (30 minutes)

★ **MOVIE LOCATIONS TOUR**
435/259-8825

There are several brochures available at the visitors center in Moab that give details for self-guided hiking, biking, driving, and floating tours in the region. Movie buffs will particularly enjoy the movie locations tour. Many Westerns have been filmed here over the years, some starring legendary actors like John Wayne (*Rio Grande*) and Henry Fonda (*Warlock*). More recently, films like *Thelma and Louise* and *Indiana Jones and the Last Crusade* were filmed in the region. The brochure tells you where scenes were shot and what happened in the scenes.

Details: (time spent depends on the tour you choose)

★ **SCOTT M. MATHESON WETLANDS PRESERVE**
North of Kane Creek Rd., near the Colorado River
435/259-4629

West of Moab, along the Colorado River, the Moab Slough has been a home to wildlife for centuries. Today, trails lead through the 875 acres that are owned and jointly managed by the Nature Conservancy and the Utah Division of Wildlife Resources. The preserve was named after a former governor of Utah who was a conservation advocate.

Details: Open daily sunrise to sunset. Naturalist-guided walks Mar–Oct Sat 8 a.m. (half day)

FITNESS AND RECREATION

Moab features the best in all sorts of outdoor recreational activities. River runners, whether looking for flat water or white water, have been coming to Moab for decades. Several companies that specialize in float and rapid trips, four-wheel-drive trips, horseback riding, and biking have brochures at the visitors center in Moab.

The **Slickrock Bike Trail** attracts mountain bikers from all over the world, but it's a very difficult trail to ride. Other popular trails include the **Monitor and Merrimac Trail**, **Gemini Bridges Trail**, and **Hurrah Pass Trail**. Bring your own bike, or rent one at any of the several bike shops in town.

Numerous easy and difficult hikes can be found in Arches National Park. The trails in Canyonlands National Park, however, tend to be much longer and harder—some require extensive backcountry knowledge and several days of backpacking. The **Devils Garden Trail** is a popular hike past several arches in Arches National Park. Short hikes in the Island in the Sky district of Canyonlands include the **Mesa Arch Trail**, **Upheaval Dome Overlook**, and **Grand View Trail**. More difficult hikes in that district include **Neck Spring Trail** and **Lathrop Trail**. The **White Rim Road** is a very popular 100-mile four-wheel-drive road. The **Elephant Hill Trailhead** in the Needles district offers several options for hiking and four-wheeling into the back coun-

MOAB

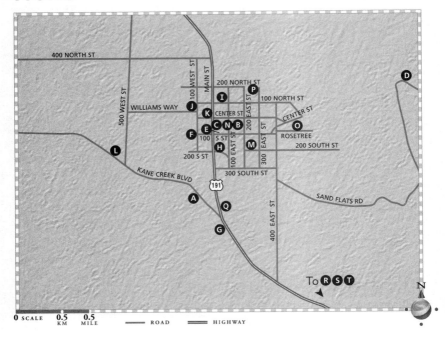

try. A popular hike from there is the one to Druid Arch. Other popular hikes around Moab include **Negro Bill Canyon, Hidden Valley Trail**, and **Corona Arch Trail**. Four-wheel-drive enthusiasts will like the **Moab Rim Trail** and **Poison Spider Mesa**.

It gets very hot in much of the red rock country, and park rangers recommend that hikers carry at least one gallon of water per person. Don't ignore their advice. People have died from a combination of the heat, exposure, and a lack of water in this part of the country.

The nearby La Sal Mountains offer a variety of hiking and cross-country skiing opportunities as well as fishing and hunting.

Rock climbing is quite popular here. **Fisher Towers** and **Castle Valley** are popular destinations among sandstone climbers. But if you're looking for more traditional recreation, try tennis on the public courts at **Grand County Middle School**, 217 East Center Street, or golf at **Moab Golf Course**, 435/259-6488. You can keep cool during the summer in the pools at **King World Water Park**, 1500 North U.S. Highway 191, 435/25-WATER.

FOOD

Moab has lots of great places to eat. But keep in mind that Moab is a tourist mecca and prices are likely to reflect that.

The **Moab Diner**, 189 South Main Street, 435/259-4006, is a fun little café frequented by locals with a craving for good home cooking. They open at

---

SIGHTS

- Ⓐ Arches Winery
- Ⓑ Dan O'Laurie Museum
- Ⓒ Moab to Monument Valley Film Commission and Museum
- Ⓓ The Slickrock Bike Trail

FOOD

- Ⓔ Eddie McStiff's
- Ⓕ Fat City Smokehouse
- Ⓖ Moab Brewery
- Ⓗ Moab Diner
- Ⓘ Poplar Place
- Ⓙ Rio Colorado
- Ⓚ Slickrock Cafe

LODGING

- Ⓛ Blue Heron Bed-and-Breakfast
- Ⓜ Dream Catcher Inn
- Ⓝ Hotel Off Cent'r
- Ⓞ Mayor's House Bed-and-Breakfast
- Ⓟ Sunflower Hill B&B Inn

CAMPING

- Ⓠ Canyonlands Campground
- Ⓡ Moab KOA
- Ⓢ Moab Valley RV and Campark
- Ⓣ Slickrock Campground

Cryptobiotic Soils

Much of the dirt in southeastern Utah—from Capitol Reef to Lake Powell—is alive. It won't bite you, but your footprint can kill it. Called "cryptobiotic" or "cryptogamic," the soil is composed of several species of mosses, lichens, fungi, and algae. They protect the soil from erosion, absorb moisture, and provide nitrogen and other nutrients for plant growth. These living organisms form a dark, cruddy-looking crust that covers much of the terrain of untrampled desert areas. Avoid these areas when hiking or biking. It takes decades for trampled areas of cryptobiotic soil to grow back. Stay on the slickrock sandstone as much as possible. If you have to venture off the rocks, try to follow washes, where the cryptobiotic soil is unlikely to be. (But remember to be cautious about flash floods.) For more information about this soil, ask rangers at any state or national park in the Moab area, or check at the Moab Information Center.

6 a.m. and specialize in breakfast, which is served all day long. For years, **Eddie McStiff's**, 57 South Main Street, 435/259-BEER, was the only microbrewery in town. But **Moab Brewery**, 686 South Main Street, 435/259-6333, opened a few years ago and competes to quench the thirsts of Moab's active outdoors people. Eddie McStiff's features pizzas, pastas, and salads, while Moab Brewery offers steaks and seafood. Both have typical pub fare and vegetarian dishes. The **Slickrock Cafe**, at the corner of Center and Main Streets, 435/259-8004, and **Poplar Place**, 11 East 100 North, 435/259-6018, also serve typical pub food in contemporary settings. If you're craving something barbecued that will just melt in your mouth, try **Fat City Smokehouse**, 36 South 100 West, 435/259-4302. The **Rio Colorado**, 2 South 100 West, 435/259-6666, features good southwestern food and dancing in the adjoining private club. But if you're looking for something fancy and quiet, drive 16 miles south of town to the **Pack Creek Inn**, on the La Sal Loop Road, 435/259-5505. It features steaks, quail, salmon, and vegetarian fare. Sunday evenings are set aside for a Western barbecue supper.

LODGING
The **Hotel Off Cent'r**, 96 East Center Street, 435/259-4244, is an older building that was once the region's energy office during the height of the uranium

boom. Today, it has nine economical guest rooms, including a dormitory-style room with four single beds for those on a supertight budget. The **Lazy Lizard International Hostel**, 1213 South U.S. Highway 191, 435/259-6057, is a bargain place to stay if you're willing to share. In addition to the dormitory, the hostel has private rooms and cabins, and you might even find a tepee.

Moderately priced accommodations include the **Mayor's House Bed-and-Breakfast**, 505 East Rose Tree Lane, 435/259-6015, which was just that—it was the mayor's house for 16 years, until 1998. Owners of the **Dream Catcher Inn**, 191 South 200 East, 435/259-5998, are experienced hikers, bikers, and boaters in the region. They're available to answer questions for their guests and will let you browse through the inn's library of guidebooks and maps.

Additional choices for moderately priced lodging include the **Sunflower Hill B&B Inn**, 185 North 300 East, 435/259-2974, which is a restored farmhouse and a quaint Cape Cod–style cottage with a wrap-around porch. The **Blue Heron Bed-and-Breakfast**, 900 Kane Creek Boulevard, 435/259-4921, is one mile southwest of the center of Moab and adjacent to the Matheson Wetlands Preserve. And if you want to escape the crowds in Moab, head out to Castle Valley and stay at the **Castle Valley Inn**, off the La Sal Mountain Loop Road, 435/259-6012. It features five rooms in the main building and three bungalows.

CAMPING

The National Park Service operates one campground in Arches National Park, **Devils Garden**, 435/259-8161, and two in Canyonlands National Park, **Squaw Flat** in the Needles district, 435/259-4711, and **Willow Flat** in Island in the Sky, 435/259-4712. Devils Garden and Squaw Flat have drinking water. The Park Service campgrounds are open year-round and do not have RV hookups. There are 21 sites with RV hookups at **Dead Horse Point State Park**, 435/259-2614. The **Bureau of Land Management**, 435/259-6111, operates several campgrounds in the Moab area, including five campgrounds that are north of U.S. Highway 191 along the Colorado River. All of the BLM campgrounds have RV hookups and tent sites.

There are numerous private campgrounds in the area, including **Canyonlands Campground**, 555 South Main Street, 435/259-6848; **Moab KOA**, 3225 South U.S. Highway 191, 435/259-6682; **Moab Valley RV and Campark**, 1773 North U.S. Highway 191, 435/259-4469; and **Slickrock Campground**, 1301½ North U.S. Highway 191, 435/259-7660. Each of these campgrounds has more than 100 sites, including some with RV hookups.

NIGHTLIFE

Moab Brewery, 868 South Main Street, 435/259-6333; **Eddie McStiff's**, 57 South Main Street, 534/259-BEER; and **Rio Colorado**, 2 South 100 West, 435/259-6666, are popular nighttime hangouts where you can get a good drink. At the Rio you can dance to live rock, reggae, or jazz on most weekends during the summer. Country-and-western music is on tap at the **Sportsman's Lounge**, 1991 South U.S. Highway 191, 435/259-6585. Old West gunfights are still taking place at the **Bar-M Chuckwagon**, 435/259-2276, which offers a "cowboy supper" and live Western stage show with comedy and music. In September the **Moab Music Festival**, 435/259-7003, features classical chamber music in various outdoor settings throughout the region. A unique way to see the Colorado River and its adjacent red rock canyon walls is to take a **Canyonlands by Night** tour, 435/259-5261. During the summer boats take visitors along the river while giant lights illuminate the canyon walls.

13
CASTLE VALLEY

Castle Valley is nestled between the Wasatch Plateau to the west, the San Rafael Swell to the southeast, and the West Tavaputs Plateau and the Book Cliffs to the northeast. The largest of the Castle Valley communities is Price, at the crossroads of Utah Highway 10 and U.S. Highways 6 and 191. It serves as a gateway to the canyon country of southeastern Utah.

Price was likely named for a Mormon bishop who explored the region in 1869. The coal mines made Price and its neighboring communities what they are today. After the railroad was built through the area in 1883, Price was quickly transformed from an isolated farming community to a commercial hub—a retail, political, educational, and cultural center for the area. Thousands of foreign-born, non-Mormon immigrants descended into the valley to work in its mines.

Life was not easy for those early coal miners. Modern equipment and techniques have now replaced the thousands of workers it took to extract coal from the ground. Their camps have long since disappeared, but the endless lines of coal-laden railroad cars remind us of Castle Valley's heritage.

The miners were of various nationalities, including Greek, Italian, Austrian, and Japanese, making Price a very diverse community—and that diversity is still alive today. The community celebrates its diversity each year with several events, including International Days and the Greek Festival.

Remnants from dinosaurs, early Native Americans, explorers, and the people who tamed the Old West are found throughout Castle Valley, a region rich in history.

A PERFECT DAY IN CASTLE VALLEY

Start in Helper's Western Mining and Railroad Museum, then check out a few of the art studios in Helper's downtown business district. Drive down to Price for lunch at the Greek Streak before cruising over to the College of Eastern Utah's Prehistoric Museum. If there's time, it's worth the drive south to the Cleveland-Lloyd Dinosaur Quarry, where some of the bones at CEU were discovered. Or, spend the day venturing into Nine-Mile Canyon on a highway that was used by early Native Americans, stage coaches, mail couriers, freighters, and ranchers—a place to really step back in history.

SIGHTSEEING HIGHLIGHTS

★★★★ CLEVELAND-LLOYD DINOSAUR QUARRY
435/636-3600

More than 12,000 bones from 70 different animals have been excavated at this site, including an egg containing a fossilized dinosaur embryo. Dinosaur bones from this quarry are on display in museums across the United States, Europe, and the Far East. About 147 million years ago, this area was a shallow freshwater lake with a muddy bottom. Plant-eating dinosaurs and the meat-eaters who preyed upon them occasionally became trapped in the mud. In 1929 University of Utah scientists conducted the first dig at the site. Between 1939 and 1941, Princeton University did some extensive work in the quarry, financed by Malcomb Lloyd. Because of the proximity to Cleveland, it became known as the Cleveland-Lloyd Quarry. It was designated as a national natural landmark in 1966. It's still possible today to occasionally see scientists working in the quarry. The Bureau of Land Management operates a visitors center here.

Details: *Near Cleveland (south of Price on Hwy. 10 and Hwy. 155); after turning onto 155, follow the signs to the dinosaur quarry; the last 8 miles are gravel road. Open Easter–Memorial Day Sat, Sun 10–5; then daily until Labor Day. $2 adults, $1 students and ages 6–17. (half day)*

★★★★ NINE-MILE CANYON
The road between Wellington and Myton was built in 1886 by the U.S. Ninth Cavalry, a regiment of African American men formed

GREEN RIVER AND
THE SAN RAFAEL SWELL

Geologic upheavals formed a giant dome of rock in the east-central Utah desert. Eventually, the harsh elements beat against the dome until it collapsed into a wild, broken array of multicolored sandstone. Wind and water then carved the jumble of rock into the buttes, canyons, pinnacles, and mesas that make the San Rafael Swell one of the most ruggedly beautiful areas in the Southwest.

The Swell is crisscrossed by numerous roads that are best travelled by four-wheel-drive vehicles. The Swell is a great place for desert camping and hiking. Make sure you bring enough gasoline and drinking water.

The **Wedge Overlook** provides a spectacular view of the canyon formed by the San Rafael River—a "little Grand Canyon." To get there, drive east of Highway 10, about one mile north of Castle Dale, for 13 miles. At the junction, head south for six miles through pinyon pines and junipers until you reach the overlook.

The Green River forms the eastern boundary of the Swell. The town of Green River, near the junction of Interstate 70 and U.S. Highways 6 and 191, developed because it was the only spot within 200 miles with a bridge over the mighty river. Ute Indians used the crossing for centuries and it was part of the old Spanish Trail (first used in 1830) between Santa Fe, New Mexico, and Los Angeles, California.

The **John Wesley Powell Museum**, 885 East Main Street, Green River, 435/564-3427, was named after the man who charted the Green and Colorado Rivers. He also mapped much of the region near those rivers in 1869 and 1871. The museum features journal excerpts from early explorers and displays of their boats, as well as a 20-minute video on Powell's adventures.

Green River is a hub for boaters. Some sections of the river offer calm canoe rides, others roaring Class IV rapids. North of town, the river runs through **Desolation Canyon**, which was designated a national historic landmark. The Bureau of Land Management office in Price can help with a list of professional river-guiding companies, 435/636-3600.

Something just as spectacular, but not quite as gut wrenching, is **Crystal Geyser**, a cold-water geyser that erupts three to four times a day on the east bank of the Green River. Directions can be obtained at the visitors center inside the Powell Museum.

CASTLE VALLEY

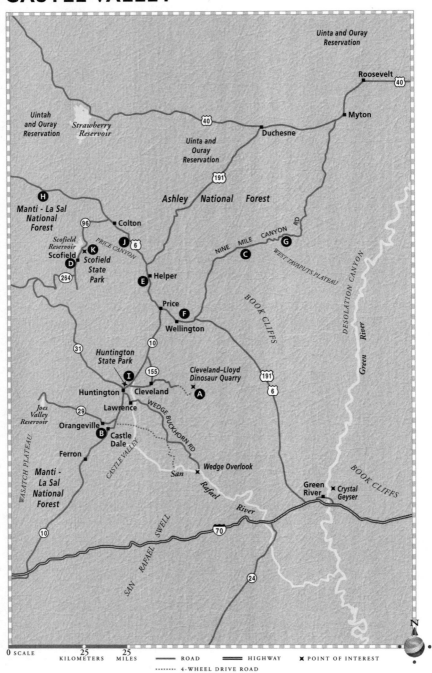

Uinta and Ouray Reservation

Roosevelt
40

Myton

Uintah and Ouray Reservation

Strawberry Reservoir

40

Duchesne

Uinta and Ouray Reservation

191

Ashley National Forest

H

Manti - La Sal National Forest

96

Colton

J
6

PRICE CANYON

Scofield Reservoir

K

Scofield

D

264

Scofield State Park

E

Helper

NINE MILE CANYON RD

C

G

WEST TAVAPUTS PLATEAU

BOOK CLIFFS

DESOLATION CANYON

Green River

Price

F

Wellington

10

31

Huntington State Park

155

Cleveland–Lloyd Dinosaur Quarry

191

6

I

Huntington

Cleveland

A

Lawrence

WEDGE BUCKHORN RD

Joes Valley Reservoir

29

Orangeville

B

Castle Dale

Ferron

CASTLE VALLEY

San

Rafael

Wedge Overlook

River

BOOK CLIFFS

Green River

Crystal Geyser

WASATCH PLATEAU

Manti - La Sal National Forest

10

SAN RAFAEL SWELL

70

24

N

0 SCALE
KILOMETERS   25   25   MILES

ROAD   HIGHWAY   ✖ POINT OF INTEREST
·········· 4-WHEEL DRIVE ROAD

after the Civil War. The road and adjacent telegraph line, which followed an old Indian trail, were built to support the military post at Fort Duchesne. It is believed to have been the most heavily traveled road in eastern Utah until about 1910, bringing mail, freight, and homesteaders through the canyon. But its history goes back even further than that. Indians once lived here as far back as 12,000 years ago. More recently, the Fremont people farmed land in the canyon about 1,000 years ago and left their marks on many of the sandstone cliff faces. It has been called the world's longest art gallery, and it is one of the largest concentrations of Native American pictographs and petroglyphs in Utah. It was called Nine-Mile Canyon after one of John Wesley Powell's map-makers recorded a creek near his ninth mile marker. The canyon is about 40 miles long, and the trip between Price and Myton is 78 miles.

There are several good guidebooks and pamphlets that detail where most of the historically significant sites are located. *The Pioneer Saga of the Nine Mile Road* and *Utah's Nine-Mile Canyon* are free pamphlets available at most local visitors centers. The former gives details about miners, freighters, and settlers who used the road; the latter tells where the major rock art sites are.

Details: *Drive 7.5 miles southeast of Price on U.S. Hwy. 191/6 through Wellington, turn left (northeast). The paved road should be marked by a Back Country Byway sign. The pavement ends after 12 miles, and the first rock art panels are located about 22 miles from the highway*

SIGHTS

A Cleveland-Lloyd Dinosaur Quarry
B Emery County Pioneer Museum
B Museum of the San Rafael
C Nine-Mile Canyon
D Scofield Cemetery
E Western Mining and Railroad Museum

FOOD

F Cowboy's Kitchen
E Pinnacle Brewing Co.

LODGING

G Nine Mile Ranch

CAMPING

A Cleveland-Lloyd Dinosaur Quarry
H Manti-La Sal National Forest
I Millsite Huntington State Park
F Mountain View RV Park
G Nine Mile Ranch
J Price Canyon Recreation Area
K Scofield State Park

Note: Items with the same letter are located in the same place.

turnoff. There are no services—including gas and water—in Nine-Mile Canyon. Check road conditions with the Bureau of Land Management before you start, 435/636-3600. (full day)

★★★★ WESTERN MINING AND RAILROAD MUSEUM
296 South Main St., Helper, 435/472-3009

It seems only appropriate that this museum be in Helper, which was named after the "helper" locomotives that were stored here and added to trains to help them over the steep Soldier Summit grade on their way to the Wasatch Front. Four floors of a 1913 hotel display exhibits on the region's mining and railroading days, from the late 1800s to the early 1900s. The museum also features outdoor displays of mining and railroading equipment.

Details: *Open summer Mon–Sat 9–5; winter Tue–Sat 11–4. Donations encouraged. (2 hours)*

★★★ COLLEGE OF EASTERN UTAH PREHISTORIC MUSEUM
155 East Main St., Price, 435/637-5060

Here's where you'll find the largest collection of dinosaur tracks in the world. Many were found in the local coal mines. Six complete dinosaur skeletons from the Jurassic and Cretaceous periods have been reconstructed and are on display, and you'll even find a Utah raptor. A large Columbian mammoth, which roamed the area more than 10,000 years ago, is also on display. Several artifacts from the region's Fremont Indian culture round out the displays. The museum is operated by the College of Eastern Utah, which was established in 1937. It was the first state-supported, two-year college in Utah. Vocational-technical programs, including nursing programs, have always been important at CEU.

Details: *Open Apr 1–Sep 30 daily 9–6; Oct 1–Mar 31 Mon–Sat 9–5. Donations encouraged. (2 hours)*

★★ EMERY COUNTY PIONEER MUSEUM
At the corner of 100 North and 100 East, Castle Dale, 435/381-5154

This museum focuses on the pioneer settlement of the region. It features an early home, store, and school. In fact, the museum is housed in the 1909 Castle Dale School. A visit here will give you a sense of what it was like to build farms and communities in the late 1800s and early 1900s.

Details: *Open Mon–Fri 10–4, Sat noon–4. Donations encouraged. (2 hours)*

★★ MUSEUM OF THE SAN RAFAEL
64 North 100 East, Castle Dale, 435/381-5252

This museum features the geology, history, and animal and plant life of the high desert country of the nearby San Rafael Swell. It includes dinosaurs and Native American artifacts, including the Sitterud Bundle, an Indian tool-making kit dating from A.D. 1250 to 1450 that was found in the local area in 1968. Arts and craft shows are often held at the facility.

Details: *Open Mon–Fri 10–4, Sat noon–4. Donations encouraged. (1 hour)*

★ SCOFIELD CEMETERY

Death was a grim fact of life around coal mines in the late 1800s and early 1900s. On the east side of Scofield, which is 32 miles northwest of Price, is a cemetery that contains the graves of 149 of the 200 victims of the Winter Quarters Mine Disaster in 1900. At the time, it was the worst coal mine disaster in the country's history. The disaster led to calls for greater mine safety and was cited as one of the causes of subsequent labor strikes. Some of the original wooden markers are still standing in the cemetery.

Details: *(1 hour)*

FITNESS AND RECREATION

There are a lot of opportunities for hiking and biking in and around Castle Valley. Nine-Mile Canyon offers numerous places to stretch your legs and explore. But remember: there's a lot of private land in the canyon. Ask permission before entering someone's property. The road through the canyon is popular among mountain bikers.

Price Canyon Recreation Area, off U.S. Highway 6 in Price Canyon north of Helper, offers camping, picnicking, and nature trails. At 7,600 feet, **Scofield State Park**, 435/448-9449, is Utah's highest state park. Fishing and boating are popular here during the summer, while ice fishing, cross-country skiing, and snowmobiling are favorites in the winter. **Joe's Valley Reservoir** is a popular fishing spot 18 miles west of Orangeville and nearby Castle Dale. It is the largest lake in Emery County. **Skyline Drive**, above the reservoir, is an unpaved road across the top of the Wasatch Plateau that provides access to the many hunting, fishing, camping, hiking, and other recreational activities in the mountains above Castle Valley. The reservoir at **Huntington State Park**, two miles north of

PRICE

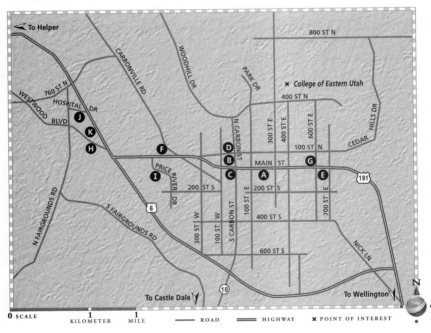

Huntington, is an ideal place for water-skiing and fishing. Further south, near Ferron, is **Mill Site State Park** and a multipurpose reservoir that, among other things, serves the nearby Hunter Power Plant.

The third fairway of the **Millsite Golf Course**, 435/384-2887, runs along the length of the Millsite Dam. **Carbon Country Club Golf Course**, 435/637-2388, is an older course between Helper and Price.

Price Park, 500 North 300 East, 435/637-7946, has tennis courts and a swimming pool and wave pool that are open year-round.

FOOD

At one time Price had a very strong Greek community. Times have changed, but there's still one place in town where gyros, lamb, and baklava are permanent choices on the menu—**Greek Streak**, 30 West 100 North, 435/637-1930. Enjoy authentic but inexpensive Greek cuisine in a casual café setting. Italians helped settled the region too, so savor some pasta at **Fairlainos**, 87 West Main Street, Price, 435/637-9217. With roots in Fiore, Italy, the restaurant specializes in sumptuous Italian meals, which are served only Wednesday through Saturday from 5 p.m. to 9 p.m. You can catch breakfast or lunch, including Fairlainos's famous hamburgers, Monday through Saturday from 7 a.m. to 2 p.m. **Ricardos**, 655 East Main Street, Price, 435/637-2020, next to the Greenwell Inn, features Mexican, American, and seafood dishes. If you're aching for a burger and a good hand-crafted beer, grab a table at the **Pinnacle Brewing Company**, 1653 North Carbonville Road, Helper, 435/637-2924. The brewpub features typical pub fare as well as heartier items like ribs and filet mignon. But if you're looking for a real hunk of beef, steaks are a specialty at the

---

SIGHTS

Ⓐ College of Eastern Utah Prehistoric Museum
Ⓑ Price Historic District

FOOD

Ⓒ Fairlainos
Ⓓ Greek Streak
Ⓔ Ricardos

LODGING

Ⓕ Budget Host Inn
Ⓖ Best Western Carriage House Inn
Ⓔ Greenwell Inn
Ⓗ Holiday Inn
Ⓘ National 9 Inn
Ⓙ Super 8

CAMPING

Ⓚ Budget Host RV Park

Note: Items with the same letter are located in the same place.

Cowboy's Kitchen, 31 East Main Street, Wellington, 435/637-4223. They even offer a one-and-a-half-pound sirloin.

LODGING

Since Nine-Mile Canyon is a popular place to explore, it only seems natural to spend the night there. **Nine Mile Ranch**, 25 miles northeast of Wellington, 435/637-2572, is nearly 1,000 acres along the road that stage coaches, Indians, and freighters used more than 100 years ago. A four-bedroom cottage that was once used in one of the region's mining camps was moved to the location and now serves as a bed-and-breakfast inn. Prices for rooms and campsites are very reasonable. The ranch also offers Dutch-oven dinners, horseback riding, and hayrides.

Two economical choices in Price include the **Greenwell Inn**, 655 East Main Street, 435/637-3520, a full-service hotel with convention and banquet facilities; and the **Best Western Carriage House Inn**, 590 East Main Street, 435/637-5660, just down the block from the Greenwell. Both have indoor pools, but the Greenwell also has amenities such as a lounge, gymnasium, and a horseshoe pit for lazy, sunny afternoons.

Price also offers a number of national chain hotels, including **Holiday Inn**, 838 Westwood Boulevard, 435/637-8880; **Super 8**, 180 North Hospital Drive, 435/637-8088; **National 9 Inn**, 641 West Price River Drive, 435/637-7000; and **Budget Host Inn**, 145 North Carbonville Road, 435/637-2424.

CAMPING

In addition to the camping at **Nine Mile Ranch**, as mentioned above, there are several campgrounds in Castle Valley and along the nearby Wasatch Plateau. **Millsite Huntington** and **Scofield State Parks**, 800/322-3770, have campgrounds with water and toilets. Scofield also has showers for campers. The **Bureau of Land Management**, 435/636-3600, operates campgrounds in the **Price Canyon Recreation Area** and near the **Cleveland-Lloyd Dinosaur Quarry**. The **Forest Service**, 800/280-2267, operates campgrounds in the nearby **Manti-La Sal National Forest**. Joe's Valley has the most facilities. Other Forest Service campgrounds include **Ferron Reservoir**, **Fish Creek Trailhead**, **Forks of Huntington**, **Indian Creek**, and **Old Folk's Flat**.

Private campgrounds include the **Budget Host RV Park**, 145 North Carbonville Road, Price, 435/637-2424, and **Mountain View RV Park**, 50 South 700 East, Wellington, 435/637-7980.

NIGHTLIFE

There are several popular taverns in Price: **Big Dog's**, 27 North 100 West, 435/637-0940, and **Silver Dollar Sports**, 36 West Main Street, 435/637-9446 are two of the most popular. And don't forget about the brewpub at **Pinnacle Brewing Company**, 1653 North Carbonville Road, Helper, 435/637-2924.

14
UINTA BASIN

The cities of Vernal, Roosevelt, and Duchesne (Doo-SHANE) sit at the base of the Uinta Mountains, one of the only major mountain ranges in North America that runs east-west. The state's highest summit—13,528-foot Kings Peak—is located in this stage. Dinosaurs lived and died in the swamps that used to cover the land below the mountains in this area, now straddling the Utah-Colorado border. The first major discovery of dinosaur fossils was in 1877, in Morrison, Colorado, setting off a rush to find more evidence of the prehistoric creatures. In August 1909 several large dinosaur vertebrae were found emerging out of the weathered sandstone near Jensen, Utah. Over the next 15 years, paleontologists excavated the area, sending dinosaur bones to the Smithsonian Institution and the University of Utah, and more than 350 tons of fossils to the Carnegie Museum in Pennsylvania. The resulting quarry was designated a national monument in 1915, and the park was expanded in 1938 to include more than 300 square miles of beautiful scenery.

But dinosaurs aren't the only ancient inhabitants that attract people to the Uinta Basin. Fremont Indians lived in the area between A.D. 200 and 1300. Impressive displays of petroglyphs and pictographs—symbols etched or painted on rocks—can be seen throughout the area.

The Fremont people were replaced by Ute Indians, who occupied the area when Dominguez and Escalante explored the region in 1776. Trappers and traders entered the area in the early 1800s. Reed Trading Post in Whiterocks was one of the first trading posts in Utah. Famed trapper Antoine Robidoux owned the post from the 1830s until 1844, when it was burned to the ground by enraged Utes.

In 1861 President Abraham Lincoln designated a major portion of the Uinta Basin as an Indian reservation. Today, the Uintah and Ouray Reservation (John Wesley Powell apparently dropped the "h" in "Uintah" when he mapped the area) is the largest Indian reservation in the state. President Theodore Roosevelt subsequently opened some of the reservation lands to homesteading in 1905, which led to the development of several communities in the basin, including his namesake.

Oil, water, and agriculture are important industries today in the Uinta Basin, an area that retains much of its rural character and charm. The basin communities host several festivals and events throughout the year, including the month-long Outlaw Trail Festival, with outdoor music, storytelling, a parade, and an art show, between mid-June and mid-July, and the Ute Pow Wow in early July.

A PERFECT DAY IN THE UINTA BASIN

Although the quarry near Jensen is no longer being excavated, it's a good place to start a tour of the Uinta Basin. After seeing the more than 1,600 fossilized dinosaur bones that form a relief in the hillside, pick up a road guide for the self-guided Tour of the Tilted Rocks along Cub Creek Road. It's a 24-mile round-trip. After stopping to see the rock art, the beautiful Green River, and the Josie Morris homestead cabin, head into Vernal and catch a glimpse of the area's "outlaw" past at the Western Heritage Museum. Don't forget to pose for a picture next to the big pink dinosaur at the Dina-A-Ville Motel.

SIGHTSEEING HIGHLIGHTS
★★★★ DINOSAUR NATIONAL MONUMENT/DINOSAUR QUARRY VISITOR CENTER
7 miles north of Jensen (east of Vernal) on Hwy. 149
435/789-2115

The world's largest quarry featuring fossilized bones from the Jurassic period is located seven miles north of Jensen and 20 miles east of Vernal. The quarry was discovered in 1909 and was subsequently named a national monument. Bones from apatosaurus, camarasaurus, diplodocus, barosaurus, camptosaurus, stegosaurus, allosaurus, and ceratosaurus were found in the quarry. It's believed that the animals congregated along a river during a drought, died, and were washed by flash floods to a spot where they piled up—and were later uncovered.

The quarry's visitors center was built in 1958. It provided shelter for paleontologists working on the 200-foot-wide hillside and allowed visitors to see the excavation work where more than 1,600 dinosaur bones have been uncovered and remain embedded in the sandstone. For the most part, work is finished at the quarry. But there are numerous exhibits that explain the history of the quarry and provide details about the dinosaurs whose bones have been found there. Workers can sometimes be seen cleaning and preparing fossils in the adjacent laboratory. Brochures can be purchased for 50¢ at the visitors center that describe the various stops on the 24-mile round-trip, self-guided Tour of the Tilted Rocks along Cub Creek Road. This is a great educational trip for the whole family. The tour stops at sites with remarkable Fremont rock art, gives you a view of Split Mountain (where it looks as if the Green River split the mountain in half), and ends at the Josie Morris cabin. Morris built the homestead cabin in 1914 and ran a ranch from it for the next 50 years.

See Dinosaur National Monument/Park Headquarters Visitors Center below for additional information and sites within the park.

Details: *From Memorial Day–Labor Day you may be required to park in a lot and take a shuttle bus to the quarry. Open summer 8–7 p.m.; the rest of the year 8–4:30. $10/vehicle, good for 7 days, includes admission to the quarry and Park Headquarters Visitors Center in Colorado. (1–2 hours for the quarry, another 1–2 hours for the driving tour)*

★★★ DRY FORK PETROGLYPHS

The Fremont Indians decorated several miles of walls in Dry Fork Canyon, north of Vernal. Some of the symbols are as large as nine feet tall. Hundreds of petroglyphs are located on the canyon wall above McConkie Ranch, about three miles beyond Remember the Maine Park. This is private property, and you should ask permission before entering the ranch. Follow the road another two miles, turn right at the junction, and continue another three miles to Dry Fork Village, a ghost town from the early settlement of the Ashley Valley.

Details: *Drive north of Vernal on 500 West, turn west onto 500 North, follow signs to Remember the Maine Park, and continue for 3 miles. (2–3 hours)*

★★★ UTAH FIELD HOUSE OF NATURAL HISTORY
235 East Main St., Vernal, 435/789-3799

Dinosaur fossils and minerals from the local area are featured here in downtown Vernal. The museum has a spectacular collection of Native American artifacts, particularly from the Fremont and Ute cultures. The most popular feature is the outdoor Dinosaur Gardens, where 17 life-size dinosaurs and creatures from the Mesozoic period are on permanent display. The gardens are separated into the swamp, lake, and rock environments that existed in this region from 65 to 150 million years ago. Ask about a souvenir dinosaur hunting license.

Details: *Open summer 8 a.m.–9 p.m.; the rest of the year 9–5. $2/person or $5/family. (1–2 hours)*

★★★ TRIASSIC DINOSAUR TRACKWAY
4335 North U.S. Hwy. 191, about 10 miles north of Vernal 435/789-4432

UINTA BASIN

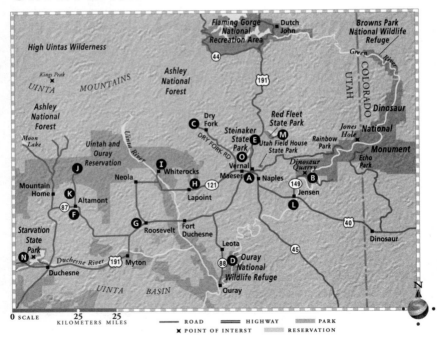

Walk in the footprints left by dinosaurs 200 million years ago. They are located at Red Fleet State Park, north of Vernal, on a slab of rock that slants down into the water across the reservoir from the park's boat ramp. The park has been described as a "little Lake Powell." You can see the greatest number of tracks when the water is at its lowest point, generally from late summer through winter. You can hike or boat to the tracks. Check with rangers for the best directions for the hike.

Details: *Open summer 6 a.m.–10 p.m.; winter 8–5. $3/day. (1–3 hours if you hike)*

★★★ WESTERN HERITAGE MUSEUM
300 East 200 South, Vernal, 435/789-7399
This is one of the few museums in the Uinta Basin where you won't find dinosaurs. Instead, the museum houses memorabilia from the area's "outlaw" past—Butch Cassidy and the likes—as well as a large collection of Native American artifacts and exhibits detailing life in the Old West.

Details: *Open summer Mon–Sat 9–6; the rest of the year 9–5. Free. (2 hours)*

★★ DINOSAUR NATIONAL MONUMENT/PARK HEADQUARTERS VISITORS CENTER

SIGHTS
- **A** Dinosaur National Monument/Park Headquarters Visitors Center
- **B** Dinosaur National Monument/Dinosaur Quarry Visitors Center
- **C** Dry Fork Petroglyphs
- **D** Ouray National Wildlife Refuge
- **E** Triassic Dinosaur Trackway

FOOD
- **F** Falcoln's Ledge
- **G** Frontier Grill
- **H** The Stockman

LODGING
- **G** Cedar Trail Ranch
- **F** Falcoln's Ledge
- **I** J/L Ranch
- **J** Moon Lake Resort
- **K** Rock Creek Guest Ranch

CAMPING
- **G** Classic RV Park
- **B** Dinosaur National Monument
- **L** Dinosaur Village
- **M** Red Fleet State Park
- **N** Starvation State Park
- **O** Steinake State Park

Note: Items with the same letter are located in the same place.

At the junction of U.S. Hwy. 40 and Harpers Corner Rd. 970/374-3000

In 1938 the monument was expanded beyond just the quarry (see above). It now covers 325 acres in Utah and Colorado, encompassing the confluence of the Green and Yampa Rivers. The headquarters visitors center is located near Dinosaur, Colorado. It features exhibits, lectures, and an audiovisual program about the park. The visitors center is also the start of a 62-mile round-trip scenic drive on Harper's Corner Road. The road provides fantastic views of the gorges cut by the Green and Yampa Rivers.

Details: *2 miles east of Dinosaur, Colorado. Open summer daily 8–4:30; the rest of the year Mon–Fri. $10/vehicle, good for 7 days, includes admission to the visitors center and quarry. (1 hour)*

★★ OURAY NATIONAL WILDLIFE REFUGE
Utah Hwy. 88, southwest of Vernal, 435/545-2522

Extending 12 miles along the Green River, the 11,827-acre wetland refuge is home to hundreds of species of migratory birds during the spring and fall. There's an observation tower and 10-mile driving loop.

Details: *Open one hour before sunrise–one hour after sunset. Free. (half day)*

★ DAUGHTERS OF UTAH PIONEERS MUSEUM
500 West 200 South, Vernal

Contains artifacts and historic photographs of the region from the mid-1800s. It is housed in an 1887 tithing office where livestock and produce were collected and distributed as part of the 10 percent tithe Mormons made to their church.

Details: *Open summer Mon–Sat 1–7 p.m.; closed the rest of the year. Donations encouraged. (1 hour)*

★ LADIES OF THE WHITE HOUSE DOLL COLLECTION
155 East Main St. (located in the Uintah County Library) Vernal, 435/789-0091

Dolls dressed in miniature replicas of the inaugural ball gowns worn by each of the first ladies.

Details: *Open Mon–Thu 10–8, Fri–Sat 10–6. Free. (30 minutes)*

★ ZIONS BANK
3 West Main St., Vernal, 435/789-7082

FLAMING GORGE NATIONAL RECREATION AREA

*From Vernal, a 41-mile drive leads to **Flaming Gorge Reservoir**, a 91-mile-long lake formed along the Green River that is popular for fishing and boating. The dam was completed in 1963, and the man-made lake straddles the Utah-Wyoming border. The colorful rocks surrounding the lake take on a spectacular red brilliance with the rising and setting sun. Record-breaking trout have been caught in the lake, including a 51-pound Mackinaw in 1988. The area around the reservoir is popular for hiking, biking, and camping. There are also two historic ranches nearby, the **Swett Ranch** and the **John Jarvie Ranch**. Oscar and Emma Swett raised nine children on their 397-acre ranch, where they used only horse- and man-powered equipment between 1909 and 1970. It is located near the intersection of U.S. Highway 191 and Utah Highway 44. Jarvie Ranch includes an old country store where cowboys and outlaws bought provisions after Jarvie settled in Brown's Park in 1880. The ranch is 22 miles east of U.S. Highway 191, where it meets the Wyoming border. The drive includes steep 17 percent grades through **Jesse Ewing Canyon**.*

Formerly the Bank of Vernal, it is believed to be the only building in the world that was delivered by parcel post. At the time the bank was built, around 1920, the closest city where the textured bricks were available was Salt Lake City. Because railroad freight costs were higher than postal rates, the bank president opted to have the bricks mailed to Vernal. They were sent to several addresses in the city because postal regulations allowed only so many pounds to be delivered to one address. It is still being used as a bank today.

Details: *(30 minutes)*

FITNESS AND RECREATION

There are almost limitless hiking and backpacking opportunities in the Uinta Basin and Uinta Mountains. The state's highest mountain, **Kings Peak**, can be climbed from the basin side, but most opt for a route that starts on the northern flank of the range.

RESPECT FOR LAND AND PEOPLES

Much of the land throughout the **Uinta Basin** is rich with fossils and Native American artifacts. But remember, if you take something away, you are depriving the next person of the opportunity to see it in its natural state. It is also against the law. Utah Antiquity Laws protect all Indian artifacts. Items should be left as they are and the State Historical Society should be notified of large finds. The removal of invertebrate fossils (from creatures without backbones) for private collecting is often allowed on lands outside state and national parks. Fossilized vertebrates of any kind, however, are protected and cannot be removed. Finds should be reported to the Utah Field House of Natural History in Vernal.

Present-day Native American culture should also be respected. The Utes have several colorful celebrations throughout the year that visitors are welcome to attend. You should not take pictures or shoot videos of the people or ceremonies without first asking permission. Some ceremonies are very sacred, and photographs are not permitted. For more information about the Ute people and their ceremonies, visit the **Ute Tribal Museum** at Fort Duchesne, 435/722-4992.

In **Dinosaur National Monument**, the scenic drives on Cub Creek Road and Harper's Corner Road provide access to several trailheads. The **Sound of Silence Trail** and **Desert Voices Nature Trail** are both two miles long and start at points along Cub Creek Road. The **Cold Desert Trail** and **Plug Hat Nature Trail** are both a quarter-mile long and are accessed from Harper's Corner Road. The two-mile **Harper's Corner Trail** is at the end of the road of the same name.

Bicycle Utah Vacation Guides publishes a free mountain bike guide for the Basin, including routes in Dinosaur National Monument, the Uinta Mountains and nearby Flaming Gorge National Recreation Area. They are available at most places that distribute tourist information.

Fishing holes and streams are plentiful in the Uinta Basin. Reservoirs at **Steinaker** and **Red Fleet State Parks**, both less than 11 miles north of Vernal, have trout and bass that are sought by anglers year-round.

Starvation Reservoir State Park, four miles west of Duchesne, is also open year-round to anglers. **Moon Lake** is the largest and one of the most popular of the thousands of natural lakes in the Uinta Mountains. The mountains also feed several streams favored by anglers. Purchase a special fishing permit, available at most local sporting goods stores, if you're going to try your luck on streams within the Uintah and Ouray Indian Reservation.

River rafting is popular on the Green and Yampa Rivers. A list of authorized outfitters is available at the Dinosaur National Monument visitors centers and at regional tourist information centers. Several outfitters arrange horseback-riding trips in the basin and mountains.

Closer to town, golfers might try the links at **Vernal's Dinaland Golf Course**, 675 South 2000 East, 435/781-1428, or **Roosevelt Golf Course**, 1115 Clubhouse Drive, 435/722-9644. **Spring Creek Park**, 1781 West 1000 South, Vernal, 435/781-0088, has batting cages and miniature golf. Vernal also has a swimming pool, 600 West 100 South, and the **Hydrosaurus Water Slide**, 1701 East 1900 South.

During the winter, snowmobilers roar along the groomed trails at the **Uinta Basin Snowmobile Complex**, 14 miles north of Vernal. A trail guide is available from the Forest Service and state parks. The local tourism agency also puts out a cross-country ski trail guide.

FOOD

The Uinta Basin is home to restaurants with interesting monikers. **Hog Heaven**, 2750 West U.S. Highway 40, Vernal, 435/789-3738, offers barbecue ribs, chicken, and prime rib. But don't expect to find a T-bone here. The **Crack'd Pot**, 1089 East Main Street, Vernal, 435/781-0133, offers burgers and other sandwiches, but it's more of an upscale restaurant, with Mexican food, pasta, steaks, and lobster. The restaurant includes a lounge with a full bar. If you're looking for something tony with a Western atmosphere, try **Falcon's Ledge**, P.O. Box 67, Altamont, 435/454-3737. It's a small lodge northeast of Roosevelt that offers an elegant seven-course dinner for $35 a person. Another restaurant worth dressing up for is the **Curry Manor**, 189 South Vernal Avenue, 435/789-2289. But don't fret if your wallet isn't full enough for fancy food. The **Frontier Grill**, 65 South 200 East, 435/722-3669, serves turkey pie, steak, or prime rib for under $13. And **The Stockman**, in the small town of Lapoint, 435/247-2300, is a café with great steaks and Mexican food. The locals suggest making reservations on the weekend.

LODGING

It may not be the greatest hotel in the area, but who can resist a giant pink dinosaur? The economical **Dine-A-Ville Motel**, 801 West Highway 40, Vernal, 435/789-9571, is a throwback to the old Route 66 days, when roadside signs and buildings were real characters. **Moon Lake Resort**, P.O. Box 510070, Mountain Home, 435/454-3142, has cabins that sleep four to six people for one low price. They include the basics, but patrons should bring their own bedding, towels, and kitchen utensils.

More moderately priced accommodations include the **Landmark Inn**, 288 East 100 South, Vernal, 435/781-1800, which is an 11-room bed-and-breakfast in a renovated Baptist church. If you're looking for a country setting near town, try the **Hillhouse Bed 'N Breakfast**, 675 West 3300 North, Vernal, 435/789-0700, but don't expect a Victorian. The four- to five-room home was built in the 1960s. The **Weston Plaza Hotel**, 1684 West Highway 40, Vernal, 435/789-4874, is probably the largest full-service hotel in the Basin and is the only one with an indoor pool.

A little pricier is the **Falcon's Ledge**, P.O. Box 67, Altamont,

VERNAL

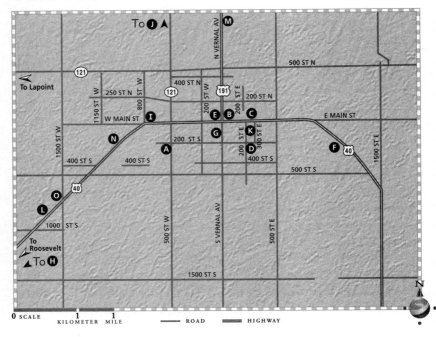

435/454-3737, which is an eight-room lodge northeast of Roosevelt that caters to people who like luxury accommodations, fine dining, and fly-fishing. The fishing is, of course, optional.

The Uinta Basin also offers several unique guest ranches. Prices vary depending on the custom package you select. Many offer fishing and hunting trips as well as horseback riding and cattle drives. Guest ranches in the area include: the **J/L Ranch**, P.O. Box 129, Whiterocks, 435/353-4049; **Cedar Trail Ranch**, Route 3 Box 3052 A, Roosevelt, 888/852-6706; **Rock Creek Guest Ranch**, P.O. Box 510060, Mountain Home, 435/454-3332; and **Rocky Meadows Ranch Adventures**, which can be reached through Shawn White, 5584 West Townsend Way, Kearns, 801/966-7650.

CAMPING

Because the Uinta Basin butts up against the Ashley National Forest and the Uinta Mountains, there is an abundance of campgrounds in the region. The **Forest Service** operates several campgrounds out of its district offices in Vernal, 435/789-1181, Roosevelt, 435/722-5018, and Duchesne, 435/738-2482. Most Forest Service campgrounds have toilets, and about two-thirds of them have drinking water. **Dinosaur National Monument** has three campgrounds in Utah and three in Colorado. Only **Rainbow Park**, near the quarry in Utah, is open year-round. But it has only four sites for RVs or tents. **Green River**, just east of the quarry, has 77 sites. There are also several camp sites at **Red Fleet**, **Starvation**, and **Steinaker State Parks**, 800/322-3770. Each has approximately 30 RV sites and a handful of tent sites.

SIGHTS

- **A** Daughters Of Utah Pioneers Museum
- **B** Ladies of the White House Doll Collection
- **C** Utah Field House of Natural History
- **D** Western Heritage Museum
- **E** ZionS Bank

FOOD

- **F** Crack'd Pot
- **G** Curry Manor
- **H** Hog Heaven

LODGING

- **I** Dine-A-Ville Motel
- **J** Hillhouse Bed 'N Breakfast
- **K** Landmark Inn
- **L** Weston Plaza Hotel

CAMPING

- **M** Campground Dina
- **N** Fossil Valley RV
- **O** Vernal KOA

Commercial campgrounds in the region include the **Vernal KOA**, 1800 West Sheraton, Vernal, 800/KOA-7574, which is open only during the summer; **Campground Dina**, 930 North Vernal Avenue, Vernal, 800/245-2148; **Dinosaur Village**, Jensen, 435/789-5552; **Classic RV Park**, 145 South 500 East, Roosevelt, 435/722-2294; and **Fossil Valley RV**, 999 West Highway 40, Vernal, 435/789-6450.

PERFORMING ARTS

Vernal is home to the **Outlaw Trail Theater**, 435/789-6932, which stages outdoor Western musicals and melodramas in the **Western Park Amphitheater**, 302 East 200 South. Performances include a pre-show of old-fashioned cowboy music. Be prepared for the weather—the show has been stopped only once in 10 years because of rain.

Scenic Route: Flaming Gorge-Uinta's Scenic Byway

This 67-mile drive, which has been called **"Drive Through the Ages"**—and more recently, **"Wildlife Through the Ages"**—stretches north from Vernal to Flaming Gorge Reservoir on U.S. Highway 191 and west to Manila on Utah Highway 44. Interpretive signs along the way explain the various geological formations as the road cuts through the heart of the **Uinta Mountains**. The oldest rocks are nearly 1 billion years old. This was one of the first designated national scenic byways in the country.

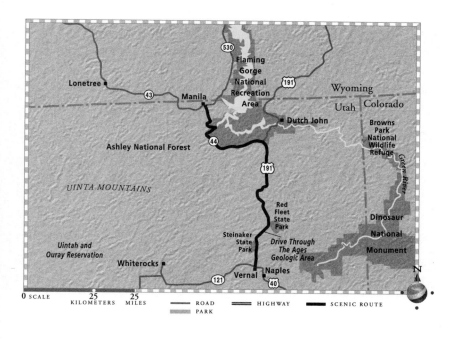

15
PARK CITY

From the very beginning, Park City has gone from rags to riches time and time again. One of its first settlers was Parley Pratt, a Mormon apostle who moved to Utah with Brigham Young in 1847. Pratt found a prime area where his livestock could graze. He called that area "Parley's Park." But a few years later, he was called to another church assignment and moved away.

In 1869 the first mining claim was filed in Park City, which took its name from Parley's Park. By 1872 the city had gained a reputation as a great silver mining camp. The Ontario Mine alone reportedly produced $50 million in ore. The mine was flourishing in 1879, and houses were springing up everywhere in the canyon. In December 1882 a fire destroyed many of the young town's principal buildings. But the buildings were rebuilt, and the town boomed once again. The economic panic of 1893 slowed the city's growth, but it was another devastating fire in June 1898 that destroyed Park City's commercial district. Main Street was in ruins and 200 or so houses were razed.

The townspeople had done it before, and they did it again—they rebuilt the city. Mining production dwindled during the Great Depression and picked up again to meet war demand during the 1940s. But by the 1950s, mining—the city's life blood—was all but gone.

Then, somebody got the idea that Park City's annual blanket of snow might have a silver lining. It did, and the popularity of skiing and other winter sports provided Park City with a rebound the likes of which had never been seen before. Today, snow is a multimillion dollar industry in Park City, which is home to three major ski resorts and the Utah Winter Sports Park—where Olympic athletes train and compete in ski jumping, luge, and bobsled. The historic Main Street still maintains the character and charm of its mining-town heritage, complete with fine shops, world-class restaurants, and fun bars.

A PERFECT DAY IN PARK CITY

If you like skiing, simply buy a lift ticket at Park City Mountain Resort and spend the day shushing down the slopes, which cover 2,200 acres of mountainside. Of course, you can only do that in the winter. The resort has more than $11 million in snow-making equipment, but it's not going to do much good in the summer. If you visit Park City during the summer, you can enjoy the shops of Main Street and either tour the silver mine or ride the Heber Valley Historic Railroad. For dinner, grab a bite to eat and a drink at Utah's oldest brewpub, and do a little dancing at the Alamo Saloon or Cisero's.

SIGHTSEEING HIGHLIGHTS
★★★★ HISTORIC MAIN STREET

Several Utah cities have ski resorts, but only Park City has a main street that attracts visitors who just want to walk up and down the steep and narrow road while poking their heads into various shops and galleries. The city's historic preservation ordinances are some of the strictest in the state—possibly the country—all in an effort to maintain the character of this nineteenth-century mining community. Most of the city's popular restaurants and bars line Main Street in historic (or historic-looking) buildings.

Details: (half day)

★★★★ UTAH WINTER SPORTS PARK
3000 Bear Hollow Dr., Park City, 435/658-4200 or 435/649-5447

This is a major venue for the 2002 Winter Olympics. Lake Placid, New York, is the only other place in the United States with a refrigerated bobsled and luge track. The $25 million park was completed not just for the elite Olympic athletes, but for the developing and recreational athletes as well. Utah's sports authorities, for example, plan to use the facility to expose youngsters to the sports of ski jumping, bobsled, and luge. The track and ski jumps are open for use by the general

---

public for a nominal fee. You can ride down the track, fly off the jumps, or simply watch the world-class athletes train and compete.

Details: (4 hours)

★★★ PARK CITY MUSEUM
528 Main St., Park City, 435/649-6104

This fun museum is housed in Park City's 1885 City Hall and Territorial Jail. The jail, in the basement, still has the original cells and leg irons, which are popular attractions. Exhibits and video presentations depict the town's history from silver mines to the ski industry.

Details: Open Mon–Sat 10–7, Sun noon–6; Apr, Oct daily noon–5. Free. (1 hour)

★★★ SILVER MINE ADVENTURE
1.5 miles south of Park City on Hwy. 224, 800/467-3828

The Ontario Mine was perhaps Park City's greatest silver mine. It reportedly made millionaires out of 22 people during its run from the 1870s to the 1980s. Today, you can put on a jacket and helmet and descend 1,500 feet into the Ontario's No. 3 shaft, then take a half-mile train ride through the tunnels of this once great mine. The tour includes interactive displays and exhibits about mining.

Details: Open daily 10–7. $17.95 adults, $12.50 seniors and ages under 12. (4 hours)

★★ ALF ENGEN SKI MUSEUM
3000 Bear Hollow Dr., Park City, 801/272-4334

Engen is credited with bringing the sport of skiing to the United States. The native of Norway won numerous national ski-jumping championships in the 1930s and 1940s, and he even set a world record. He coached the 1948 U.S. Olympic Team and directed the ski school at Alta. The museum houses a collection of photographs, skis, trophies, and other memorabilia from Engen's career.

Details: The items are on display in the Bear Hollow Day Lodge at the Utah Winter Sports Park; eventually, the collection may be housed in a permanent museum. Free. (1 hour)

★★ KIMBALL ART CENTER
638 Park Ave., Park City, 435/649-8882

The center has two galleries: one concentrating on national exhibits, the other focusing on the works of professional local and regional

PARK CITY

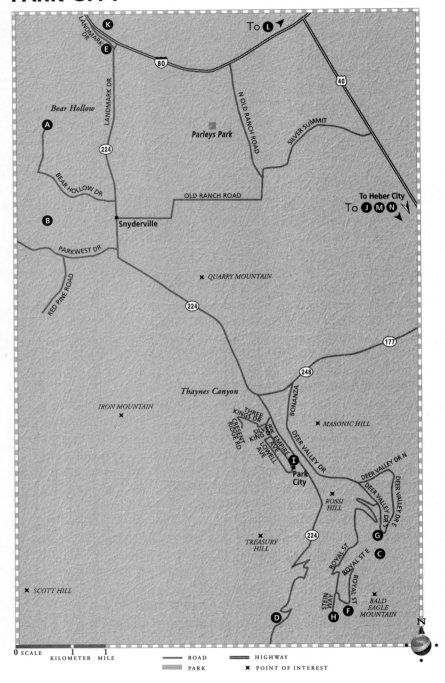

artists. The Kimball Art Center also hosts classes and workshops throughout the year.

Details: Open Mon–Sat 10–6, Sun noon–6. Free except during special events. (2 hours)

★ FACTORY OUTLETS
6699 North Landmark Dr., 435/645-7078

Bargain hunters know where Park City is. Just outside town, near the freeway, are dozens of factory outlets clustered into one center.

Details: Located along a frontage road near I-80. (half day)

RESORT SIGHTSEEING HIGHLIGHTS

There are three major ski resorts in Park City: Park City Mountain Resort, Deer Valley Resort, and The Canyons. All three resorts have activities throughout the year, including concerts.

★★★ PARK CITY MOUNTAIN RESORT
1310 Lowell Ave., 800/222-7275

From its humble beginning in 1963, Park City Mountain Resort has grown from one tram and two lifts to become one of Utah's largest winter resorts. It is the venue for alpine skiing and snowboarding competitions in the 2002 Winter Olympics. Today, there are 93 trails over 2,200 acres of skiable terrain around many of the old mining buildings from Park City's past. (A map that describes shows

---

SIGHTS
- Ⓐ Alf Engen Ski Museum
- Ⓑ The Canyons
- Ⓒ Deer Valley Resort
- Ⓓ Silver Mine Adventure
- Ⓐ Utah Winter Sports Park

FOOD
- Ⓔ Baja Cantina
- Ⓕ The Mariposa
- Ⓖ Seafood Buffet

LODGING
- Ⓔ Lodge at Resort Center
- Ⓗ Stein Eriksen Lodge
- Ⓘ Washington School Inn

CAMPING
- Ⓙ Echo Reservoir
- Ⓚ Hidden Haven Campground
- Ⓛ Holiday Hills Campground
- Ⓜ Jordanelle State Park
- Ⓝ Rockport State Park

Note: Items with the same letter are located in the same place.

HEBER VALLEY

The Heber Valley, including the towns of Heber and Midway, is only a 20-minute drive away from Park City. With the explosion of growth in Park City, Heber Valley—like it or not—is becoming a suburb of sorts of the historic mining center. Along one side of the valley, **Wasatch Mountain State Park** *is the venue for biathlon and cross-country skiing events in the 2002 Winter Olympics.* **Homestead Resort,** *adjacent to the park, has fine restaurants, a resort hotel, an 18-hole championship golf course, and pretty much everything else, from horse-drawn buggy rides to scuba diving. The community's main claim to fame is the* **Historic Heber Valley Railroad,** *435/654-5601, Utah's only steam railroad. The railroad features restored vintage coaches and a steam locomotive dating back to 1907. Vintage diesel engines are also used for excursions along the same line that was used by the Utah Eastern Railway (Rio Grande Western) in 1899 between Heber and Provo. Today, trips are made to nearby* **Deer Creek Dam** *or through Provo Canyon to Vivian Park.*

and historical sites on the mountain is available at ticket windows.) At the top of the mountain, there are 650 acres of wide-open bowls for skiing. Three six-passenger high-speed lifts, two quad lifts, five triples, and four doubles carry a combined total of 26,600 skiers per hour. One of the lifts and two of the ski runs even drop into Park City's historic district.

Details: *(full day)*

★★ DEER VALLEY RESORT
2250 Dear Valley Dr. S., 800/424-3337

This is one of Utah's most elite ski resorts. Its clientele consists of movie stars and world leaders. It is also the host of the slalom, combined slalom, mogul, and aerial events in the 2002 Winter Olympics. Deer Valley's 68 trails on 1,200 acres are served by three high-speed detachable quad lifts, nine triples, and two doubles.

Details: *(full day)*

★★ THE CANYONS
800/754-1636

This resort has undergone a number of name and ownership changes in the last few years. It has one gondola tram, three high-speed detachable quad lifts, three fixed-grip quads, and two doubles, providing a total capacity of 16,280 skiers per hour. The resort has more than 2,000 acres of skiable terrain.

Details: *(full day)*

FITNESS AND RECREATION

There's skiing, of course. But what do you do when the snow melts? The **Alpine Slide**, 435/649-8111, at **Park City Mountain Resort** is a half-mile-long track like a scaled-down bobsled run that snakes down the hillside. Thrill-seekers young and old ride down on sleds during the summer.

A free hiking and biking trail guide is available at visitors centers and some local bike shops. All three resorts have hiking and biking trails. Deer Valley even offers lift service Wednesday to Sunday. Bicyclists are required to wear helmets when they ride at any of the three resorts.

The historic **Union Pacific Rail Trail**, completed in 1993, is part of the state parks system. The relatively easy and flat trail runs from Park City to Echo Reservoir—about 30 miles. It's used by hikers and mountain bike riders. Eventually, it may connect with trails to **Jordanelle State Park**, 435/649-9540, and its large reservoir. The trail already runs by **Rockport State Park**, 435/336-2241, and its reservoir.

Park City Municipal Golf Course, 435/521-2135, doubles as the **White Pine Touring Center**, 435/649-8710, during the winter, with 12 miles of groomed cross-country skiing trails. Park City has a second golf course, **Park Meadows**, 435/531-7029, which will challenge even the best golfers.

FOOD

After a long day of skiing or mountain biking, when you just want to sit down, prop up your feet, grab a simple bite to eat, and quench your thirst with a good beer while enjoying the big screen, head to Utah's oldest brewpub—**Wasatch Brewery**, 250 Main Street, 435/649-0900. Or, if you're looking for something spicy from south of the border, check out the **Irish Camel**, 434 Main Street, 435/649-6645. This isn't a place for corned beef and cabbage. Like the sign says, this is a place for "Irish pub and Mexican grub." And watch out for that hot salsa! If you don't want to fight to find a parking place along Main Street, but you do want Mexican food, try the **Baja Cantina** at Park City Mountain Resort, 435/649-BAJA. Their huge and elaborate burritos are highly recommended. The **Claimjumper Steakhouse**, 573 Main Street, 435/649-8051, is a landmark in Park City. Half its menu is filled with steaks, the other half with prime rib and seafood.

There are several places in Park City that cater to elite palates. Few, if any, will turn you away if you're not wearing a gown or dinner jacket. Downtown Park City, in particular, specializes in casual dining. **Grappa**, 151 Main Street, 435/645-0636, has fabulous Italian food at the top of historic Main Street. Its luscious food is baked in wood-burning ovens, and the decor in the over 100-year-old building is stunning. **Alex's Bistro**, 442 Main Street, 435/649-5252, is a small French bistro featuring salmon in puff pastry and frog legs provençal. Alex's also offers appetizers and salad that serve as a light meal or a late-night snack. **Café Terigo**, 424 Main Street, 435/645-9555, specializes in contemporary European cuisine. Deer Valley caters to the rich and famous and is renowned for its fine food. Prices are high, but the food is worth it. You might want to skip lunch to save room

HISTORIC PARK CITY

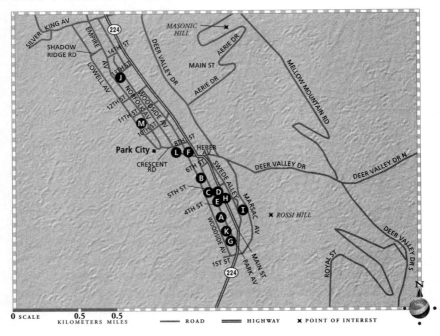

for the **Seafood Buffet**, 435/645-6632, at Deer Valley's Snow Park Lodge. Or, for a more traditional meal, try **The Mariposa** restaurant, 435/645-6715, in the resort's Silver Lake Lodge.

LODGING

Staying in any town that is based around ski resorts is likely to be expensive. Winter rates can be as much as four times higher than off-season summer rates. Park City in no exception. Some accommodations can run upwards of $1,000 or more a night during the ski season. But there's usually one or two bargains. The **Chateau Après Lodge**, for example, at 1299 Norfolk Avenue, Park City, 435/649-9372, has separate men's and women's dorm rooms for as little as $25 a night during ski season. Compare that to the **Lodge at Resort Center** at Park City Mountain Resort, 435/649-0800, with four-bedroom condos that cost $875-plus a night during the peak season.

The **Stein Eriksen Lodge** in Deer Valley, 7700 Stein Way, 435/649-5825, is flat-out expensive, even for Park City. But it is "committed to world-class luxury and pampering."

There are also several bed-and-breakfast inns in historic buildings. The **Washington School Inn**, 543 Park Avenue, 435/649-3802, has 15 country-style rooms in a three-story 1889 schoolhouse. Prices vary and range from moderate to somewhat pricey. The **Old Miner's Lodge**, 615 Woodside Avenue, 435/645-8068, also presents its guests a range in prices. The lodge was a boarding house for local miners in 1889. You still may not find a television there today. Moderately priced accommodations are also offered at **Old Town Guest House**, 1011 Empire, 435/649-2642, where visitors gather around the fireplace as guests did in 1910. And, at the top of the hill on Main Street, guests

---

SIGHTS
Ⓐ Historic Main street
Ⓑ Kimball Art Center
Ⓒ Park City Museum

FOOD
Ⓓ Alex's Bistro
Ⓔ Café Terigo
Ⓕ Claimjumper Steakhouse
Ⓖ Grappa
Ⓗ Irish Camel
Ⓘ Wasatch Brewery

LODGING
Ⓙ Chateau Après Lodge
Ⓚ Imperial Hotel
Ⓛ Old Miner's Lodge
Ⓜ Old Town Guest House

still check in at the **Imperial Hotel**, 435/649-1904, as they did when the building was built in 1904 as a boarding house for miners.

CAMPING
Jordanelle State Park, 435/649-9540, and **Rockport State Park**, 435/336-2241, have several camping sites, as does **Echo Reservoir**, 435/336-9894. Private campgrounds in the Park City area include **Holiday Hills Campground**, in Coalville, 435/336-4421, and **Hidden Haven Campground**, 220 Rassmusen Road, Park City, 435/649-8935.

NIGHTLIFE
There are several places to kick up your heels and dance in Park City. Some of the popular places with live bands include the **Alamo Saloon**, 447 Main Street, 435/649-2380, and **Cisero's Nightclub**, 306 Main Street, 435/649-6800. There are also numerous art galleries in the historic downtown section of Park City. One of the best ways to see them all is to join one of the **Main Street Gallery Strolls**, 435/649-8882, the first Friday of every month.

The **Sundance Film Festival**, although based at Sundance, utilizes most of the theaters in Park City in January to show films associated with the festival. It's a good time to rub shoulders with the stars on the streets of Park City.

PERFORMING ARTS
All sorts of music are on tap in Park City during the summer. The **Music in the Mountains** concerts in City Park, the **Saturday Afternoon Performing Arts Series**, the annual **Folk and Bluegrass Festival** at Deer Valley, the **Utah Symphony Summer Series**, the **Park City International Music Festival**, and the **Institute at Deer Valley**, which features string chamber music, are just a few of the programs. In addition, contemporary rock concerts are booked at **The Canyons'** outdoor theater, and live stage performances are featured in the historic **Egyptian Theatre**, 328 Main Street, 435/649-9371, which was first used for vaudeville and silent films in 1926.

APPENDIX

Consider this appendix your travel tool box. Use it along with the material in the Planning Your Trip chapter to craft the trip you want. Here are the tools you'll find inside:

1. **Mileage Chart.** This chart shows the driving distances (in miles) between various destinations throughout the state. Use it in conjunction with the Planning Map.
2. **Planning Map.** Make copies of this map and plot out various trip possibilities. Once you've decided on your route, you can write it on the original map and refer to it as you're traveling.
3. **Special Interest Tours.** If you'd like to plan a trip around a certain theme—such as nature, sports, or art—one of these tours may work for you.
4. **Calendar of Events.** Here you'll find a month-by-month listing of major area events.
5. **Resources.** This guide lists various regional chambers of commerce and visitors bureaus, state offices, bed-and-breakfast registries, and other useful sources of information.

UTAH MILEAGE CHART

	Brigham City	Bryce Canyon	Canyonlands NP	Capitol Reef NP	Cedar City	Fillmore	Grand Canyon NP	Logan	Moab	Ogden	Park City	Price	Provo	Salt Lake City
Bryce Canyon	316													
Canyonlands NP	360	327												
Capitol Reef NP	279	120	235											
Cedar City	306	78	354	199										
Fillmore	197	127	276	170	109									
Grand Canyon NP	437	155	409	275	354	248								
Logan	25	341	385	314	331	399	319							
Moab	294	270	66	145	288	416	46	2						
Ogden	21	295	339	268	285	382	112	239	66					
Park City	87	261	305	234	251	340	200	119	154	120				
Price	175	219	185	138	229	151	340	200	119	154	120			
Provo	101	215	215	188	205	96	336	126	193	80	120	74		
Salt Lake City	56	260	304	224	250	141	381	81	238	35	31	119	45	
Zion NP	365	84	372	204	59	168	119	390	328	344	308	269	264	309

USING THE PLANNING MAP

An important aspect of itinerary planning is determining your mode of transportation and the route you will follow as you travel from destination to destination. The Planning Map on the following pages will allow you to do just that.

First, read through the destination chapters carefully and note the sights that interest you. Then photocopy the Planning Map so you can try out several different routes that will take you to these destinations. (The mileage chart that follows will allow you to calculate your travel distances.) Decide where you will be starting your tour of Utah. Will you fly into Salt Lake International Airport, or will you start from somewhere in between? Will you be driving from place to place or flying into major transportation hubs and renting a car for day trips? The answers to these questions will form the basis for your route design.

Once you have a firm idea of where your travels will take you, copy your route onto one of the additional Planning Maps in the appendix. You won't have to worry about where your map is, and the information you need on each destination will always be close at hand.

Planning Map: Utah

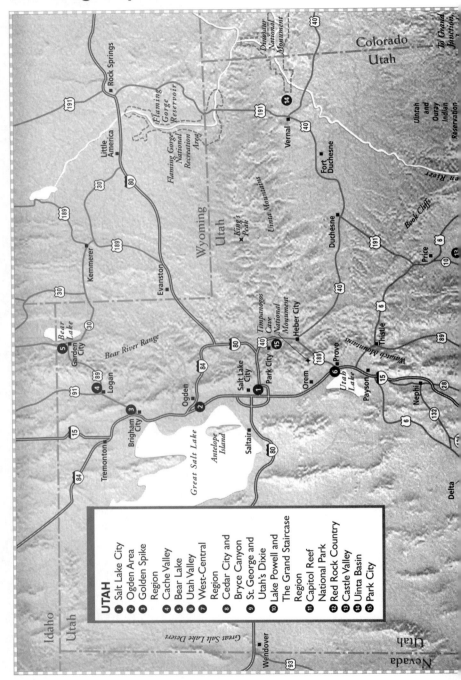

UTAH

1. Salt Lake City
2. Ogden Area
3. Golden Spike Region
4. Cache Valley
5. Bear Lake
6. Utah Valley
7. West-Central Region
8. Cedar City and Bryce Canyon
9. St. George and Utah's Dixie
10. Lake Powell and The Grand Staircase Region
11. Capitol Reef National Park
12. Red Rock Country
13. Castle Valley
14. Uinta Basin
15. Park City

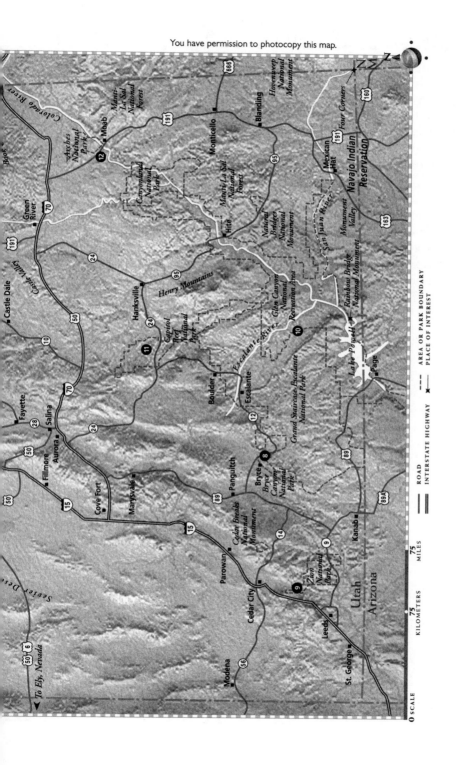

SPECIAL INTEREST TOURS

With the *Utah Travel•Smart* guidebook, you can plan a trip of any length—a one-day excursion, a getaway weekend, or a three-week vacation—around any special interest. To get you started, the following pages contain seven suggested itineraries geared toward a variety of interests. For more information refer to the chapters listed—chapter names are bolded and chapter numbers appear inside black bullets. You can follow a special interest tour in its entirety, or shorten, lengthen, or combine parts of each, depending on your starting and ending points.

Discuss alternative routes and schedules with your travel companions—it's a great way to have fun, even before you leave home. And remember: don't hesitate to change your itinerary once you're on the road. Careful study and planning ahead of time will help you make informed decisions as you go, but spontaneity is the extra ingredient that will make your trip memorable.

BEST OF UTAH TOUR

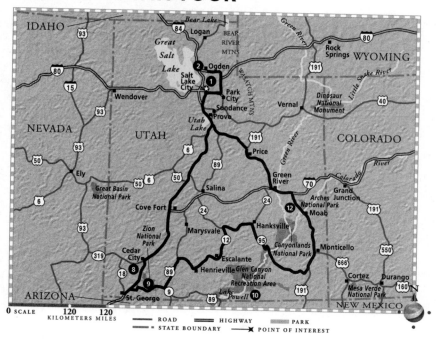

❶ **Salt Lake City** (Temple Square, Utah Museum of Natural History, Snowbird)

❷ **Ogden Area** (Union Station, Antelope Island)

❽ **Cedar City and Bryce Canyon** (Bryce Canyon National Park)

❾ **St. George and Utah's Dixie** (Zion National Park, Downtown St. George)

❿ **Lake Powell and the Grand Staircase Region** (Lake Powell, Rainbow Bridge)

⓬ **Red Rock Country** (Arches National Park, Canyonlands National Park, Slickrock Trail)

Time needed: two to three weeks

NATURE LOVERS' TOUR

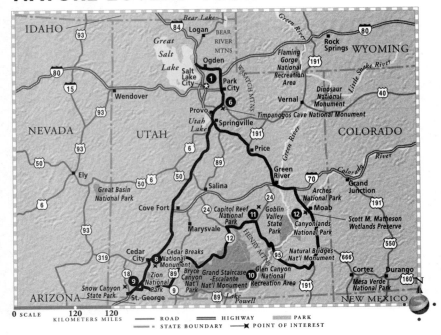

Utah offers endless opportunities for people who love nature, wildlife, and the outdoors. The state is home to numerous national parks, monuments, and forests, as well as spectacular rivers and state parks.

❶ Salt Lake City (Utah Museum of Natural History, Red Butte Garden and Arboretum, Great Salt Lake)

❻ Utah Valley (Timpanogos Cave National Monument, Bridal Veil Falls)

❽ Cedar City and Bryce Canyon (Bryce Canyon National Park, Cedar Breaks National Monument)

❾ St. George and Utah's Dixie (Zion National Park, Snow Canyon State Park)

❿ Lake Powell and the Grand Staircase Region (Glen Canyon National Recreation Area, Kodachrome Basin State Park)

⓫ Capitol Reef National Park (Goblin Valley State Park, Henry Mountains)

⓬ Red Rock Country (Arches National Park, Canyonlands National Park, Dead Horse Point State Park, Scott M. Matheson Wetlands Preserve)

Time needed: two weeks

ARTS AND CULTURE TOUR

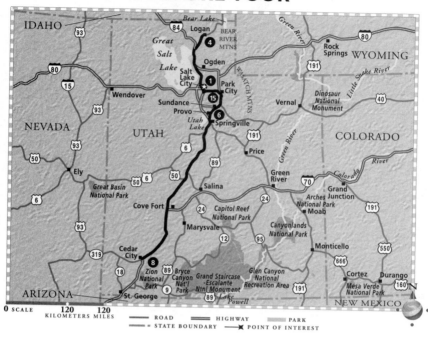

Utah's arts and cultures date back to prehistoric times when rock walls were the artistic canvas for Native Americans. Today, the state boasts many fine art museums. Its diverse cultural heritage is also preserved and displayed in pioneer museums throughout the state.

❶ Salt Lake City (Pioneer Memorial Museum, Hellenic Cultural Museum, Utah Museum of Fine Arts)

❹ Cache Valley (Nora Eccles Harrison Museum of Art, American West Heritage Center)

❻ Utah Valley (Springville Museum of Art, Sundance, Orem Heritage Museum, BYU Museum of Art)

❽ Cedar City and Bryce Canyon (Utah Shakespearean Festival, Braithwaite Fine Arts Gallery)

⓯ Park City (Kimball Art Center, Park City Museum, Alf Engen Ski Museum)

Time needed: two weeks

FAMILY FUN TOUR

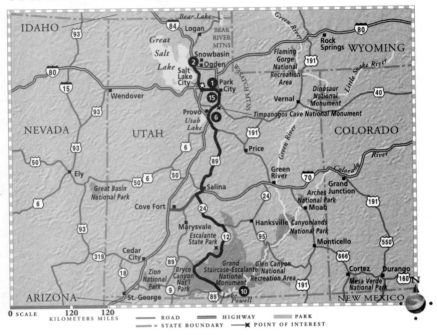

Utah is well known for its strong emphasis on family-oriented activities. Most destinations have something every member of the family will enjoy. But there are some specific sights that will bring out the kid in everyone.

❶ Salt Lake City (Hansen Planetarium, Children's Museum of Utah, Hogle Zoo, Tracy Aviary)
❷ Ogden Area (Hill Aerospace Museum, George S. Eccles Dinosaur Park, Lagoon)
❻ Utah Valley (Seven Peaks Resort Water Park, Trafalga Family Fun Center, Peppermint Place)
❿ Lake Powell and the Grand Staircase Region (Lake Powell)
⓯ Park City (Utah Winter Sports Park, Silver Mine Adventure, Alpine Slide)

Time needed: two weeks

SKI TOUR

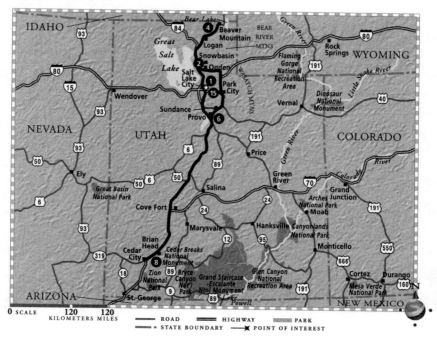

For years, Utah's license plates have promoted the state's multimillion dollar skiing industry. Touted as the best powder on earth, Utah's snow attracts skiers from all over the world. Some of the resorts are well known, like Snowbird and Park City, but others—like Beaver Mountain and Brian Head—are lesser-known secrets guarded by locals.

❶ Salt Lake City (Alta, Brighton, Snowbird, Solitude)
❷ Ogden Area (Snowbasin, Powder Mountain)
❹ Cache Valley (Beaver Mountain)
❻ Utah Valley (Sundance)
❽ Cedar City and Bryce Canyon (Brian Head, Elk Meadows)
❶❺ Park City (Park City Mountain Resort, Deer Valley, The Canyons)

Time needed: one week

DINOSAUR TOUR

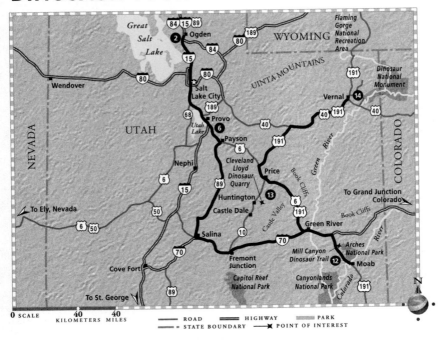

Dinosaurs called Utah home long before the state was called Utah. Their giant footprints are still visible today, and scientists keep digging up their fossilized bones in hillsides throughout the state. These large and mighty creatures that once roamed the earth continue to intrigue generations of visitors.

❷ **Ogden** (George S. Eccles Dinosaur Park)
❻ **Utah Valley** (BYU Earth Science Museum)
⓬ **Red Rock Country** (Mill Canyon Dinosaur Trail)
⓭ **Castle Valley** (Cleveland-Lloyd Dinosaur Quarry, CEU Prehistoric Museum, Museum of the San Rafael)
⓮ **Uinta Basin** (Dinosaur National Monument, Utah Field House of Natural History, Triassic Dinosaur Trackway)

Time needed: two weeks

OLYMPIC VENUES TOUR

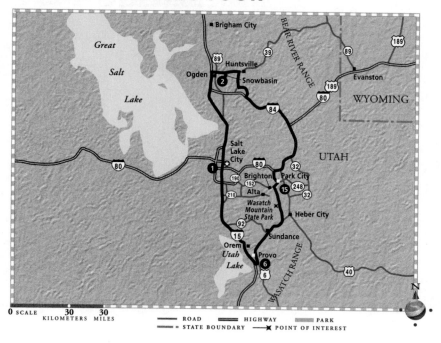

After Utah was selected to host the 2002 Winter Games, new facilities were built along the Wasatch Front and several existing facilities were upgraded to serve the needs of the Olympic competitions. The facilities are expected to be used by future generations of athletes, and they will continue to serve as venues for additional national and world competitions.

❶ **Salt Lake City** (Olympic Village)
❷ **Ogden Area** (Snowbasin, Ice Sheet)
❻ **Utah Valley** (Ice Sheet)
⓯ **Park City** (Utah Winter Sports Park, Park City Mountain Resort, Deer Valley Resort, Wasatch Mountain State Park)

Note: As pre-Olympic competitions are held at these sites leading up to 2002, organizers may change the locations where some Olympic events will be held.

Time needed: one week

CALENDAR OF EVENTS

January
Sundance Film Festival, Slamdance Film Festival, Park City
Utah Winter Games, statewide

March
St. George Arts Festival, St. George

April
Jeep Safari, Rod Benders Car Show, Moab
Semi-annual LDS World Conference, Salt Lake City
Spring Carnival, Brian Head

May
Golden Spike Anniversary, Promontory

June
ATV Jamboree, Fillmore
Scottish Highland Festival, Utah Arts Festival, Salt Lake City
Utah Summer Games, Utah Shakespeare Festival (through August), Cedar City

July
Bear Lake Raspberry Days, Garden City
Cache Valley Cruise In, Festival of the American West, Logan
Dinosaur Days, Vernal
Independence Day and Pioneer Day (July 24) celebrations, statewide
International Days, Price
Torrey Apple Days, Torrey

August
county fairs, statewide
International Festival, Salt Lake City
Park City Arts Festival, Park City
Timpanogos Storytelling Festival, Provo

September
Octoberfest (through October), Snowbird
Peach Days, Brigham City
Utah State Fair, Salt Lake City

October
Buffalo Roundup, Antelope Island
Canyonlands Fat Tire Festival, Moab
St. George Marathon, World Senior Games, St. George
Semi-annual LDS World Conference, Salt Lake City

November
World Cup Ski Races, Park City

December
Festival of Trees, Salt Lake City
Railroaders Film Festival and Winter Steam Demonstrations, Promontory

RESOURCES

Avalanche Forecast and Mountain Weather Reports
- — Logan, 435/797-4146
- — Ogden, 801/621-2362
- — Park City, 435/649-2250
- — Provo, 801/374-9770
- — Salt Lake City, 801/364-1581

Bicycle Utah, 801/649-5806

Bureau of Land Management, Utah State Office, 801/539-4001

Emergencies, 911

Great Salt Lake Travel Region, 801/521-2822

Multi-Agency Information Center, 801/627-8288

National Weather Service, 801/524-5133

Park City Chamber of Commerce, 435/649-6100

Raft Utah/Utah Guides and Outfitters, 801/566-2662

Salt Lake Visitor Information Center, 801/521-2868

Ski Utah, 800/SKI-UTAH, www.skiutah.com

U.S. Forest Service Intermountain Region Office, 801/625-5306

Utah Department of Transportation, 801/964-6000

Utah Highway Patrol, 801/965-4505

Utah Hotel and Lodging Association, 801/359-0104

Utah State Chamber of Commerce, 801/467-0844

Utah State Parks and Recreation, 801/538-7220

Utah Travel Council, 801/538-1030, 800/200-1160, www.utah.com

INDEX

MAP INDEX

You'll Feel like a Local When You Travel with Guides from John Muir Publications

CiTY·SMarT™ GUIDEBOOKS

Pick one for your favorite city: *Albuquerque, Anchorage, Austin, Calgary, Charlotte, Chicago, Cincinnati, Cleveland, Denver, Indianapolis, Kansas City, Memphis, Milwaukee, Minneapolis/St. Paul, Nashville, Pittsburgh, Portland, Richmond, Salt Lake City, San Antonio, St. Louis, Tampa/ St. Petersburg, Tucson*

Guides for kids 6 to 10 years old about what to do, where to go, and how to have fun in: *Atlanta, Austin, Boston, Chicago, Cleveland, Denver, Indianapolis, Kansas City, Miami, Milwaukee, Minneapolis/St. Paul, Nashville, Portland, San Francisco, Seattle, Washington D.C.*

TRAVEL✦SMART®

Trip planners with select recommendations to: *Alaska, American Southwest, Carolinas, Colorado, Deep South, Eastern Canada, Florida Gulf Coast, Hawaii, Illinois/Indiana, Kentucky/Tennessee, Maryland/Delaware, Michigan, Minnesota/Wisconsin, Montana/Wyoming/Idaho, New England, New Mexico, New York State, Northern California, Ohio, Pacific Northwest, Pennsylvania/New Jersey, South Florida and the Keys, Southern California, Texas, Utah, Virginias, Western Canada*

Rick Steves' GUIDES

See *Europe Through the Back Door* and take along guides to: *France, Belgium & the Netherlands; Germany, Austria & Switzerland; Great Britain & Ireland; Italy; Russia & the Baltics; Scandinavia; Spain & Portugal; London; Paris;* or the *Best of Europe*

ADVENTURES IN NATURE

Plan your next adventure in: *Alaska, Belize, Caribbean, Costa Rica, Guatemala, Honduras, Mexico*

JMP travel guides are available at your favorite bookstores. For a FREE catalog or to place a mail order, call: 800-888-7504.

John Muir Publications ✦ P.O. Box 613 ✦ Santa Fe, NM 87504

Cater to Your Interests on Your Next Vacation

The 100 Best Small Art Towns in America
3rd edition
Discover Creative Communities, Fresh Air, and
Affordable Living
U.S. $16.95, Canada $24.95

The Big Book of Adventure Travel
2nd edition
Profiles more than 400 great escapes to all corners
of the world
U.S. $17.95, Canada $25.50

Cross-Country Ski Vacations
A Guide to the Best Resorts, Lodges, and Groomed
Trails in North America
U.S. $15.95, Canada $22.50

Gene Kilgore's Ranch Vacations, 5th edition
The Complete Guide to Guest Resorts, Fly-Fishing,
and Cross-Country Skiing Ranches
U.S. $22.95, Canada $35.50

Indian America, 4th edition
A traveler's companion to more than 300 Indian
tribes in the United States
U.S. $18.95, Canada $26.75

Saddle Up!
A Guide to Planning the Perfect Horseback
Vacation
U.S. $14.95, Canada $20.95

Watch It Made in the U.S.A., 2nd edition
A Visitor's Guide to the Companies That Make Your
Favorite Products
U.S. $17.95, Canada $25.50

The World Awaits
A Comprehensive Guide to Extended Backpack
Travel
U.S. $16.95, Canada $23.95

**JMP travel guides are available
at your favorite bookstores.
For a FREE catalog or to place a
mail order, call: 800-888-7504.**

ABOUT THE AUTHOR

Michael R. Weibel grew up in San Diego, California. He moved to the Midwest in 1982, where he later earned a bachelor's degree in journalism at the University of Nebraska-Lincoln. Since then, Mike has worked for newspapers in Nebraska, Oklahoma, and Utah. He is currently the senior reporter at *The Herald Journal* in Logan, Utah. An avid outdoorsman, he co-authored *High in Utah, A Hiking Guide to the Tallest Peak in Each of the State's Twenty-nine Counties* (University of Utah Press). Mike and his wife, Lora, live in Hyde Park, Utah.

ABOUT THE AUTHOR

Michael R. Weibel grew up in San Diego, California. He moved to the Midwest in 1982, where he later earned a bachelor's degree in journalism at the University of Nebraska-Lincoln. Since then, Mike has worked for newspapers in Nebraska, Oklahoma, and Utah. He is currently the senior reporter at *The Herald Journal* in Logan, Utah. An avid outdoorsman, he co-authored *High in Utah, A Hiking Guide to the Tallest Peak in Each of the State's Twenty-nine Counties* (University of Utah Press). Mike and his wife, Lora, live in Hyde Park, Utah.